MW00784451

The Dyscalculia Solution

Teaching number sense

Jane Emerson and Patricia Babtie

Foreword by Brian Butterworth

Bloomsbury Education
An imprint of Bloomsbury Publishing Plc

50 Bedford Square
London
WC1B 3DP
UK

1385 Broadway
New York
NY 10018
USA

www.bloomsbury.com

First published 2014

British Library Cataloguing-in-Publication Data
A catalogue record for this book is available from the British Library.

ISBN:
PB: 9781441129512

Library of Congress Cataloging-in-Publication Data
A catalog record for this book is available from the Library of Congress.

10 9 8 7 6

Printed by CPI Group (UK) Ltd, Croydon, CR0 4YY

This book is produced using paper that is made from wood grown in managed, sustainable forests. It is natural, renewable and recyclable. The logging and manufacturing processes conform to the environmental regulations of the country of origin.

To view more of our titles please visit www.bloomsbury.com

Also available now:

The Dyscalculia Assessment is the award-winning resource for investigating pupils' numeracy abilities, designed to inform the personalised teaching programme that *The Dyscalculia Solution* features.

To find out more or to purchase *The Dyscalculia Assessment* visit www.bloomsbury.com/education.

ISBN: 9781408193716

Acknowledgements

Our ideas on how to help people with dyscalculia to understand numeracy are constantly evolving as we collaborate with pupils and colleagues. The SEN world is a generous one in which people freely share ideas in the quest to make learning possible and enjoyable for all. We would like to thank everyone who has helped and encouraged us over the years to refine the multi-sensory approach described in this book.

The late Dorian Yeo developed the Dot Patterns to 10, which are the key feature of this teaching approach, at Emerson House. She was inspired by Steve Chinn's work in teaching numeracy at Mark College, and Brian Butterworth's research at University College London into how the brain learns mathematics. They have both been long-standing supporters of the authors. Encouragement has also come from Chris Messenger who managed the Harrow Dyscalculia Project which was set up by Brian Butterworth. Generous support has also been given by Sue Gifford at Roehampton University and Diana Laurillard at the Institute of Education.

The teachers at Emerson House in London have contributed an enormous amount. Emerson House is a specialist centre; the challenge was to transfer these ideas from a specialist setting into mainstream schools. The staff and pupils at St Richard's CE Primary School, Richmond, have been amazingly supportive over many years as they patiently tried out and adapted many of the ideas in this book for classroom use. Carmen Palmer, Headmistress, Angela King, SENCO, Sian Murphy, and Tom Saunders made this possible. The children also trialled digital manipulatives, developed by Diana Laurillard and Hassan Baajour at the Institute of Education, London, which were based on these ideas. Jenny Aviss of the Alpha Plus Group kindly arranged for staff at their schools to be trained in the use of this approach. The feedback they provided has been immensely valuable. Jane Trapmore of the Cornwall Dyslexia Service has been a staunch supporter in making this approach available in mainstream classrooms. Mature student Emma Fullerton pointed out that this book is helpful for assessment and the development of a plan to help adults with dyscalculia.

Siock Kheng Ang, Ann Babtie, Alan Fraser, Jane Lees-Millais and Caroline Wentzel have kindly read and commented on various drafts and Henrietta Hunt helped with the preparation of drawings. At Bloomsbury Helen Diamond and Holly Gardner cheerfully guided us through the publishing process. Emily Wilson has been an amazing additional editor whilst Steve Evans and Marcus Duck patiently sorted out the diagrams and design.

Finally, thank you to Andrew Walker and William Babtie for all their support and encouragement.

Jane Emerson and Patricia Babtie

Contents

Foreword – From assessment to teaching

The importance of mathematics instruction has been stressed, quite rightly, in many official reports in the UK, the US and other nations. Napoleon famously said that mathematics is 'intimately connected with the prosperity of the state'. In his foreword to the Cockcroft report on maths teaching in 1982, Sir Keith Joseph, Secretary of State for Education and Science, wrote, 'Few subjects are as important to the future of the nation as mathematics'. Since Cockcroft, in the UK alone, there has been Professor Adrian Smith's report on post-14 maths, and Sir Peter Williams's report on primary maths. Poor maths has consequences for the lives of individuals. A UK survey found that learners with poor maths are more likely to be unemployed, depressed and in trouble with the law. The accountancy firm, KPMG, estimated the cost to the UK of the bottom 10% of maths achievers in terms of lost direct and indirect taxes, unemployment benefits, justice costs, and additional educational costs, was £2.4 billion per year. Therefore, successful methods for raising the level of the lowest attainers can have direct benefit not only to the sufferers, but also to society as a whole. Nevertheless, the lowest attainers, the dyscalculic learners, who probably make up about 5% of school and adult population, are neglected. As Sir John Beddington and colleagues wrote in 2008, 'Developmental dyscalculia is currently the poor relation of dyslexia, with a much lower public profile. But the consequences of dyscalculia are at least as severe as those for dyslexia.'

In 2010, Jane Emerson and Patricia Babtie, two of the most experienced teachers of dyscalculia in the country, published *The Dyscalculia Assessment*. This presented a thorough and systematic procedure for identifying specific difficulties in young learners, especially dyscalculic learners. It also gave many suggestions for interventions, based on the findings from assessment.

This new book, *The Dyscalculia Solution*, describes in detail the work that has been carried out at Emerson House in London UK, over many years, based on the work of Dorian Yeo. The approach is based upon multi-sensory principles similar to those used to help dyslexic learners. The pupil is encouraged to hear, see, touch and talk about carefully selected real objects including specially designed equipment designed to make explicit those concepts that most young learners seem to absorb implicitly. However, dyscalculic learners lack this inbuilt capacity to make sense of numbers.

Maths symbols and expressions gain meaning through their grounding in the perceptual and motor systems of the body. The close connection between maths thinking and action – and the neural basis of this connection – has been known to neuroscientists for many years. Now, findings from neuroscience suggest that tasks involving the manipulation of concrete objects make number concepts meaningful by providing an intrinsic relationship between *the goal of an action*, the *result of the action* and *informational feedback* about the difference between the result and the goal. In *The Dyscalculia Solution*, Emerson and Babtie put forward an approach to intervention that enables the learner to develop visual representations of numbers based on actions with concrete materials. Only when the learner is competent and confident with concrete materials, can there be progress to symbolic and abstract concepts of number and arithmetic.

This special equipment cannot be carried around in a suitcase for ever, so the aim is to guide any numerically vulnerable pupils to form meaningful images in their mind that they can call upon through visualisation when needed, in order to recapture the images of quantities, concepts, strategies and procedures to facilitate efficient calculation linked to real problem solving involving number.

This seemingly prescriptive approach can of course be adapted to individual needs and circumstances. However, the grand challenges remain: to work towards an understanding of how individual differences in brain development interact with formal education as well as with specialist interventions and also how learning pathways can adapt to individual needs.

Brian Butterworth
Institute of Cognitive Neuroscience, UCL, and the Centre for Educational Neuroscience.

Getting started

The Dyscalculia Solution

The Dyscalculia Solution shows how pupils can learn to understand numbers so that they can use them with confidence and enjoyment. Pupils use concrete materials and talk about what they see and do as well as recording their thinking in a variety of written forms. They develop conceptual understanding and strong visual images from which to derive calculation strategies.

The basis of numeracy is number sense: understanding what numbers represent and how they can be used to solve problems. Pupils with dyscalculia lack number sense and have difficulty acquiring arithmetical skills. Dyscalculia is a specific learning difficulty; however the term dyscalculia is also often used as an umbrella term to describe a range of difficulties in acquiring numerical skills. The term is used in a general way in this book. Pupils with dyscalculia can achieve numerical competence if they are taught appropriately using a structured, multi-sensory approach.

The Dyscalculia Solution offers practical guidance for teachers, teaching assistants and special educational needs co-ordinators who work with individual pupils and can also be adapted for classroom use. It will be useful for parents who want to help their own children.

The teaching programme described in The Dyscalculia Solution was developed at Emerson House, which is a specialist centre in London, supporting pupils with difficulties in numeracy and literacy. Pupils learn to think about the meaning of numbers using concrete materials and to express their ideas verbally, using diagrams, number lines, equations and standard written methods. They learn essential facts and procedures but they are not expected to learn by rote. Word problems form an integral part of teaching from the earliest stages. Ideally they should concern topics that interest the pupils – whether they involve real or fantasy worlds. Word problems should involve a process of discovery by the pupils. Too often they are given a very restricted range of word problems which 'limits their conceptual understanding in number work and contributes to inflexible thinking patterns.' (Yeo 2003)

Effective problem solving depends on asking pertinent questions. The detailed guidance explains how to teach pupils to do this by developing their language and visualisation skills. Much of The Dyscalculia Solution is written as a script which models the simple, direct language that is required from the teacher and fostered in the pupil. The words are not a prescription, they are a guide. Teachers may vary their language provided that questions and instructions are kept short and clear. Pupils must express their ideas in their own words. Initially they may find this very difficult and explanations may be cumbersome. They should not be told to use the pupil wording in the script. It is provided as a guide to the kind of thinking habits that pupils need to acquire in order to reason logically. There is much repetition. This is intentional and necessary as the teacher models the language which the pupil will eventually acquire. Games are an integral part of the approach as they foster a positive attitude towards numeracy as well as developing and practising knowledge and skills.

Structure of The Dyscalculia Solution

- There are two sections: Part 1: Foundations of numeracy: mental maths; Part 2: Formal Numeracy.
- Individual topics deal with each numerical step in detail starting with understanding counting.
- Each topic starts with a list of objectives.
- There is important information and guidance for teaching each topic.
- The teaching instructions provide a detailed script describing how to teach. This is for guidance.
- Pupils should always express their thinking in their own words. Allow pupils plenty of time to respond and accept any explanation that conveys their understanding.
- Games and activities develop understanding and provide practice. They also put numbers in contexts.
- Examples of word problems for each topic are provided in Chapter 10 (p216). It is essential that pupils solve word problems at each stage.
- A checklist at the end of each topic reiterates the goals that pupils should have achieved.

Key concepts and skills

Counting - number names and the number sequence; number representing a quantity (cardinal value) and the relationships between numbers

Dot patterns - distinct and memorable images of the numbers to 10 emphasising doubles and near doubles bonds

Key facts - bonds of all the numbers to 10; the inverse relationship between addition and subtraction

The base 10 structure - emphasising repeated groups of 10; the principle of exchange; representing numbers using equipment; numbers to 100

Calculation strategies - applying key facts and knowledge of the structure of the number system to use strategies including partitioning, bridging through 10, and complementary addition

Multiplication and division - the concepts of grouping, arrays and area; the division concepts of grouping and sharing; the inverse relationship between multiplication and division

Essential multiplication facts - learn 10 times a number; reason to derive all the other multiplication facts.

Number lines - understanding a number as both a point on a line and the distance from the origin; understanding the difference between counting numbers (shown on a number track) and measuring numbers (shown on a number line)

Place value - the structure of the place value system into hundreds, tens and units (HTU); zero as a place holder; the repeated pattern of HTU within each of the larger categories of thousands and millions; exchange between place value columns

Formal written methods - use base 10 equipment to model the structure of formal written methods then work abstractly

Word problems - use numbers in context; move from discussing concrete materials to visualising numbers in other situations; tackle word problems of increasing complexity. Word problems should be an integral part of each stage of teaching.

Numeracy

Numeracy is an essential life skill. 'Being numerate is about appreciating number relationships and interpreting answers, and not just about doing calculations.' (National Numeracy 2013) In the 21st century, numbers are a feature of everyday life. People need to assess numerical information generated by computers and presented in many different forms, and decide whether the answers are sensible, or even possible.

'The key components of number sense ... include an awareness of numbers and their uses in the world around us, a good sense of place value concepts, approximation, estimation, and magnitude, the concept of numeration, and an understanding of comparisons and the equivalence of different representations and forms of numbers.' (New Jersey Mathematics Coalition 1996)

Numerate people understand the basis of the number system – that a number represents a fixed quantity (the cardinal value) and that numbers have a stable relationship to each other. They have a store of basic knowledge which they use to reason about numbers. They can identify the patterns in, and relationships between, numbers and then generalise this knowledge to solve problems by reasoning. For example, they realise that if 2 + 3 = 5 they can generalise this knowledge to work out 200 + 300, or 50 – 20. Numerate people also understand the difference between the counting numbers (discrete numbers) and the measuring numbers (continuous numbers).

The number system is a place value system, which means that the value of each digit depends on its position in the written number. In the base 10 system, all numbers are formed by combining the digits 0, 1, 2, 3, 4, 5, 6, 7, 8 and 9 in different ways. Understanding how these abstract symbols are derived and abstracted from real objects is crucial to developing numeracy. However, for those with dyscalculia the symbols 0 to 9 can be meaningless, either because the symbols themselves have no meaning for them, or because they have no sense of the quantities they represent, or the relationship between them.

Dyscalculia

'Developmental dyscalculia is a condition that affects the ability to acquire arithmetical skills. Dyscalculic learners may have difficulty understanding simple number concepts, lack an intuitive grasp of numbers, and have problems learning number facts and procedures. Even if they produce a correct answer or use a correct method, they may do so mechanically and without confidence.' (DfES 2001)

Dyscalculia is also known as Specific Disorder of Arithmetical Skills and 'involves a specific impairment in arithmetical skills that is not solely explicable on the basis of general mental retardation or of inadequate schooling.' (International Classification of Diseases 10, 2010) Research indicates that dyscalculia may be caused by a brain deficit in the parietal lobe (Butterworth 1999, 2011, Simmons 2011). Dyscalculia may be developmental, a congenital condition with which the child is born, or acquired as a result of brain damage. The prevalence of dyscalculia in school-age children is about 5 per cent (Gifford 2005). Dyscalculia may also co-exist with other conditions such as dyslexia, dyspraxia, attention deficit disorder (ADD) and attention deficit hyperactivity disorder (ADHD). These are known as co-occurring conditions and are discussed in more detail in The Dyscalculia Assessment. Numeracy difficulties can cause maths anxiety which will exacerbate the problem.

People with dyscalculia lack the ability to subitise, which is the innate ability to recognise how many objects there are in a randomly arranged group without having to count them. Most people can quickly identify up to 4 objects that are randomly scattered. Some people with dyscalculia cannot manage even 2. Difficulties include inaccurate counting, inability to count backwards, difficulty sequencing, weak pattern recognition, as well as spatial and directional problems. Even when they do learn the counting sequence, they may think of numbers as a random string of sounds, or see them as 'clumps' of ones. They do not understand the value of a number, or realise that each number is composed of smaller numbers. For example, the number 4 denotes a quantity of four which can be seen as 3 and 1 or 2 groups of 2. This lack of basic understanding makes it impossible to develop efficient calculation strategies without suitable intervention to build the foundations of number sense .

Pupils with dyscalculia can become numerically competent if they start at the beginning, with counting and pattern awareness, and learn to understand the structure of the number system. This approach has the advantage that pupils need to learn relatively few facts since they can reason from known facts to derive new facts. However this can only occur if they are allowed the time to develop their thinking.

Learning and memory

New concepts are built on previously learned information which has been stored in long-term memory. The process of constructing useful memories involves a complex interplay between perception and language which causes brain changes to take place. The stronger the neural connections made, the more enduring the memory. Visual images play a particularly important part in memorisation and making memories accessible.

Meaning plays an important role as you cannot remember something with ease if it has no meaning for you. The more meaningful the material the easier it is to learn. Constructing meaning and remembering requires three elements: perception, language and time. In simple, colloquial terms this means having something to think about, an ability to express your thoughts, and sufficient time to think.

In learning about the world, young children begin by exploring physical objects, discussing them in words and so develop visual images linked to those words. The same process occurs when learning about numbers: exploring real objects and talking about them develops meaningful concepts. Later pupils depict their ideas in drawings and diagrams, and finally learn the abstract symbolic notation. Too often teaching starts at the abstract, symbolic level before pupils have grasped the patterns within numbers and the relationships between them.

Tell me what you see

Traditional numeracy teaching often moves quickly to the use of abstract symbols - too quickly for many pupils. The best way to teach so that pupils can understand and remember is to use a multi-sensory approach. This can be summarised as: 'Tell me what you see.' Concrete objects provide the opportunity for pupils to investigate and discuss numerical ideas. The word 'tell' need not be restricted to spoken language; the thinking process should also be conveyed in diagrammatic and written forms. First pupils draw pictures, and then progress to pictograms, tally charts, and tables; later they will use graphs. The symbolic forms include informal numerical recording, number lines and equations as well as the standard algorithms.

Concrete materials provide the opportunity for early word problems, which are an integral part of the teaching process, though too often taught as a separate topic. Pupils use equipment to model the elements of the question, and talk about what they see and do. For example: 'There are 4 counters. Add 6 more counters. How many counters can you see?' It is a small step to generalise the information by imagining that the counters represent other items such as pets, goals scored, or TV programmes watched.

The importance of the pupil learning to ask questions cannot be overemphasised. Too often problem solving is seen as getting the correct answer; in fact problem solving requires the ability to ask the right questions. Initially the teacher will prompt discussion and direct thinking by asking questions such as 'How many are there?', 'What do you need to do?' However the aim is for the pupil to learn to ask their own questions, in their own words, in order to understand what the problem is about. Games and activities provide opportunities to develop this kind of thinking in an informal way.

Teaching

Successful teaching requires a planned, structured approach. Assess the pupil, summarise the results and use this to prepare teaching plans. Set specific objectives for each term, or a series of lessons. It encourages pupils to know that they have specific goals to reach, and can give them a sense of accomplishment when they reach them. The goals should be realistic and measurable such as 'Counting to 10' or 'Know the 10 times table'.

Do not be afraid of starting at an apparently 'basic' level. Pupils who are struggling with numeracy may be unable to access the curriculum at the expected level because they have not mastered basic concepts. They develop the problem solving skills required to analyse information and reason about larger numbers while working on small numbers and basic calculations.

Always be aware of laying solid foundations for future concepts. If pupils learn to think and reason about small numbers, they will be able to generalise this approach to larger whole numbers, to fractions, and to algebra.

Three questions help to plan effectively.
• What am I going to teach?
• How am I going to teach it?
• How will I know that the pupils have learned it?

What am I going to teach?

It is imperative that pupils develop confidence in their own ability. Experience has shown that it is best to start by investigating the numbers to 10. It is strongly advised that all pupils study the dot patterns as the work in this section develops essential reasoning skills and concepts.

Pupils need to know a limited number of key facts, and learn to derive other facts from these by using their understanding of the number system. They also need to be able to calculate using a few 'big-value' strategies that can be universally applied, such as partitioning, and bridging through 10.

Assess the pupil to find out what they know and how they think about numbers. The aim is to find the starting point which is just before understanding has broken down. It is important that teaching starts at a point of secure knowledge and then build on that. The accompanying book The Dyscalculia Assessment is a detailed guide to conducting an assessment and interpreting the results. (Emerson and Babtie 2013).

Summarise the findings in the Summary Numeracy Profile (Template p229) and use the information to draw up a Teaching Plan Summary (Template p230). This defines the topics to be taught in a specified length of time. A realistic guide is to allow about 10 lessons to teach 3 topics. However the rate of progress will depend on the severity of the each pupil's difficulties.

Draw up an Individual Lesson Plan for each lesson (Template p231). Set specific goals for each lesson. Clearly state the concept being taught as well as any subsidiary aims. For example, for the concept Counting to 10 the initial goals are oral counting, counting objects, and ordering objects in a line. Keep the structure of each lesson consistent so that pupils know what to expect. Start by reviewing the previous topic as learning occurs by building on information already in the memory. Then consolidate understanding or introduce the next related topic, practice it and do an activity or play a game. Be prepared to change the plan if the pupil has forgotten the previous work, or is unsure.

How am I going to teach it?

Use multi-sensory teaching methods. Pupils manipulate the equipment themselves. The teacher's role is to provoke thinking, not to demonstrate results.

Pupils need experience with real objects before they can understand the abstract concepts that numbers represent. Learning takes place as the pupil talks about and manipulates the equipment. They draw diagrams of what they see. This is a crucial stage in developing visual images which can be used later for deriving calculation strategies. Once they have mastered the written numerals, they represent their thinking in equations and standard algorithms.

Word problems and games are essential features of the teaching approach: word problems put numbers in context and develop analytical skills; games provide repetition and reduce maths anxiety if they are pitched at the correct level.

The key to success is to encourage the pupil to talk about what they are seeing and doing. Teachers help pupils develop their reasoning skills by careful questioning using the appropriate vocabulary. It is essential to use simple words and short sentences, and only to ask one question at a time. However, the aim is for pupils to take responsibility for framing questions to help them tackle problems. The Dyscalculia Solution provides detailed guidelines for showing how to approach each topic. As mentioned earlier, the teacher scripts are given to show the kind of clear, simple language required, and the pupil's scripts show the kind of response they may give. They are not intended as a prescriptive blueprint. Pupils use their own words.

How will I know that the pupils have learned it?

On-going assessment forms part of the teaching process. Asking pupils to explain what they are doing and why, during the lesson, will elicit much helpful information. Be ready to change the lesson plan if the pupil cannot answer review questions at the beginning of the lesson. The teacher will then need to give the pupil more time to work with that topic until it is secure.

Concrete materials

Base 10 equipment
Base 10 equipment is also known as Dienes equipment. Wooden or plastic cuboids represent the relationships in the metric system: unit 1 cm³, rod 10 cm long, square 10 cm², cube 10 cm³. They should all be the same colour.

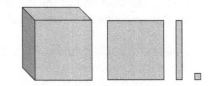

Bead strings
Unnumbered beads that can be easily moved along a piece of string. This reinforces the strategy of touching or moving each item as it is counted. The colours clearly show alternating groups of 10. Use bead-strings with 20 beads and 100 beads.

Cards
Packs of cards which show numbers in different forms: dot patterns, numerals and words. There are also packs of question cards for specific games. Each pack should be a different colour. This is for practical reasons.

1 - 10
Number cards Pattern cards

1 - 10
Word cards

Counters
Small objects of the same size and the same colour. Plastic or glass nuggets are recommended as they are easy to pick up.

Cuisenaire rods
Coloured cuboids of proportional lengths, based on 1 cm², represent the numbers from 1 to 10.

Dice
Dice numbered 1 - 3, conventional dice with patterns 1 to 6, 10-sided dice numbered 0 to 9, blank 6-sided dice to customize for games, adapted 10-sided dice to provide dice numbered 1 to 10, and dice numbered 11 to 20.

Pencil, paper and coloured pencils
Use squared paper with 1 cm squares to help pupils organise their work systematically. Plain paper is required for drawing score sheets for some of the games, and for drawing Place Value grids. Some pupils prefer plain paper because they find the lines on squared paper distracting, especially when they are drawing diagrams. Coloured pencils to match the colours of the Cuisenaire rods.

Ruler
Metric rulers with the whole numbers marked at the lines showing the intervals. Do not use rulers that show the numbers in the space between the intervals.

Additional useful equipment
Stern blocks and Dual Boards
This is a comprehensive system for investigating numbers and their relationships. Coloured rods denote the numbers 1 to 10 and base boards provide additional structure. The principle of the Stern materials is similar to Cuisenaire rods, however the pieces are larger. They are useful for young children and pupils with motor difficulties.

Part 1:
Foundations of Numeracy: Mental Maths

Counting is the foundation of numeracy. Part 1 deals with numbers to 100. Pupils learn to count accurately and flexibly, learn key facts, and apply those facts to calculations using the four operations.

The base 10 structure is implicit in all the activities in this section but formal place value is not introduced until pupils are secure with both counting and number facts to 100.

First pupils work with the numbers to 10. Pupils learn to count to 10 and learn the number bonds, which are key facts. By working with these apparently simple numbers, pupils develop numeracy concepts and reasoning skills which are the foundation of all numeracy work. These include the relationships between numbers, the components of numbers, and the vocabulary required to describe numbers in terms of their size and position.

There are step-by-step instructions for teaching pupils to count using multi-sensory methods. Dot patterns establish memorable images that can be used for calculation. Pupils learn the key number facts: bonds of 10, doubles and near doubles, as well as the bonds of all the numbers to 10.

In the section on the numbers to 20 the importance of number location and the ability to count flexibly forwards and backwards is introduced. Pupils explore the link between number tracks and number lines to make the distinction between counting and measuring numbers explicit. They apply knowledge of number facts to develop calculation strategies for addition and subtraction.

Finally pupils work with the numbers to 100. Pupils explore the principle of exchange and decomposition using base 10 equipment and learn to partition numbers into tens and units. Number sequences lead on to the concept of multiplication as repeated addition to 10 x 10. Pupils learn the 10, 5 and 2 times tables. They learn to derive all the other tables by reasoning from the 10 times table.

1

Numbers to 10: Counting

Counting is much more than being able to say number names in sequences by rote. Pupils need to learn to count flexibly, which means understanding how the numbers are related to each other, and realising that numbers are made of smaller numbers. The aim is to enable pupils to use their counting knowledge flexibly as a tool to solve problems.

Learning to count requires co-ordination of action and thought. Pupils need to recite number names in the correct order, whilst synchronising each number word with a particular object in a collection. This is called one-to-one correspondence. Counting is used to find out the total number of items in a collection. This is the cardinal value. Counting also identifies the position of an item in a sequence. This is the ordinal value.

Pupils with dyscalculia have difficulty remembering the number names, they have difficulty saying the numbers in sequence, and they tend to think of numbers as 'clumps' of ones. They may not understand that the last number in a count represents the total number of items in the set. Some counting errors are caused by auditory discrimination difficulties. It is essential that pupils learn to articulate the counting words correctly.

Equipment

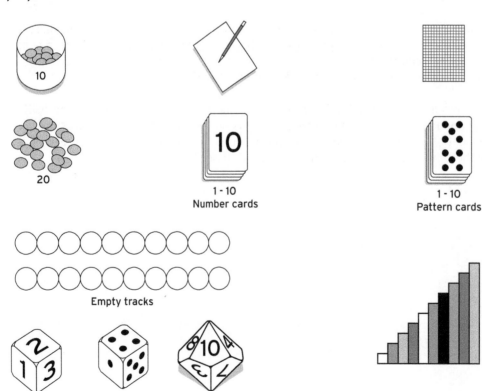

10

20

1 - 10
Number cards

1 - 10
Pattern cards

Empty tracks

Counting to 10: comparing quantities

Objectives
- Compare quantities in terms of relative size
- Use the terms more than and less than
- Structure counters in a line
- Use the words more, less, bigger, smaller, same, one, two, three

Pre-count skills
Counting with understanding requires the ability to relate numbers to each other. This entails comparing quantities. Before starting number comparisons, ensure that pupils can sort objects according to different criteria such as colour, shape and size.

Comparative size can be a difficult concept to grasp. Start by discussing non-count comparative quantities such as some, a few, a lot; for example *some water, a few children, a lot of counters* before moving on to the relative size of the quantities. (Grauberg 1998)

It is particularly important that pupils can use comparative language such as *same, different, bigger, smaller, more than*, and *less than*. Pupils will not be able to understand the relationships between numbers, which underpin numeracy, if they do not understand these relative concepts.

More than and *less than*
The concepts of *more* and *less* can be difficult for pupils to understand. Establish the concept of *more than* before investigating *less than*. *More* and *less* are imprecise quantities, and in everyday usage the words may have connotations which obscure their meaning. *More* will probably be associated with meal times. *Do you want some more?* In this context the word *more* means another, or second, helping. The second helping is likely to be smaller than the original quantity (which has been eaten so is no longer available for comparison). The mathematical idea of an increase in size is lost. Young children's cognitive abilities are not sufficiently developed to be able to hold two distinct quantities in mind when comparing them so it is important to introduce early work on *more than* and *less than* by comparing two quantities which remain visible all the time.

The difficulty is compounded by introducing comparative number work by adding *one more*. One is a small number; an association is made between *one* and *small*. This is the opposite of the idea of *more* meaning *greater than*.

Teaching
Introduce the idea of comparing quantities in a structured way by playing 'The More or Less Game' and encourage pupils to talk about which player has more or less counters (p10).

The More or Less Game

Vocabulary of more and less

Aims
- To compare quantities
- To practice comparative language: more than, less than, the same as
- To count to 3

Equipment
- Counters - 10 for each player
- Dice (1 to 3)
- Board with one 'track' for each player

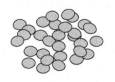

Player A ◯◯◯◯◯◯◯◯◯◯

Player B ◯◯◯◯◯◯◯◯◯◯

Activity

Players take turns. Work on the term *more than* initially. When pupils are secure using *more than*, introduce *less than*. On each turn, players say who has more counters than their opponent. Players use full sentences and proper names rather than 'you'.

Note that players are not expected to count the number of counters on the track; they need to focus on comparing the quantity that they have with their opponent's quantity. At this stage, asking players to count the counters will interfere with the task, which is to take in the quantity as a whole and compare it with another quantity.

Player A throws the dice and counts out the number of counters indicated, then places them on the track. (See example below).

Player B has a turn and compares the quantities using the word *more*.

The winner is the first player to reach the end of their track.

Example showing play:

Round 1 Player A throws 3. Player B throws 2.

Player A ●●●◯◯◯◯◯◯◯   Player A: *I have more counters than Player B.*

Player B ●●◯◯◯◯◯◯◯◯   Player B: *Player A has more counters than me.*

Round 2 Player A throws 1. Player B throws 2.

Player A ●●●●◯◯◯◯◯◯   Player A: *I have the same number of counters as Player B.*

Player B ●●●●◯◯◯◯◯◯   Player B: *I have the same number of counters as Player A.*

Checklist - Counting to 10: comparing quantities

Pupils can:
- ☐ Compare quantities in terms of relative size
- ☐ Use the terms more than and less than
- ☐ Structure counters in a line
- ☐ Use the words more, less, bigger, smaller, same, one, two, three

Counting to 10: number names and one-to-one correspondence

Objectives
- Recite the number names to 10
- Articulate the sounds clearly, especially the initial sounds in 'three', 'four' and 'five'
- Synchronise number names with objects counted
- Order objects in a line as they are counted

Teach the number names by counting objects. Most children can recite the number words to 10 when they start school. However they may not realise that each word refers to a specific place in a sequence (the ordinality principle) and that the final word refers to the total number of objects in the count (the cardinality principle). Some children may not know the number words. Pupils cannot continue until they can say the sequence to 10 fluently without hesitation. Traditional nursery rhymes can help children acquire fluency in reciting the number names.

Some pupils may say the number words as a flow of sound but fail to link them to quantities of objects. Use real objects and train them to touch each object as it is counted, and to move the objects into a line. It is important that the objects are the same colour. Some pupils may be able to remember only two or three newly introduced number names in a sequence. Work at the pupils' pace, start with three objects and when they have learnt to count to three off-by-heart, gradually add more items to the sequence. This can take some time. However it is absolutely essential that the pupil learns the number names to 10 before moving on.

Do not ask pupils to count backwards until they are absolutely secure in counting and sequencing the numbers forwards to 20.

Auditory discrimination errors
These can occur on the letters 'f' 'v' and 'th' in counting the numbers 'three', 'four' and 'five'.

Many people, even adults, confuse the sounds 'f' and 'th' as in 'fin' and 'thin', as well as 'v' and 'th' as in 'van' and 'than'. A further confusion arises because the digraph 'th' represents two different sounds, one voiced and one voiceless, as in 'this' and 'thin'.

The initial sounds in 'fin' and 'thin' are made voicelessly, that is without the 'voice box' or larynx vibrating until the onset of the following vowel sound. Conversely, the initial sounds in 'van' and 'than' are voiced sounds made with the larynx vibrating.

It is very important that these confusions are resolved or at least brought to the pupil's attention, in order to avoid future difficulties with the number words 'thirteen', 'fourteen' and 'fifteen', as well as 'thirty', 'forty' and 'fifty' etc. through the decades. These confusions can also cause difficulties when pupils work on reading the number words involving these sounds.

Only the voiceless 'th' occurs in the counting sequence in 'three', 'thirteen' and 'thirty' etc. and can be referred to as the quiet 'th' to help the pupil become aware of the breath which can be felt by holding a hand up in front of the mouth as the tongue is brought forwards for the 'th' sound. A useful visual clue in the form of a small pink tongue can be drawn under any initial 'th' sound in the counting sequence.

Some pupils start to omit 'f' sounds and change them all to 'th' sounds in the mistaken belief that the 'f' sound is always an error.

If these confusions persist, even with some initial help, refer the pupil to a speech therapist for a short course of intervention.

Teaching

Oral counting: number names
Teacher models the counting sequence to 10, reciting the number names slowly and clearly.
The teacher and pupil recite the numbers to 10 together.
If pupils are successful, ask them to count to 10 on their own.

Concrete counting: one-to-one correspondence
Give the pupil a bowl of more than 10 counters. (Prepare these before the lesson. Do not count them out in front of the pupil.)

Teacher: *Count 10 counters into a line. Say the numbers aloud.*

Placing items in a line helps pupils to count accurately, as they avoid counting items twice or leaving items out of the count. Make sure that each number name is synchronised exclusively with one counter in the sequence. This is called one-to-one correspondence. Pupils with dyscalculia often have difficulty understanding this. If the pupil is not successful, model the counting sequence by counting the counters with the pupil. Note any pronunciation problems such as 'f' for 'th' so that the pupil says 'free' instead of 'three.

Ask the pupil to draw a diagram showing the line of counters. Pupils need to learn to record information systematically in diagrammatic form.

Checklist – Counting to 10: number names and one-to-one correspondence
Pupils can:
- ☐ Recite the number names to 10
- ☐ Articulate the sounds clearly, especially the initial sounds in 'three', 'four' and 'five'
- ☐ Synchronise number names with objects counted
- ☐ Order objects in a line as they are counted

Estimate up to 10

Objectives

- Make a reasonable estimate for up to 10 objects
- Check the estimate by counting systematically

The ability to estimate quantities helps develop a 'feel' for the size of numbers, which is an important part of number sense, and essential for checking calculations.

Teaching

Estimating Activity

Aims
- To develop a sense of the size of quantities
- To practise counting numbers up to 10

Equipment
- A bowl of 10 counters (do not count them out in front of the pupil)
- Blank sheet of paper

Activity

Take at least five counters from the bowl and put them in a pile on the table. Let pupils look at them for a few seconds but not for long enough to be able to count them. Cover them with a sheet of paper. Teacher asks the pupil to estimate the amount: *How many are there?*

Then let pupils see the counters again.
Teacher: *Can you check how many there are?*
The pupil counts the counters.

Do pupils have a counting strategy? Do they touch each counter? Do they count them methodically? Do they count them into a line?

When they have finished the count, remember to ask: *How many are there?*

Teach pupils to put the counters in a line as they count them. If they are not accurate, say: *Let's count them together. Touch each counter as you say the number.*

The teacher sets the pace so that pupils focus on each counter as they touch it  and say the number word.

Continue this estimating activity until the pupil can give reasonable estimates for up to 10 items.

Checklist – Estimate up to 10

Pupils can:

- ☐ Make a reasonable estimate for up to 10 objects
- ☐ Check the estimate by counting systematically

Read and sequence numbers

Objectives
- Read the numbers to 10
- Link oral numbers to numerals
- Order the numbers to 10
- Describe the position of numbers in relation to each other
- Use the words between, next to, after, before, beginning, end

When pupils can count to 10 accurately, link oral counting to the written digits. Teach pupils to read numerals by ordering number cards and saying the number words.

It is important to be able to place cards in order without reciting the sequence from 1 each time a card is placed. Pupils also need to describe the relative position of numbers using comparative terms such as *between*, *before* and *after*. Pupils need to be able to fill in missing numbers in a written sequence.

The concept of zero needs to be very carefully taught (see p181). At this stage, pupils only need to use zero for writing the zero in the number ten. If necessary tell them that ten is written as a one and a zero. Many pupils know this without understanding what the two digits mean.

Teaching

Reading numbers: link oral numbers to numerals
Explain that the cards have a special order. Use the digit cards 1, 2 and 3. The teacher models the order by laying out the sequence and saying the number names *slowly and clearly*, pointing to each card to make the link between the word and the symbol explicit.

Ask the pupil to point to each card as they say the number word.

Start by teaching the correct order up to 5. When the pupil can do this consistently, introduce the numbers up to 10.

Ask the pupil to lay out number cards in order to develop the ability to sequence automatically.

When the pupil can lay out the sequence confidently, introduce the comparative terms *next to*, *between*, *after*, and *before* to describe relative positions. Start with the word *between*. Teacher models the language, then points to a number and asks the pupil to describe the position.

Teacher points to 7 and says: *7 is next to 6 and 8.*
7 is between 6 and 8.

Teacher points to 5 and asks: *Tell me about 5. Which numbers are next to it?*

5 is next to 4 and 6. 5 is between 4 and 6.

What is the number between 8 and 10? Point to it.

Pupil points to 9.
9 is between 8 and 10.

When pupils can confidently use the term *between,* introduce *after.*

Teacher points to 4 and says: *4 is next to 3.*
4 comes after 3.

Teacher points to 6 and asks: *Look at 6.*
What is the number after 6?

Teacher points to 8.
What is the number after 8?

Pupil points to 6.
6 is next to 5. 6 comes after 5.

Pupil points to 8.
8 is between 7 and 9.
9 is the number after 8.

When pupils can confidently use the term *after,* introduce *before.*

Teacher points to 8 and says:
8 is between 7 and 9. 7 comes before 8.

Look at 3. What is the number before 3?

Pupil points to 3.
3 is between 2 and 4.
2 comes before 3.
2 is the number before 3.

Order Numbers to 10

Aims
- To learn the numerical symbols 1 to 10
- To link number words and symbols
- To practise ordering numbers to 10
- To use comparative language

Equipment
- Cards numbered 1 to 10

1 - 10
Number cards

Activity

Shuffle the cards and ask the pupil to read each number and put it on the table to form the sequence 1 to 10.

At first the pupil may have to search through the pack to find 1, then 2 and so on. As they become familiar with the sequence, ask them to put the cards out in roughly the appropriate place, even though other cards are missing at this point.

Encourage them to use comparative language to work out where the cards go in relation to each other. For example: 5 is smaller than 7 so 5 goes before 7.

If pupils make mistakes, allow them time to find the error before helping them to do so.

Some pupils find it very difficult to sequence cards from a randomly ordered pack. It is important that they practise and learn to do this.

Checklist - Read and sequence numbers
Pupils can:
- ☐ Read the numbers to 10
- ☐ Link oral numbers to numerals
- ☐ Order the numbers to 10
- ☐ Describe the position of numbers in relation to each other
- ☐ Use the words between, next to, after, before, beginning, end

Write digits 0 to 9

Objectives
- Write numbers clearly and comfortably
- Write numbers without reversing digits (e.g. 3 not Ɛ)
- Use the words top, down, clockwise, anti-clockwise

It is very important to write digits clearly. Untidy and idiosyncratic formations of written numbers can lead to calculation and communication errors. Take time to teach the correct way to write numbers. Good handwriting is easy to read, and comfortable and quick for the writer to produce. Teach pupils to write all the digits from 0 to 9. Use the word zero to describe 0; do not use the terms nothing, or nought.

Clear handwriting starts with good posture. The desk and chair need to be the correct height for the writer. Place feet slightly apart, back straight and one arm resting on the desk so that the weight is evenly distributed and the writing hand is free to move across the page. Give pupils practice in pencil control without having to think about number formation. Activities such as colouring, dot-to-dot, and tracing are a few ways of doing this.

Reversing numbers is a common problem with younger pupils. All digits apart from 0, 1 and 8 may be reversed. It is normal for young children to reverse letters and numbers, however, continued reversals may be a sign of visuo-spatial difficulties.

Avoid reversals by relating numbers to a vertical line and giving pupils plenty of practice in writing numbers as a handwriting exercise. This means they can concentrate on the number formation without thinking about their numerical value. Most digits are formed with a continuous line; the pencil is not lifted from the paper, 4 and 5 are the only exceptions.

Number by number

0 is formed from a continuous line to make a circle or an oval. Start at the top and move the pencil in an anti-clockwise direction. It is easier to form an anti-clockwise movement than a clockwise movement if the pupil is right-handed. However a left-handed pupil will find it easier to make a clockwise movement and they should be allowed to do so if they wish.

1 is a single vertical line. Some pupils put a serif on it. This is unnecessary and can lead to confusion with the number 7 if the digits are not clearly written.

2 is formed from a curve and a straight horizontal line. A single continuous curve is incorrect.

3 is formed from two curves. It can also be formed by a combination of straight and curved lines as in 3. It is better to discourage this formation until pupils are more experienced as it is harder to write clearly than the more conventional 3.

4 is formed by a downward stroke, then a horizontal line to form an L shape. The pupil then lifts the pen and makes a short vertical stroke. Four is often printed as 4 and some pupils try to write it like that. Discourage this formation as it requires starting from the bottom of the number which causes confusion for many young children. Of course, if a pupil is able to write it clearly then do not attempt to change it.

5 is formed by a short downward stroke leading to a curve to the right. Then the pupil lifts the pencil, returns to the original starting point and draws a horizontal line at the top. Some pupils use a continuous curve to form S. This is incorrect and often resembles the letter 's'.

6 is formed from a continuous curve. Make sure that the space in the lower half of the digit is a circle.

7 is formed from a straight line which moves from horizontal to diagonal. Young children and pupils with directional weaknesses may find it difficult to draw a diagonal line.

8 is formed by a continuous curved line. It is important that the pupil makes a figure of 8 rather than forming the 8 from two circles.

9 is formed from curved and straight lines. It is important to draw the circular part of the 9 first, then the downward stroke. This prevents confusion with the letter 'p' which is formed by a downward stroke followed by a circle.

Teaching

Start at the left hand edge of the page so that pupils can only write numbers in the required position. The exception is 9 where the vertical line will be inside the edge of the page (see diagram). Later, pupils will write numbers adjacent to a vertical line.

All digits start from the top. Most of them can be formed by working to the right of the vertical line. 9 is the only digit that is formed by a circle to the left of vertical.

☆ Shows the starting point

⟶ Shows the direction of the first pen stroke

Guess My Number

Aim
- To practise correct number formation

Equipment
- Pencil and paper

Activity
This activity is for two pupils. Pupil A sits at a desk ready to write a number on an A4 sheet of paper. Pupil B stands behind Pupil A and uses a finger to draw a large, single digit on the back of Pupil A. Pupil A writes the number they have 'felt' on their back.

Pupils switch places and continue the activity.

This exercise encourages the production of large motor movements which help pupils recall the correct formation of the digit. Interpreting the feeling of the digit drawn on their back also helps recall the correct orientation of the digit.

Checklist - Write digits 0 to 9

Pupils can:
- ☐ Write numbers clearly and comfortably
- ☐ Write numbers without reversing digits (e.g. 3 not Ɛ)
- ☐ Use the words top, down, clockwise, anti-clockwise

Read and spell number words

Objectives
- Read number words from one to ten
- Write number words from one to ten

Make sure that pupils can read and write the number words from one to ten. It is particularly important to spell 'two' correctly to avoid confusion with the preposition 'to' and the adverb 'too'.

Teaching

Teach pupils to read and spell number words correctly by using the Look, Say, Cover, Write method. (p236)

The list of number words is presented on a worksheet with spaces for pupils to write the word three times.
- Read the first word aloud then copy it once and check the spelling.
- Read the word again. Cover up the word with a piece of paper. Write the word again.
- Check the spelling. Cover up the word. Write the word again.

Pupils need to take responsibility for checking their own spelling and correcting errors. Pupils practise this method until they can spell the words correctly.

Look, Say, Cover, Write
Say the first word. Copy it. Cover it up and write it. Check the spelling. Write it again.

Say	Copy	Cover and write	Check and write
one			
two			
three			
four			
five			
six			
seven			
eight			
nine			
ten			

Checklist - Read and spell number words
Pupils can:
- ☐ Read number words from one to ten
- ☐ Write number words from one to ten

Dot patterns 1 to 10: doubles and near doubles

Objectives
- Recognise, recall and draw the dice patterns 1 to 6
- Construct dot patterns for numbers 7, 8, 9, 10
- Use the terms double and half to describe the relationship between a doubles number and its components
- Draw accurate dot patterns of doubles and near doubles patterns
- Describe the relationship between doubles numbers and near doubles numbers
- Sequence the dot patterns from 1 to 10
- Match numerals to dot patterns

Pupils need visual images of the size of numbers. They need to develop the concept of relative size and to think in terms of components.

Pattern recognition and the relationship between numbers lie at the heart of understanding numbers. Pattern recognition and recall is an essential cognitive skill. It is important for being able to process quantitative information and then derive other information from it. The distinction between recognition and recall of information is an important one. To recognise means to know something when you see it. For example, a pupil may be able to recognise a number 4 when they can see it but not necessarily be able to recall what 4 looks like when it is not present. To recall information means to remember it. Recall is much more difficult than recognition as it requires pupils to retrieve information from memory.

The dot patterns provide distinctive visual images of the numbers from 1 to 10. Exploring numbers using dot patterns draws attention to the internal structure within numbers, knowledge which is essential for developing effective calculation strategies. They show clearly how all quantities greater than 1 are made up of smaller quantities. Inherent in the structure of the dot patterns are the number bonds for the core patterns of doubles and near doubles. They can be used to introduce the idea of double and half, and to make the relationship between numbers explicit, such as *less than*, *more than*, *before* and *after*.

Pupils develop language, reasoning and problem-solving skills by constructing the patterns and describing the relationships between them. Initially the teacher models questions to prompt pupils to investigate the numbers but encourages the pupils to start asking questions for themselves as soon as possible. The ability to ask pertinent questions is essential for analysing information in order to solve problems.

Dot patterns showing doubles and near doubles

The numbers 1 to 6 are the conventional dice patterns. The numbers 7 to 10 are derived in a structured way to show the core patterns of doubles and near doubles. A doubles number is formed by adding a number to itself. For example, 6 is double 3. A near doubles pattern is one more or one less than a doubles number. 5 is one more than 4; it is also one less than 6. For clarity, the patterns for all the numbers from 1 to 10 are referred to as the dot patterns. Doubles numbers are even numbers; near doubles numbers are odd numbers. Do not teach the terms odd and even at this stage as it can cause confusion. (See p117)

Pupils need to be able to use counters to show the dot patterns from 1 to 6, without looking at the dice, and draw the pattern from memory. Do not develop dot patterns until they can do this. Pupils with very poor pattern recognition skills may need specialist visuo-spatial training from an occupational therapist.

Drawing objects is an important step in relating concrete objects to their pictorial representations. Drawing also helps create visual images which can be recalled and used to generalise knowledge to larger numbers. Some pupils find it difficult to represent data in the clear, systematic way that is required for successful problem solving. Presenting information diagrammatically helps clarify concepts.

Teaching

Patterns of numbers 1 to 6

Show the pupil a conventional dice. Point to each pattern and ask: *How many dots are there?*

Teacher removes the dice and now puts out a single counter and says: *This is the pattern of 1.*

Then the teacher puts out two more counters aligned vertically or diagonally and says:
This is the pattern of 2. Use counters to show what the other dice patterns look like.

If pupils construct all the numbers in a linear form, this may indicate poor pattern recognition skills. It may also be that they did not fully understand the instruction. Show them the dice and ask them to copy the patterns.

Some pupils place counters too far apart. This indicates poor pattern recognition. Teach pupils to make patterns that are reasonably compact to ensure that patterns are easily distinguishable.

Give the pupil a sheet of squared paper.

Draw the dot pattern of 2.

If pupils find it difficult to draw, they can use sticker dots to create the patterns.

What did you draw?

If the pupil says 'drawed' instead of 'drew', do not correct them. Say: *Yes, you drew the pattern of 2.*

Ask the pupil to draw the patterns of 3, 4, 5 and 6.

Pupil says how many dots there are on each pattern.

Pupil constructs the patterns.
Pupils with poor pattern recognition skills may need to count each dot as they look at a pattern; allow them to do so. They may need to do this repeatedly until they are able to recognise the pattern without counting.

Pupil draws two dots to show 2. Note that the orientation of the dots does not matter; they do need to be reasonably close together.

I drew the pattern of 2.

Doubles patterns 2, 4, 6, 8, 10

Allow pupils plenty of time to think as many pupils find this a difficult task.

Teacher makes the dice patterns from 1 to 6, placing the patterns of 2 and 3 in a vertical orientation.

Teachers points to the pattern of 2.

Look at 2. Two is made of 1 and 1.

If the pupil queries the vertical representation of the pattern of 2, explain that the way the counters are orientated does not affect the value. Putting the counters vertically makes it easier to compare the components of numbers.

Teacher points to the pattern of 4.
Look at 4. What can you see?
What is 4 made of?

I can see 4 counters.
4 is made of 2 and 2. 2 and 2 is 4.
2 twos make 4.
Any sensible explanation is acceptable.

Teacher points to the pattern of 6.
Look at 6. What can you see?

I can see 6 counters. 6 is made of 3 and 3.
3 and 3 makes 6.
2 threes make 6.

Give pupils a bowl of counters. Encourage pupils to talk about what they doing as they carry out the instruction.

4 and 6 are called doubles numbers. A doubles number is made by adding a number to itself. I want you to make some more doubles numbers.

Make the pattern of 8.
Make a pattern of 4, then make another pattern of 4 underneath it.

Pupil makes two patterns of 4 leaving a slight gap between the top and the bottom patterns. It is important that the pattern of 8 is clearly seen as a repeat of the pattern of 4 rather than two vertical lines of 4 each.

What can you see?

I can see 8 counters.
8 is made of 4 and 4, so 4 and 4 makes 8.
2 fours make 8.

Make the pattern of 10.
Make a pattern of 5, then make another pattern of 5 underneath it.

It is important that a small gap is left between one 5 and the other so that it is easy to see that the pattern of 10 is double 5.

What can you see?

I can see 10 counters.
10 is made of 5 and 5. 5 and 5 makes 10.
2 fives make 10

10 is a doubles number. It is made of 5 and 5.

Near doubles patterns 3, 5, 7, and 9

Discuss the patterns that are *1 more than*, or *1 less than* a double; always point to the dot pattern that is being discussed.

3 and 5 are near doubles numbers. A near doubles number is between two doubles numbers. It is one more than the smaller doubles number. It is one less than the bigger doubles number.

Teacher puts out dot patterns to 6, and points to each number as it is mentioned.

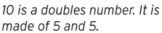 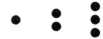

Look at the pattern of 3. 3 is between 2 and 4. 2 is a doubles number. 4 is a doubles number. 3 is one more than 2. 3 is one less than 4.

Look at the pattern of 5.
Can you tell me about 5?

Pupil describes 5 in terms of the numbers next to it, pointing to each number as it is said.
5 is between 4 and 6.
5 is one more than 4.
5 is one less than 6.

Develop the pattern of 9 by relating 9 to 8.

Make the pattern of 8.

Pupil makes the pattern of 8 and explains that it is made of 4 and 4.

Which number is one more than 8?

One more than 8 is 9.

How can you change 8 into 9?
Add one more counter to show the pattern of 9.

I can add one more to 8 to make 9.

Pupil places one more counter to show how the patterns of 4 and 5 make 9.
4 and 4 makes 8 so 4 and 5 makes 9.

Develop the pattern of 9 by relating 9 to 10

If the pupil found it easy to do the task above, suggest they derive the pattern of 9 from the pattern of 10. If the pupil had difficulty, do not confuse them by exploring this alternative method.

Make the pattern of 10.
How can you change 10 into 9?

I can take one away from 10 to make 9.
9 is one less than 10. If I make the pattern of 10 and take away one, I will have 9 counters.
9 is made of 5 and 4.

Pupils put the patterns of 8, 9 and 10 in the correct place in the sequence when they have derived them.

Develop the pattern of 7 by using the patterns of 4 and 3.

Which number is one more than 6?

7 is one more than 6.

Which number is one less than 8?

7 is one less than 8.

Make the pattern of 8.
How many counters are there?

There are 8 counters.

Take away 1 counter. How many counters are there?

I take away 1 counter so there are 7 counters.
7 is made of 4 and 3.

Move the counters to show that 7 is made of the pattern of 4 and the pattern of 3.

If pupils have difficulty, the teacher demonstrates the pattern of 7.

If pupils prefer to show 7 as 3 and 4 allow them to do so but only teach one orientation.

Draw the dot patterns

Give pupils squared paper. Ask them to write each number from 1 to 10 and draw the dot pattern.
Pupils with spatial difficulties may need guidance as to where to start each pattern on the page.
Pupils who find drawing very difficult can create the dot patterns using dot stickers.

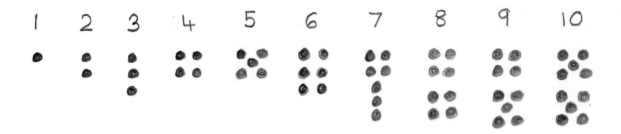

Developing dot patterns

The Canonical Dice Patterns

Dot Patterns

DOUBLES

Making 4 from twos

This is the pattern of 2.
If I add 2 more, I will have 4 counters.

This is the pattern of 4.
I can see a 2 and a 2 inside the pattern of 4.
4 is made of 2 and 2.
2 and 2 makes 4.
4 is double 2, so double 2 is 4.

Making 6 from threes

This is the pattern of 3.
If I add another 3, I will have 6 counters.

This is the pattern of 6.
I can see a 3 and a 3 inside the pattern of 6.
6 is made of 3 and 3.
3 and 3 makes 6.
6 is double 3, so double 3 is 6.

Making 8 from fours

This is the pattern of 4.
If I add 4 more, I will have 8 counters.

This is the pattern of 8.
I can see a 4 and a 4 inside the pattern of 8.
8 is made of 4 and 4.
4 and 4 makes 8.
8 is double 4, so double 4 is 8.

Making 10 from fives

This is the pattern of 5.
If I add another 5, I will have 10 counters.

This is the pattern of 10.
I can see a 5 and a 5 inside the pattern of 10.
10 is made of 5 and 5.
5 and 5 makes 10.
10 is double 5, so double 5 is 10.

NEAR DOUBLES

Making 9 - one more than 8

This is the pattern of 8.
If I add one more to 8, I will have 9.

This is the pattern of 9.
9 is made of 5 and 4.
5 and 4 makes 9.
9 is made of 4 and 5.
4 and 5 is 9.

Making 7 from 4 and 3

This is the pattern of 4.

This is the pattern of 3.

This is the pattern of 7.
7 is made of 4 and 3.
4 and 3 makes 7.
7 is made of 3 and 4.
3 and 4 is 7.

Pattern Match 1 to 10

Aims
- To recognise dot patterns
- To sequence numbers from 1 to 10

Equipment
- Number cards 1 to 10 (one set for each player)
- Pattern cards 1 to 10 (one set for each player)
- 1 to 10 dice

1 - 10
Number cards

1 - 10
Pattern cards

How to play
Players put their number cards in sequence in a line. Place the pattern cards face up, randomly in the middle of the table.

Player A rolls the dice and takes the pattern card that matches the number. Player puts the card in the correct position on their number sequence.

Player B has a turn.

If a player throws a number that they have already thrown, they miss a turn.

The winner is the first person to cover all the numbers in their sequence.

Cards in play:

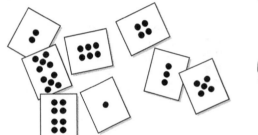

Player A rolls 7 and puts the pattern of 7 over the number card in the sequence.

| 1 | 2 | 3 | 4 | 5 | 6 | ⋮ | 8 | 9 | 10 |

Checklist - Dot patterns 1 to 10: doubles and near doubles
Pupils can:
- ☐ Recognise, recall and draw the dice patterns 1 to 6
- ☐ Construct dot patterns for numbers 7, 8, 9, 10
- ☐ Use the terms double and half to describe the relationship between a doubles number and its components
- ☐ Draw accurate dot patterns of doubles and near doubles patterns
- ☐ Describe the relationship between doubles numbers and near doubles numbers
- ☐ Sequence the dot patterns from 1 to 10
- ☐ Match numerals to dot patterns

Compare numbers using Cuisenaire rods

Objectives

- Sequence numbers to 10 using Cuisenaire rods
- Demonstrate that each number in the sequence is 1 more, or 1 less, than the adjacent number
- Explain how each number in the sequence is 1 more, or 1 less, than the adjacent number
- Use the words order, size, length

When pupils can count reliably to 10, introduce Cuisenaire rods. This equipment helps pupils move away from 'ones based thinking' towards cognitive and conceptual models which can be used for calculation. For example, they see the 'fiveness' of 5, rather than a 'clump' of five ones. Provide a box of Cuisenaire rods for each pupil. Initially pupils should play with the rods. They will discover the relationships between them by making structures and patterns, then drawing the patterns (see Appendix (p237) for preliminary Cuisenaire activities).

The dot patterns show how the sequence of numbers becomes larger as it progresses from 1 to 10. Each number has a distinct and memorable pattern; however the fact that each number is 1 more or 1 less than the numbers adjacent to it is not immediately apparent in the images. Cuisenaire rods make this property of the sequence of counting numbers clear.

The dot pattern work showed the discrete aspect of numbers; the Cuisenaire rods represent numbers in continuous form. They provide a link between the counting numbers and the measuring numbers. Although the rods are compatible with standard metric units, do not introduce the concept of formal measurement at this stage. When pupils are familiar with the rods, they can be used in structured ways for comparing and sequencing numbers, for adding, subtracting, multiplying and dividing, and later for fraction work.

Teaching

Sequencing numbers to 10

Give pupils a box of Cuisenaire rods. Pupils build the sequence of rods and talk about them in relative terms. Do some of the introductory exercises described in Appendix 3 (p237).

Take one rod of each colour. Put them next to each other in order of size. The pattern will look like a staircase.

When pupils have made the pattern, ask them to name each rod from 1 (white) to 10 (orange).

Point to 5.

What is one more than 5?

Pupils may find this difficult. If they make errors, ask them to use the unit cubes (white) to help them measure the other rods. Offer encouragement and allow them plenty of time to explore the relationships.

Pupil points to the 5 rod (yellow).

5 and 1 is 6 so 6 is one more than 5.

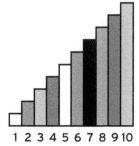

1 2 3 4 5 6 7 8 9 10

Cuisenaire rods showing the numbers 1 to 10

The Staircase Game

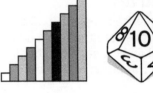

Aims
- To build a sequence using Cuisenaire rods
- To develop the concept of comparison
- To develop a strong visual image of comparative size

Equipment
- Cuisenaire rods (1 to 10) for each player
- 1-10 dice

How to play
Players compete to build their own sequences of rods.

Player A throws the dice and takes the matching Cuisenaire rod.

Player B has a turn.

If a player throws a number they have already taken, they miss a turn.

The winner is the first person to build a sequence of 4 consecutive rods.

Example of play:

Player A

Player B

A winning sequence - 7, 8, 9, 10.

Player A wins with 7, 8, 9, 10. They have also thrown 1 and 3 during the game and placed these in the correct positions.

(The game can be continued by playing the first to get 5 rods in sequence. For a longer version play the first to get 10 rods in a row.)

Checklist - Compare numbers using Cuisenaire rods
Pupils can:
- ☐ Sequence numbers to 10 using Cuisenaire rods
- ☐ Demonstrate that each number in the sequence is 1 more, or 1 less, than the adjacent number
- ☐ Explain how each number in the sequence is 1 more, or 1 less, than the adjacent number
- ☐ Use the words order, size, length

2

Numbers to 10: Calculation

Calculation to 10 is the bedrock of all future calculation. It is imperative that pupils know the key facts, which are the doubles and near doubles bonds, and the bonds of 10. Efficient calculation strategies with larger quantities rely on reasoning from these basic number facts. The strategies of generalisation, bridging through 10, and partitioning are discussed in detail in Chapter 4 and Chapter 6.

Provided that they understand how the components of numbers are related to each other, pupils only need to learn a few key facts. All the other number facts can be derived by reasoning from these. The doubles and near doubles bonds are implicit in the dot patterns. Then pupils learn the bonds of 10. Addition is a commutative operation which means that the order in which numbers are added does not affect the outcome. If pupils know that 1 + 9 = 10 they also know that 9 + 1 = 10. Subtraction is not commutative; the order in which the numbers are subtracted is critical. 7 - 2 = 5 whereas 2 - 7 will give a negative result. Addition and subtraction are inverse operations; this means that they have the opposite effect on each other so that 2 + 3 = 5 can also be expressed as 5 - 2 = 3 and 5 - 3 = 2.

Pupils use informal methods to record their thinking. The triad, sometimes called a number triple, shows the relationship between a number and its components. Pupils use counters and Cuisenaire rods to investigate the relationships between numbers. They develop logical reasoning skills by talking about what they are doing and recording their thinking in pictures, diagrams, triads and equations. Pupils should also solve and construct simple word problems to place numbers in context. (See Word Problems p216)

Do not rush this work. Establishing a sound knowledge of the key number bonds takes time.

Equipment

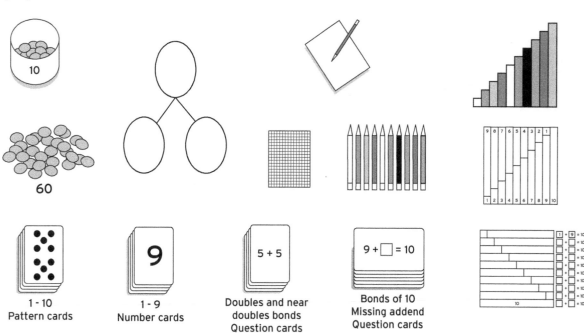

1 - 10
Pattern cards

1 - 9
Number cards

Doubles and near
doubles bonds
Question cards

Bonds of 10
Missing addend
Question cards

Early calculation: add 1 or 2, subtract 1 or 2

Objectives
- Add 1
- Add 2
- Subtract 1
- Subtract 2
- Vocabulary of addition: add, plus, increase, more
- Vocabulary of subtraction: subtract, take away, minus, decrease, difference, less

Early calculation is the ability to add 1 or 2 to a number, or subtract 1 or 2 from a number. Plenty of time spent consolidating this point will avoid many problems in calculation later. It is particularly important that pupils learn to record their work in equations.

Start by working on addition until pupils can confidently add 1 or 2 to a number. Then work on subtract 1 and subtract 2.

Pupils who have a grasp of the forward number sequence can quickly name the number that is 1 or 2 more than a number. If they are not able to do this, do more counting activities and sequencing with number cards. (See Chapter 1, p14.) Counting forward or backward a short distance may be a fall back strategy when pupils forget more sophisticated ways of calculating.

Potential sources of difficulty are:
- confusion about where to start when counting on, or back, in the number sequence
- lack of understanding of the concept of 'more than' and 'less than' (see p9 for activities to teach comparative vocabulary)
- the language of addition and subtraction
- writing equations for subtraction.

Many different words are used to describe the operations of addition and subtraction. It is important that pupils learn to use this vocabulary when they are working with small numbers. It is particularly important that pupils learn to use the word 'subtract' as well as 'take away' in the early stages. Subtraction is the operation used when a quantity is removed from an amount, and to find the difference between two quantities. Pupils who only associate the subtraction sign (-) with the term 'take away' may find it difficult to work with calculations involving the concepts of difference and equalising. This is discussed on p85-86.

Teaching

Oral revision: 1 more, 2 more
Start by checking 2 more as this will uncover any confusion the pupil may have about the starting point. Pupils should be able to respond rapidly without having to use their fingers or counting from the beginning.

What is 2 more than 7?

Check a few more examples using 1 more and 2 more.

What is 1 more than 4?
What is 2 more than 6?
What is 1 more than 9?
What is 2 more than 7?

Pupils may say 9, or count on aloud saying 8, 9. Either is acceptable. However, some pupils say 8 instead of 9 because they are confused about where to start in the count because they are not sure whether to include 7 and so count 7, 8. They need to work with counters until they are sure about where to start the count.

Concrete work: add 1, add 2

Give pupil a handful of counters (less than ten).

Put the counters in a line. How many are there?

Add 1 more. How many are there now?

Do several more concrete examples.

Give pupil some counters.
Count these. How many counters are there?

Add 2 more. How many are there?

> Pupil puts the counters in a line and says:
> *There are [number of] counters.* They recount to check if necessary.
> Pupil should be able to place one more counter and immediately say how many there are.
>
> Pupil puts the counters in a line and says:
> *There are [number of] counters.*
>
> Pupils should be able to answer quickly without using their fingers to count on. If they have to return to the beginning and count all the counters from the beginning, they will need plenty of practice before moving on.

Mental maths: add 1, add 2

Ask oral questions using a variety of language. Pupils should write the equation as well as giving the answer verbally.

What is 5 add 1? Write the equation.
Teacher demonstrates if necessary.

What is 1 more than 7?

Add 1 to 4.
What does 3 and 1 make?
Find 1 more than 9.
Increase 6 by 1.
What is 2 more than 5?
Add 2 to 6.
Count on 2 from 4.
Find 2 more than 8.
Increase 5 by 2.

> Pupil says the answer in a sentence: *5 add 1 is 6.* Then they write the equation $5 + 1 = 6$.
>
> Note that addition is commutative so it does not matter whether the pupil writes $1 + 7 = 8$ or $7 + 1 = 8$.
>
> Allow pupils to start with the smaller number if they wish to do so and are able to do so. Do not insist that pupils always start with the larger number. They need to learn that the order in which numbers are added does not affect the result.

Oral revision: 1 less, 2 less

Begin work with 1 less to make sure that pupils are clear about the meaning. Pupils should be able to respond rapidly without using their fingers or counting the whole sequence.

What is 1 less than 7?

Check a few more examples using 1 less and 2 less.

What is 1 less than 8?
What is 2 less than 7?
What is 1 less than 5?
What is 2 less than 9?

> Pupils may say 6, or count back aloud saying: *7, 6 so the answer is 6.* Either is acceptable.
>
> However, some pupils may be slow to give an answer. Ask them how they did it. Some pupils may count the whole sequence, starting from 1. When they reach 7 they realise that 6 came before 7, therefore 1 less than 7 will be 6. Pupils often do this silently, or subtly move their fingers. If they have difficulty at this point, do more work on sequencing (see p9).

Concrete work: subtract 1, subtract 2

Give pupil a handful of counters (less than 10).

Put the counters in a line. *How many are there?*

Take away 1. *How many are there now?*

Do a few more concrete examples subtracting 1 and subtracting 2.

Give pupil some counters.
Count these. How many counters are there? Take away 2. How many are there?

Pupil puts the counters in a line and says: *There are [number of] counters.* They recount to check if necessary.

Pupil should be able to remove 1 counter and immediately say how many there are. If they cannot do this but have to remove 1 counter and then return to the beginning and count all the remaining counters, they will need plenty of practice before moving on.

Mental maths: subtract 1, subtract 2

Ask oral questions using a variety of language for subtraction. Pupils should write the equation as well as giving the answer verbally. This is important for subtraction where the order of the numbers in the question may be different to the order they are written in the equation. Pupils need to understand that a question such as *What is 2 less than 8?* requires the operation 8 subtract 2.

What is 9 take away 1?

What does 3 subtract 1 make?
Find 1 less than 7.
Decrease 6 by 1.
What is 2 less than 5?
What is the difference between 9 and 7?
Take 2 away from 6.
Count back 2 from 4.
Find 2 less than 8.
5 minus 2.

Pupil says the answer in a sentence: *9 take away 1 is 8.*
Then they write the equation $9 - 1 = 8$.

Subtraction is not commutative so pupils must start with the larger number. If they do not do this, they need to use counters to demonstrate the calculation before writing the equation.

Checklist – Early calculation: add 1 or 2, subtract 1 or 2

Pupils can:
- ☐ Add 1
- ☐ Add 2
- ☐ Subtract 1
- ☐ Subtract 2
- ☐ Use vocabulary of addition: add, plus, increase, more
- ☐ Use vocabulary of subtraction: subtract , take away, minus, decrease by, difference, less

Key facts: doubles and near doubles bonds

Objectives
- Recognise the doubles and near doubles bonds in the dot patterns
- Learn the addition and subtraction facts for the doubles and near doubles to 5 + 5
- Use counters to demonstrate the meaning of number components
- Use triads to record doubles and near doubles bonds
- Write equations for doubles and near doubles bonds to 5 + 5 = 10
- Solve simple word problems (see examples p219)

Pupils learn the doubles and near doubles facts of the numbers to 10. Later these facts will be generalised for calculating with larger numbers. Pupils need to be able to recall the doubles and near doubles bonds quickly in order to use them effectively.

The dot patterns present visual images which make it clear that each number is composed of subsets. Pupils investigate and record the relationship between a number and its components. At this stage pupils only work with the doubles and near doubles components. Do not investigate all the bonds of each number, these will come later. (See p50.)

Do not rush this work. Being allowed to take the time needed to think clearly reduces anxiety. Note that the learning is in the talking and reasoning the pupils do while constructing the patterns and recording the information in diagrammatic and written form. Encourage pupils to talk through the process themselves. They should use their own words to explain what they are doing. Any clear explanation from the pupil is acceptable.

Triads
A triad is a diagram that shows how a number can be split into two components (see diagram below). The number is written in the top oval and its components are written in the lower ovals. A triad is sometimes called a triple. A triad makes the relationship between addition and subtraction clear. Addition is commutative: the order in which the quantities are added does not affect the result. Subtraction is not commutative: changing the order does affect the result. Subtraction is the inverse operation to addition. Understanding this is essential for efficient and flexible calculation. Once pupils understand the connection between addition and subtraction, they can use a variety of methods to carry out subtraction calculations.

Pupils need plenty of practice in constructing and recording triads if they are to use them for later calculations with larger numbers. Filling in partially completed triads is a good way to encourage pupils to talk about numbers. When pupils can use triads confidently, they can omit the ovals and write the numbers with the connecting lines. (Note that there is no line linking the two components to each other.)

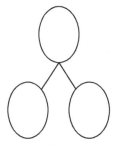

Empty triad

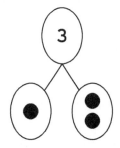

Triad showing bonds of 3

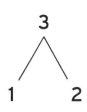

Numbers in triad formation

Equations

An equation is a statement that two expressions have the same value. The equal sign is formed from two parallel lines that are exactly the same length. The equal sign means that the term to the left has exactly the same value as the term to the right. An equation can include a quantity that is not known. The quantity can be found by 'solving' the equation to find out what the unknown quantity is.

Example: $5 = 2 + 3$ $2 + ? = 5$ $5 - 2 = ?$

Allow pupils to use the term 'number sentence' instead of 'equation' if they prefer to do so. Some pupils may feel anxious if they do not know the word equation so model the use of both terms if appropriate.

Steps in the teaching process:
- Use counters to make the number patterns on a triad.
- Move the counters on the triad mat to show the components of the number.
- Draw a diagram of the triad to record the relationships informally.
- Write the equations represented by the triad. These are $N = a + b$, $N = b + a$, $a + b = N$, $b + a = N$, $N - a = b$, $N - b = a$ where N is the whole quantity and a and b are the components.
  (At this stage the forms $a = N - b$ and $b = N - a$ are omitted as they may cause visual confusion.)
- Complete partially completed triads and do missing number exercises.

Teaching

Ask pupil to use counters to make the dot patterns from 1 to 10. They should be able to do this reasonably quickly. If they are unsure, consolidate knowledge of dot patterns before continuing.

Teacher draws a large triad mat on A4 paper and uses it to show how to split a number into its components. Teacher demonstrates whilst speaking.

Bonds of 2

This shape is called a triad. Make the pattern of 2 in the oval at the top of the triad. 2 is made of 1 and 1 so I can split the pattern of 2 into the components 1 and 1.

Teacher moves the counters into the bottom ovals of the triad. There is one counter in each of the lower ovals. Teacher points to the counters whilst saying: *2 is made of 1 and 1.*

Teacher demonstrates how to record the triads in diagrammatic and numerical form.

Draw the pattern of 2. Draw a triad. Write number 2 at the top. Draw the pattern of 1 in each of the bottom ovals. Draw another triad. Write the number 2 at the top. 2 is made of 1 and 1 so write the number 1 in the bottom ovals.

Ask the pupil to demonstrate.

Use counters to show how you can split 2 into 1 and 1 on the triad mat. Explain what you are doing. Record what you have done in your book.

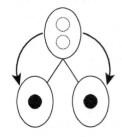

Triad of 2

It is important that the pupil explains what they are doing and thinking as they move the counters and do their recordings.

The triad form encapsulates the addition and subtraction bonds of a number. Pupils write the equations that the triad represents.

You can write equations that tell you about the numbers in the triad. What is 2 made of?

Write that as an equation. Start with 2 equals.

2 is made of 1 and 1.

Pupil writes $2 = 1 + 1$. Some pupils find it difficult to understand that the equation can be written this way. Encourage them to say 2 equals 1 and 1 as they write the equation.

Look at the counters. 1 and 1 make 2. Write an equation starting with 1 + 1 =

Teacher uses counters on the triad mat to show that 2 is made of 1 and 1.

How many counters can you see altogether?

Teacher covers one counter whilst speaking.

There are 2 counters. I take away 1. How many counters are there?

2 take away 1 is 1. Write that as an equation.

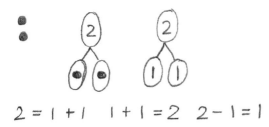

$$2 = 1 + 1 \quad 1 + 1 = 2 \quad 2 - 1 = 1$$

Triads and equations showing the bonds of 2

Pupil writes 1 + 1 = 2 and says: *1 and 1 equals 2.*

I can see 2 counters.

There is 1 counter.

Pupil writes 2 - 1 = 1 and says: *2 take away 1 equals 1.*

Bonds of 3

The pupil investigates the bonds of 3 by demonstrating with counters on a triad mat, recording the information as triads and equations. They explain each step as they do it. At first the teacher may need to help by reminding pupils of each step.

Now we will look at 3. Make the pattern of 3 on the triad mat.

Split 3 into 1 and 2.

Pupil makes the pattern of 3. Pupil moves the counters into the lower ovals so that there is 1 counter in the first oval and 2 counters in the other oval.

I split 3 into 1 and 2.

Record the triads in your book to show the patterns and the numbers.

Write the number 3 at the top of the first triad. Look at the concrete model. How many counters are in each lower oval? Draw the counters in your book.

Write the number 3 at the top of the next triad. Look at the diagram you have drawn. Write the numbers in the triad.

Write the equations. 3 is made of 1 and 2. Start with 3 equals.

Write an equation starting with 1 plus 2.

Teacher points to the concrete model.
How many counters can you see altogether?

Teacher covers the pattern of 1 whilst saying:
I take away 1. How many counters can you see?

3 take away 1 is 2. Write that as an equation.

Pupil draws the pattern of 3 and two empty triads alongside the pattern.

There is 1 counter and 2 counters.
Pupil writes 3 in the top oval and draws the pattern of 1 and the pattern of 2 in the lower ovals.

Pupils complete the diagram. It is important that the order of the numerals accurately reflect the patterns in the diagram.

Pupil writes 3 = 1 + 2
Encourage pupil to say *3 equals 1 add 2* or *3 equals 1 plus 2* as they write the equation.

Pupil writes 1 + 2= 3 and says: *1 plus 2 equals 3.*

There are 3 counters.

There are 2 counters left.

Pupil writes 3 - 1 = 2 and says: *3 take away 1 equals 2.*

Next the pupil writes the other possible equations.

The teacher points to the pattern of 2 followed by the pattern of 1. *You can also see that 3 is made of 2 and 1.*

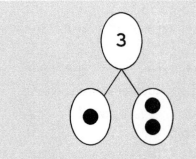

Write the equation for 3 equals 2 and 1.

Write an equation starting with 2 and 1

Teacher points to the concrete model. *How many counters can you see altogether?*

Teacher covers the pattern of 2 counters whilst saying: *There are 3 counters. I take away 2. Write the equation for 3 take away 2.*

Pupil writes 3 = 2 + 1 and says: *3 equals 2 add 1.*

Pupil writes 2 + 1 = 3 and says: *2 plus 1 equals 3.*

There are 3 counters altogether.

Pupil writes 3 - 2 = 1 and says: *3 take away 2 equals 1.*

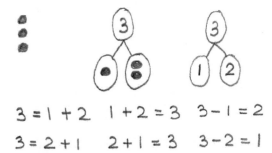

$$3 = 1 + 2 \quad 1 + 2 = 3 \quad 3 - 1 = 2$$
$$3 = 2 + 1 \quad 2 + 1 = 3 \quad 3 - 2 = 1$$

Triads and equations showing the bonds of 3

Key facts: Doubles and near doubles bonds for numbers to 10

Pupils repeat the investigation for each of the remaining doubles and near doubles patterns.

2 + 2   2 + 3   3 + 3   3 + 4   4 + 4   4 + 5   5 + 5

Pupils use counters to represent each of the dot patterns and record them in triad formation and as equations. Pupils use their own words to explain what they are doing. Any clear explanation is acceptable. When pupils are familiar with the triads, omit the ovals in the numerical recording. This both saves time and prepares them for using the triad in calculations where the use of the ovals would clutter up their working.

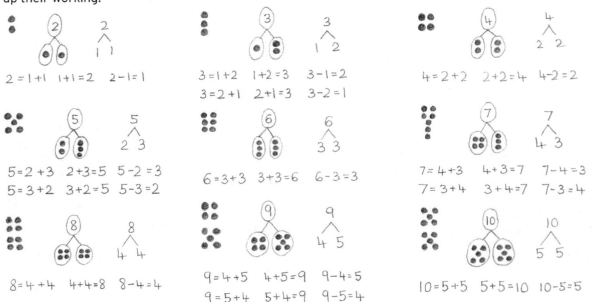

$$2 = 1 + 1 \quad 1 + 1 = 2 \quad 2 - 1 = 1$$

$$3 = 1 + 2 \quad 1 + 2 = 3 \quad 3 - 1 = 2$$
$$3 = 2 + 1 \quad 2 + 1 = 3 \quad 3 - 2 = 1$$

$$4 = 2 + 2 \quad 2 + 2 = 4 \quad 4 - 2 = 2$$

$$5 = 2 + 3 \quad 2 + 3 = 5 \quad 5 - 2 = 3$$
$$5 = 3 + 2 \quad 3 + 2 = 5 \quad 5 - 3 = 2$$

$$6 = 3 + 3 \quad 3 + 3 = 6 \quad 6 - 3 = 3$$

$$7 = 4 + 3 \quad 4 + 3 = 7 \quad 7 - 4 = 3$$
$$7 = 3 + 4 \quad 3 + 4 = 7 \quad 7 - 3 = 4$$

$$8 = 4 + 4 \quad 4 + 4 = 8 \quad 8 - 4 = 4$$

$$9 = 4 + 5 \quad 4 + 5 = 9 \quad 9 - 4 = 5$$
$$9 = 5 + 4 \quad 5 + 4 = 9 \quad 9 - 5 = 4$$

$$10 = 5 + 5 \quad 5 + 5 = 10 \quad 10 - 5 = 5$$

Key facts: doubles and near doubles bonds shown as triads and equations

Pattern Pairs

A matching and memory game

Aim
- To learn the doubles and near doubles bonds
- To develop concentration

Equipment
- Dot pattern cards
- Doubles and near doubles question cards

(Pattern cards and question cards are different colours. If there are three or more players use two packs of each set of cards.)

1 - 10
Pattern cards

Doubles and near
doubles bonds
Question cards

How to play
Spread all the pattern cards and question cards, face down, on the table. Place cards in rows and columns to make it easier to remember where cards are.

The first player turns up a question card. They read the question and say what the total is. They then turn up a pattern card. If they are a matching pair they keep them and have another turn.

If the player does not find a matching pair, they turn the cards face down. It is very important that cards always remain in the same position on the table.

The next player has a turn.

The winner is the person with the most pairs when all the cards have been collected.

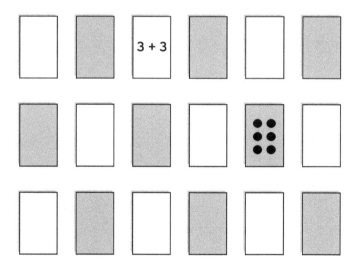

Checklist – Key facts: doubles and near doubles bonds
Pupils can:
- ☐ Use counters to demonstrate the meaning of number components
- ☐ Use triads to record doubles and near doubles bonds
- ☐ Write all equations represented by triads
- ☐ Quickly recall the doubles and near doubles bonds
- ☐ Solve simple word problems (see examples p219)

Double and half: language and concept

Objectives

- Demonstrate the concept of double as repetition of a quantity
- Demonstrate the concept of half as two equal parts of a quantity
- Use terms double and half appropriately

The word 'double' was introduced with the dot patterns. Now pupils explore the concepts of 'double' and 'half' in more detail. These concepts are very important as they are used extensively in mathematics to make calculations easier to understand.

A quantity is doubled by adding the same amount to it. To halve a quantity means to split it into two equal sized parts. Later pupils will learn that you can double a quantity by multiplying it by 2, and halve a quantity by dividing it by 2.

It is important that pupils use their own words to describe what they are doing. The kind of language they need to be able to use eventually is: *2 and 2 is 4. Double 2 is 4. Half of 4 is 2. 2 is half of 4.* Suggested scripts are used for convenience. However, pupils will learn and understand far better if they are allowed to use their own expressions rather than learning a definition. Any explanations that convey the idea of double and half are acceptable.

Teaching

Let's double it

Use counters to demonstrate double and half. The teacher points to the corresponding counters whilst modelling the appropriate language. Many pupils associate the word 'double' with the number 2 only, at first. They need plenty of practice using concrete materials and becoming familiar with the language.

We are going to talk about the numbers in another way. We will use the words double and half. To double means to add a number to itself.

Double 2

Teacher puts out 2 counters.
How many counters can you see?

I can see 2 counters.

Can you double that? Show me with counters.

Pupil puts out two more counters to make the pattern of 4.

What did you do?

I doubled 2 by adding 2 more counters.

Other ways of expressing this idea are:
4 is double 2. If you double 2 you get 4.

Double 3

Make the pattern of 3 then double it. Tell me what you are doing.

Pupil puts out 3 counters then puts out 3 more counters. *I have 3 counters: I add 3 more counters. There are 6 counters. Double 3 is 6.*

Other ways of expressing this idea are:
6 is double 3, or I doubled 3 to make 6.

Double 4

Show me 4 then double it. Tell me what you are doing.

Pupil puts out 4 counters then adds 4 more counters. *There are 4 counters.*
I add 4 more counters. There are 8 counters.
I have doubled 4. Double 4 is 8.

Other ways of expressing this idea are:
8 is double 4, I doubled 4 to make 8.

Double 5

Show me 5 then double it. Tell me what you are doing.

Pupil puts out 5 counters then adds 5 more counters explaining: *There are 5 counters. I add 5 more counters. There are 10 counters. I have doubled 5. Double 5 is 10.*

Other ways of expressing this idea are: *10 is double 5, I doubled 5 to make 10*

Let's halve it

Now we will find out what half means. To find half a number you split it into two equal parts. (At this stage do not use the word divide.)

The teacher puts out 2 counters. *I can see 2 counters. I am going to find half of 2.*

The teacher places a pencil between the counters and says: *I split 2 in half. I split 2 into 1 and 1.* Teacher points to the counters and says: *Half of 2 is 1. 1 is half of 2.*

Half of 4

Make the pattern of 4.

Can you show me half of 4?

Pupil puts out 4 counters.

The pupil demonstrates half of 4. The pupil may place a pencil between the two halves, or move the counters apart. Accept any indication that makes it clear that 2 is half of 4.

What did you do to 4?

I split 4 into 2 and 2. 2 is half of 4.

Half of 6

Make the pattern of 6. What is half of 6?

Pupil puts out the pattern of 6 and demonstrates that 3 is half of 6. *3 is half of 6. Half of 6 is 3.*

Half of 8

Make the pattern of 8. What is half of 8?

Pupil puts out the pattern of 8 and demonstrates that 4 is half of 8. *4 is half of 8. Half of 8 is 4.*

Half of 10

Make the pattern of 10. What is half of 10?

Pupil puts out the pattern of 10 and demonstrates that 5 is half of 10. *5 is half of 10. Half of 10 is 5.*

Checklist - Double and half: language and concept

Pupils can:

☐ Demonstrate the concept of double as repetition of a quantity
☐ Demonstrate the concept of half as two equal parts of a quantity
☐ Use the terms double and half appropriately

Double and half: the linear model to 5 + 5

Objectives

- Demonstrate the concept of double as repetition of a quantity using a linear model
- Demonstrate the concept of half as two equal parts of a quantity using a linear model
- Use the terms double and half appropriately
- Draw diagrams to show the doubles to 5 + 5
- Write equations for the doubles to 5 + 5 = 10

Introduce a linear model of double and half by using Cuisenaire rods.

Teaching

Doubles using Cuisenaire rods

Can you remember how you double a number?

Accept any response which contains the idea that to double a number means to add the same quantity again.

Teacher puts out a single cube (white): *This is 1. Can you show me double 1? Can you tell me what it makes?*

Pupil places another 1 cube next to it: *1 and 1 makes 2. Double 1 is 2.*

Build the next double pattern. Take a 2 rod and double it. Place it below the ones.

Pupil takes a 2 rod (red): *This is 2. I can double 2 by adding another 2 rod.*
Pupil puts the rods next to each other to form a line: *2 and 2 is 4. Double 2 is 4.*

Build double 3.
Encourage pupils to explain what they are doing. Only prompt them if they have difficulty.

Pupil uses the 3 rod (light green) to build double 3 and places it in the correct position under double 2.
This is 3. I can double 3 by adding another 3 rod. 3 and 3 is 6. Double 3 is 6.

Build double 4.

Pupil uses the 4 rod (purple) to build double 4 and places it under double 3.
This is 4. I can double 4 by adding another 4 rod. 4 and 4 is 8. Double 4 is 8.

Build double 5.

Pupil uses the 5 rod (yellow) to build double 5 and places it on the model under double 4.
This is 5. I can double 5 by adding another 5 rod. 5 and 5 is 10. Double 5 is 10.

Place the pairs of Cuisenaire rods underneath each other in a pyramid shape to emphasise the doubles patterns. Ask the pupil to draw a diagram of the doubles patterns on 1 cm² squared paper and colour it in. Some pupils may need to place the Cuisenaire rods on the paper and draw round each rod. Allow them to do this initially then encourage them to draw the diagram by counting the appropriate number of squares.

Ask the pupil to write the equation next to each doubles pattern.

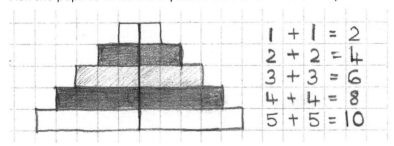

Diagram and equations showing the doubles numbers

Half using Cuisenaire rods

Can you remember how you find half of a number?

Teacher makes the Cuisenaire doubles pyramid to 5 + 5: *Look at the model. Can you split the rods in half?*

Teacher places a pencil on the midline.

Accept any response which contains the idea that to find half of a number you split it into 2 equal parts.

Pupil uses the pencil to moves the rods apart along the mid line. *I split the rods in half.*

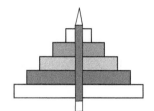

Using a pencil to show the midline

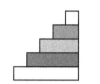

Split the rod pyramid in half

Ask the pupil to investigate each double number in turn using Cuisenaire rods to demonstrate half of each number.

Pupil puts out double 1 and says: *I can see 2.*

Pupil moves the rods apart as they say: *Half of 2 is 1. 1 is half of 2.*

Pupil puts out double 2 and says: *I can see 4.*

Pupil moves rods apart as they say: *Half of 4 is 2. 2 is half of 4.*

Pupil puts out double 3 and says: *I can see 6.*

Pupil moves rods apart as they say: *Half of 6 is 3. 3 is half of 6.*

Pupil puts out double 4 and says: *I can see 8.*

Pupil moves rods apart as they say: *Half of 8 is 4. 4 is half of 8.*

Pupil puts out double 5 and says: *I can see 10.*

Pupil moves rods apart as they say: *Half of 10 is 5. 5 is half of 10.*

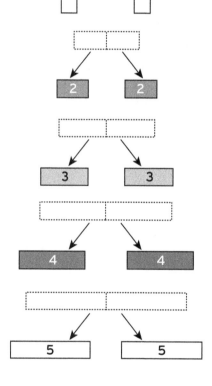

Checklist - Double and half: the linear model to 5 + 5

Pupils can:
- ☐ Demonstrate the concept of double as repetition of a quantity using a linear model
- ☐ Demonstrate the concept of half as two equal parts of a quantity using a linear model
- ☐ Use the terms double and half appropriately
- ☐ Draw diagrams to show the doubles to 5 + 5
- ☐ Write equations for the doubles to 5 + 5 = 10

Doubles and near doubles: developing logical reasoning

Objectives
- Use logical reasoning to explain the relationship between doubles and near doubles numbers
- Draw diagrams to show the doubles and near doubles to 5 + 5
- Write equations for the doubles and near doubles to 5 + 5 = 10

Logical reasoning is the basis of problem solving. This activity introduces this important thinking skill using numbers with which pupils should now be familiar.

Logical reasoning depends on the proposition that if certain information is true, then a particular result must follow. For example, 3 is one more than 2 and 5 is one more than 4. So, if 2 + 2 = 4, then 2 + 3 must equal one more than 4. Therefore, 2 + 3 = 5. If pupils do not understand this, it indicates that they have weak reasoning ability about numbers. Many pupils with poor number sense will treat 2 + 3 as a completely different problem to 2 + 2. They cannot derive a new fact from a known fact. It is quite difficult to explain this idea so allow pupils plenty of time to find their own words to convey the idea.

At this stage continue to relate numbers to each other in terms of double and near double. The concept of odd and even numbers is inherent in the Cuisenaire model. However, odd and even are not taught at this stage. They are introduced on p117.

Teaching

Near doubles
Explore the relationship between the doubles and near doubles numbers one a time. Do not attempt to demonstrate all the facts in one large model as it is visually confusing.

Teacher makes the doubles pattern for 1 + 1 = 2 then places the near doubles pattern for 1 + 2 = 3 below it.

1 and 1 makes 2. One more than 2 is 3, so 1 and 2 must be one more than 2. 1 plus 2 equals 3.

Show me double 2. Tell me what you have done.

Now show me 2 plus 3.

Look at 2 and 3. Can you see it is just one more than 2 and 2? Tell me what you did.

Leave a space then show me double 3. Tell me what you did.

Now make 3 and 4. Tell me what you did.

Pupil makes double 2.
Double 2 is 4. 4 is double 2.

Pupil puts out the Cuisenaire rods and says:
This is 2 and 3.

I know that 2 and 2 makes 4. 2 and 2 make 4 so 2 and 3 must be one more than 4. So 2 and 3 makes 5.

Pupil makes double 3.
Double 3 is 6.

I made 3 and 4.
3 and 3 makes 6, so 3 and 4 must be one more than 6. So 3 and 4 makes 7.

Leave a space then show me double 4. Tell me what you did.

Now make 4 and 5. Tell me what you did.

Pupil makes double 4. *Double 4 is 8.*

I made 4 and 5.
4 and 4 makes 8, so 4 and 5 must be one more than 8. So 4 and 5 makes 9.

4	4
4	5

Pupil draws diagrams to show Cuisenaire doubles and near doubles on squared paper (1 cm²). Leave spaces as shown to ensure that the focus is on a double and the near double that is one more. Ask the pupil to write the equation next to each pattern.

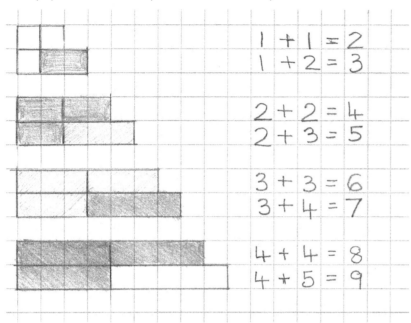

$$1 + 1 = 2$$
$$1 + 2 = 3$$

$$2 + 2 = 4$$
$$2 + 3 = 5$$

$$3 + 3 = 6$$
$$3 + 4 = 7$$

$$4 + 4 = 8$$
$$4 + 5 = 9$$

Checklist – Doubles and near doubles: developing logical reasoning
Pupils can:
- ☐ Use logical reasoning to explain the relationship between doubles and near doubles numbers
- ☐ Draw diagrams to show the doubles and near doubles to 5 + 5
- ☐ Write equations for the doubles and near doubles to 5 + 5 = 10

Key facts: bonds of 10

Objectives
- Learn bonds of 10
- Investigate bonds of 10 using counters
- Reason to derive bonds of 10 starting with dot pattern 5 + 5
- Record information in triads and equations
- Recall bonds of 10 quickly
- Solve word problems (see examples p219)

The bonds of 10 are the most important number facts because they underpin calculation throughout the number system. They are essential for mental calculation strategies such as bridging through the decade numbers. Recall of the pairs of numbers that make 10 should be automatic. Without this knowledge pupils are left with very few strategies for calculating efficiently in the higher decades. If they cannot remember them, pupils must be able to derive them from known facts quickly and efficiently.

The five pairs of numbers that add together to make 10 are: 9 + 1, 8 + 2, 7 + 3, 6 + 4, 5 + 5. If pupils know these facts and understand commutativity, they will also know that 1 + 9, 2 + 8, 3 + 7 and 4 + 6 make 10.

Teaching

Bonds of 10 using dot patterns and triads
Pupils use the triad model to investigate all the bonds of 10. Pupils need to be able to explain what the triad represents. Pupils demonstrate the bonds of 10 on a triad mat. Then they record the information in the triad form and write the equations that the triad represents. (Triads were introduced on p31.)

Summary of investigation:
- Use counters to make the number patterns on a triad mat.
- Move the counters on the triad mat to show the key facts of the number.
- Draw triads to record the relationships in diagrammatic and numerical form.
- Write the equations represented by the triad. Note that pupils do *not* write the equations in the form 5 = 10 - 5 as it often causes confusion at this early stage of developing understanding.

Triads
Give pupil counters and a triad mat.
Make the pattern of 10 on the triad? Tell me what you did.

What is 10 made of?

Split the pattern of 10 into the components 5 and 5. Move the counters onto the lower circles in the triad.

Ask the pupil to record the information. Show the pupil an example if necessary.
Draw a diagram of the pattern of 10 on the top left of the page. Draw two empty triads.

Pupil makes the pattern of 10 on a triad.
I made the pattern of 10.

10 is made of 5 and 5.

Pupil moves the counters to make the pattern of 5 in each of the lower ovals.
10 is made of 5 and 5.

Pupil draws the pattern and the triads.

Write the number 10 in the top of the first triad.
Draw the pattern of 5 in the lower ovals.
Write the number 10 in the top oval of the second triad.
Write the number 5 in each of the lower ovals.
Write the equations that the triad represents.

Pupil writes the number 10 and draws the patterns whilst saying: *10 is made of 5 and 5.*
Pupil writes the number 10 in the top oval and the number 5 in each of the lower ovals whilst saying: *10 is made of 5 and 5.*

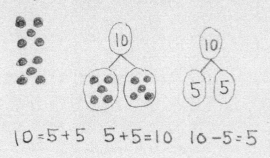

$$10 = 5 + 5 \qquad 5 + 5 = 10 \qquad 10 - 5 = 5$$

The pupil uses the same procedure to investigate the other bonds of 10. It does not matter in which order the pupil chooses to investigate the components of 10. Observe how pupils proceed. Do they work systematically? Can they see that there is a connection between the quantities of counters in the lower ovals of the triad, so that as one quantity increases the other decreases? Dyscalculic pupils often have great difficulty with this exercise as they do not see the patterns. This is an indication that they have not developed strong visual images of the patterns. Note that it is much easier to start with a larger number such as 9 and then add 1 as it is easier to visualise and understand. However pupils also need to be able to start with the smaller number and add the larger number to it.

There is a temptation to tell the pupil to work through the bonds in a systematic order. However, the pupil will learn more if they are allowed time to experiment, make mistakes and work out where they have gone wrong. The example below gives a script for suggested guidance by the teacher. This is only necessary for pupils who are struggling to proceed. Encourage the pupil to work through the examples and explain what they are doing, without the teacher's intervention if possible. They omit the ovals in the numerical representation when they are able to do so.

Make the pattern for 10. Split 10 into two other patterns. Do not use 5 and 5.

Pupil makes 10 on the triad mat, and then shows the components 9 and 1 by moving the counters into the lower ovals.
10 is made of 9 and 1.

Draw a diagram to show what you have done. Explain it as you draw.

Pupil records the information as a triad with the number 10 in the top oval and the patterns of 9 and 1 in the lower ovals.
10 is made of 9 and 1. The pupil may also say: *10 is made of 1 and 9.*

Show the bonds of 10 in numbers as a triad. Look at the model. What is 10 made of?

Pupil writes the number 10 and shows its components in triad formation.
10 is made of 9 and 1.

Equations
Write the equations that the triad represents. Start with 10 equals.

Pupil writes 10 = 9 + 1 whilst saying:
10 equals 9 and 1.

Write the equation starting with 9 plus 1.

Pupil writes 9 + 1 = 10 whilst saying:
9 plus 1 equals 10

Teacher points to the concrete model. *How many counters can you see altogether?*

I can see 10 counters.

Teacher covers the pattern of 9 and says: *I take away 9. Tell me what you see.*

I can see 1 counter.

Write the equation for 10 take away 9.

Pupil writes 10 - 9 = 1 whilst saying:
10 take away 9 equals 1.

Next the pupil writes the other equations represented by the triad.

Teacher points to the relevant counters and says:
There are 10 counters altogether. 10 is made of 9 and 1. You can see that 10 is also made of 1 and 9. Write that as an equation.

Pupil writes 10 = 1 + 9 and says:
10 equals 1 and 9.

Write the equation starting with 1 + 9.

Pupil writes 1 + 9 = 10 and says:
1 add 9 equals 10.

Show me 10 take away 1. Then write the equation.

Pupil covers up the single counter and says:
10 take away 1 leaves 9.

Pupil writes 10 - 1 = 9 and says:
10 take away 1 equals 9

The pupil investigates the three remaining bonds of 10, which are 8 + 2, 7 + 3, and 6 + 4. Encourage them to explain what they are doing as they put out the patterns, complete the triads and write the equations.

Triads and equations

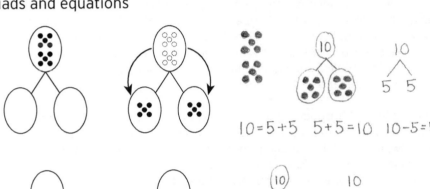

10 = 5 + 5   5 + 5 = 10   10 - 5 = 5

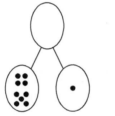 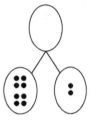

10 = 9 + 1   9 + 1 = 10   10 - 9 = 1   10 = 8 + 2   8 + 2 = 10   10 - 8 = 2
10 = 1 + 9   1 + 9 = 10   10 - 1 = 9   10 = 2 + 8   2 + 8 = 10   10 - 2 = 8

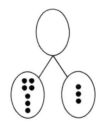 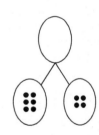 

10 = 7 + 3   7 + 3 = 10   10 - 7 = 3   10 = 6 + 4   6 + 4 = 10   10 - 6 = 4
10 = 3 + 7   3 + 7 = 10   10 - 3 = 7   10 = 4 + 6   4 + 6 = 10   10 - 4 = 6

Checklist - Key facts: bonds of 10
Pupils can:
- ☐ Learn bonds of 10
- ☐ Investigate bonds of 10 using counters
- ☐ Reason to derive bonds of 10 starting with dot pattern 5 + 5
- ☐ Record information in triads and equations
- ☐ Recall bonds of 10 quickly
- ☐ Solve word problems (see examples p219)

Bonds of 10: the linear model using Cuisenaire rods

Objectives

- Investigate bonds of 10 using Cuisenaire rods
- Make the commutative property of addition explicit
- Demonstrate the inverse relationship between addition and subtraction
- Write equations for all the bonds of 10
- Solve simple word problems (see examples p219)

Work with Cuisenaire rods establishes a visual image of the bonds of 10 which can be applied to work with larger numbers. Cuisenaire rods provide a concrete linear model which links the counting numbers to the measuring numbers. This work provides a foundation for work with number lines. Understanding that the value remains the same, whether the rod is horizontal or vertical, will be necessary for later work with graphs.

Teaching

From concrete to abstract

Use Cuisenaire rods to show the bonds of 10. Build a 'staircase' using Cuisenaire rods. Then build a second 'staircase'.

Join the staircases together. You need to turn one staircase so that it will fit onto the other one. Make sure that each pair of rods adds up to 10.

Pupil puts the rods in sequence as a 'staircase' from 1 to 10.

The teacher helps pupils who lack the manual dexterity to move the rods in this way.

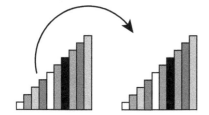 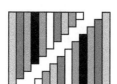

Ask the pupil to draw a diagram of the model on squared paper (1 cm²) and colour it in matching the colours of the rods. Some pupils find it very difficult to do this. In this case, give them a printed sheet to colour with the corresponding colours. (Template on p238)

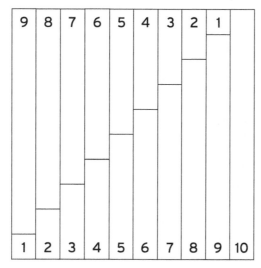

Bonds of 10 base sheet

Equations

Give pupils a printed diagram of the model of the bonds of 10 arranged horizontally. (Template on p239)

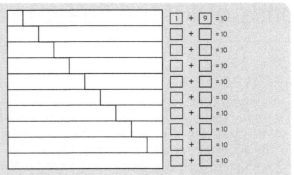

1	+	9	= 10
	+		= 10
	+		= 10
	+		= 10
	+		= 10
	+		= 10
	+		= 10
	+		= 10
	+		= 10
	+		= 10

Put the rods in the correct place on the diagram. Write the numbers of the rods in the equations alongside. Do one row at a time. Explain what you do.

Pupil puts the 1 cube and the 9 rod on the diagram and completes the equation saying:
1 and 9 makes 10.
The pupil continues until all the equations are complete.

The numbers in one column increase as the numbers in the other column decrease.

Look at the numbers in the equations. Can you see a pattern?

There are different ways of expressing this idea. Accept any reasonable explanation such as: *The numbers in the first column get bigger. The numbers in the second column get smaller.*

When pupils have completed the task, they remove the rods and colour the diagram of the rods, the colours corresponding to the Cuisenaire rods. Then pupils draw a diagram of the model on 1 cm² paper, colour it in and write the corresponding equations. They talk about what they are doing.

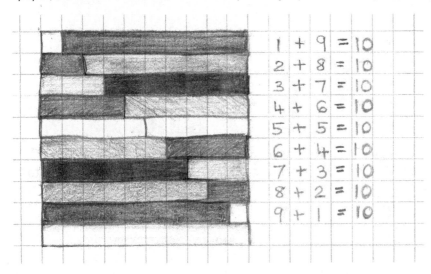

1 + 9 = 10
2 + 8 = 10
3 + 7 = 10
4 + 6 = 10
5 + 5 = 10
6 + 4 = 10
7 + 3 = 10
8 + 2 = 10
9 + 1 = 10

Checklist - Bonds of 10: the linear model using Cuisenaire rods

Pupils can:
- ☐ Investigate bonds of 10 using Cuisenaire rods
- ☐ Make the commutative property of addition explicit
- ☐ Demonstrate the inverse relationship between addition and subtraction
- ☐ Write equations for all the bonds of 10
- ☐ Solve simple word problems (see examples p219)

Bonds of 10: practice and revision

Objectives
- Recognise bonds of 10 in addition, subtraction or missing addend presentation
- Recall bonds of 10 quickly
- Solve word problems using bonds of 10 (see examples p219)

Pupils need to recall the bonds of 10 quickly. They also need to recognise the pairs of numbers that make 10. Use tracking activities to help achieve this. Allow pupils to sketch triads to help them if necessary; discourage the use of finger counting. Games play a central role in practising bonds. Memorising information requires meaningful repetition, and plenty of it. Games provide this. Enjoying the activity is also important as it fosters a positive attitude to numeracy.

Worksheets

What is the missing number?
Read the questions aloud and fill in the missing numbers. 'What' is a useful word to ask when there is an unknown signified by the empty box.

Example: $10 = 5 + ?$ Say: *10 is made of 5 and what? 10 equals 5 and 5.*

$10 = 5 + \square$	$10 - \square = 6$	$\square + 8 = 10$
$\square + 7 = 10$	$10 = 6 + \square$	$10 - 7 = \square$
$10 - 8 = \square$	$10 = 1 + \square$	$10 - 5 = \square$

Tracking worksheet
Tracking exercises reinforce recognition of the bonds of 10. Work across the page from left to right. Use a pencil to help focus attention on the numbers in each row. It is important to draw a line, pass under the bond, and then circle it with an anti-clockwise motion. (Appendix 3 p240)

Example:

$6 + 4$	$7 + 2$	$9 + 1$	$5 + 4$	$8 + 2$
$7 + 3$	$3 + 6$	$2 + 8$	$5 + 5$	$4 + 3$

Bonds of 10: Missing Addend Pairs

Aims
- To learn the bonds of 10
- To develop memory skills

Bonds of 10
Missing addend
Question cards

1 - 9
Number cards

Equipment
- One set of question cards (e.g. $9 + \square = 10$)
- One set of answer cards (1 to 9) (different colour to question cards)

How to play
Players take turns to find pairs of matching question and answer cards to complete the bond of 10.

Spread the cards face down, on the table. Placing cards in a regular pattern helps players remember where they are on the table.

Player A turns up a question card and reads it. Player then says the number that they are looking for.

Example: Card is $3 + \square = 10$. Player says: *3 plus what equals 10? I am looking for a 7.*
Or they could say: *3 and 7 equals 10, so I need to find a 7.*

Player A turns up an answer card. If the answer is the required number, the player keeps the cards and has another turn.

If the answer is not correct, the player says the number that would be required to make 10 with the answer card.

Example: Player is looking for 7 but turns up 8. Player says: *8 and 2 makes 10.*

Player turns both cards face down.
(Note: It is essential that the cards always remain in the same position on the table.)

Player B has a turn.

The winner is the person with the most cards when all the cards have been collected.

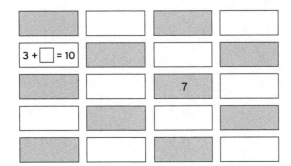

Bonds of 10: Clear the Deck

(Based on the game 'Clear the Deck' in Butterworth and Yeo 2004)

Aim
  • To practise bonds of ten

x4 sets

1 - 9
Number cards

Equipment
  • Four sets of number cards 1 to 9

How to play
The dealer shuffles the cards and places 12 cards, face up, in three rows.

Player A takes two cards that make 10. They do not have to be next to each other. The dealer then replaces the cards with two more. The next player has a turn.

Play continues until all the pairs of cards have been found.

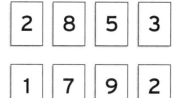

Word problems
Give pupils simple word problems to solve. Pupils summarise what the question is asking, identify relevant information, draw diagrams, write equations and write the answer as a full sentence. There is detailed information about how to tackle word problems in chapter 10 (p216). Pupils should also make up their own word problems.

Checklist – Bonds of 10: practice and revision
Pupils can:
  ☐ Recognise bonds of 10 in addition, subtraction or missing addend presentation
  ☐ Recall bonds of 10 quickly
  ☐ Solve word problems using bonds of 10 (see examples p219)

Key facts: bonds of all the numbers to 10

Objectives
- Model all the bonds of the numbers to 9 using counters
- Record all number bonds as triads and equations
- Recognise all the bonds of numbers to 9
- Recall all the bonds of numbers to 9
- Solve word problems (see examples p219)

When pupils know the bonds of 10 absolutely securely, study the numbers from 2 to 9. Pupils explore *all* the possible bonds of each number to 9. Pupils who can add or subtract 1 from a number, and have learnt the bonds of 10, and doubles and near doubles facts will already know most of the bonds for all the numbers to 10. Provided that they understand that addition is commutative, the only additional facts they need to learn are: 4+2, 5+2, 5+3, 6+2, 6+3, 7+2.

Many may be able to memorise these few new facts. However, pupils with poor auditory working memory may need to rely on deriving these facts. Pupils work through the bonds of each of the numbers to 9 using counters and recording the facts as triads and equations. They relate the new facts to the known facts of the doubles and near doubles, and the bonds of 10.

Numbers		All the bonds of numbers to 10				
2	1 + 1					
3		2 + 1				
4		2 + 2	3 + 1			
5			3 + 2	4 + 1		
6			3 + 3	4 + 2	5 + 1	
7				4 + 3	5 + 2	6 + 1
8				4 + 4	5 + 3	6 + 2	7 + 1
9					5 + 4	6 + 3	7 + 2	8 + 1
10					5 + 5	6 + 4	7 + 3	8 + 2	9 + 1

All the bonds of numbers to 10. The doubles and near doubles bonds are shown in the light grey boxes. The bonds of 10 are shown in the dark boxes.

Teaching

Investigate bonds of 2 and 3
Give pupil a triad mat.
Make the pattern of 2 on the triad mat.
Split the pattern of 2 into the components 1 and 1.

Pupil makes the pattern of 2 in the top oval and then moves the counters to show 1 and 1 in the lower ovals.

Draw the pattern of 2. Use triads and equations to record the bonds of 2. Talk about what you are doing.

Pupil draws the pattern of 2 and records the components as triads and equations.

Next ask the pupil to demonstrate the pattern of 3 and its components, and then to record the components in triads and equations. Pupils have already explored the triads and equations for the numbers 2 and 3. If they have difficulty work through them step-by-step as described in Key Facts: doubles and near doubles bonds (see p31).

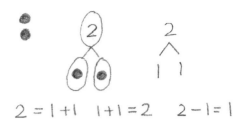

$$2 = 1 + 1 \quad 1 + 1 = 2 \quad 2 - 1 = 1$$

Bonds of 2: triads and equations

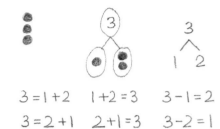

$$3 = 1 + 2 \quad 1 + 2 = 3 \quad 3 - 1 = 2$$
$$3 = 2 + 1 \quad 2 + 1 = 3 \quad 3 - 2 = 1$$

Bonds of 3: triads and equations

Investigate bonds of 4

Make the pattern of 4 on the triad mat.
Split the pattern of 4 into 2 and 2.

Pupil makes the pattern of 4 in the top oval and moves the counters to show 2 and 2 in the lower ovals. Pupil says: *4 is made of 2 and 2.* Accept any sensible explanation.

Draw the pattern of 4. Use triads to record the patterns and the numbers. Talk about what you are doing.

Pupil draws the pattern of 4 and records the components as triads in patterns and numbers. They explain the relationship between 4 and the components as they write.

Write the equations for the bonds of 4. Start with 4 equals 2 plus 2.

Pupil writes 4 = 2 + 2 and says: *4 equals 2 plus 2.*

Write the equation starting with 2 add 2.

Pupil writes 2 + 2 = 4 and says: *2 add 2 equals 4.*

There are 4 counters. I take away 2 counters. Write the equation for 4 take away 2.
[Teacher covers 2 counters whilst speaking.]

Pupil writes 4 - 2 = 2 and says: *4 take away 2 equals 2.*

Now make the pattern of 4 on the triad mat.
Split 4 into two other patterns. Do not use 2 and 2. Some pupils find this very difficult. Allow them plenty of time to experiment.

Pupil makes 4 and then moves the counters to show the components 3 and 1. The pupil says: *4 is made of 3 and 1.*

Use triads to record 3 and 1 as patterns and as numbers.

Pupil records the components 3 and 1 in the triads as patterns and numbers.

Write the equations. Start with 4 equals 3 plus 1.

Pupil writes 4 = 3 + 1 and says: *4 equals 3 plus 1.*

Write the equation starting with 3 add 1.

Pupil writes 3 + 1 = 4 and says: *3 add 1 equals 4.*

There are 4 counters. I take away 3 counters. Write the equation for 4 take away 3.
[Teacher covers the 3 counters whilst speaking.]

Pupil writes 4 - 3 = 1 and says: *4 take away 3 equals 1.*

Make the pattern of 4. Can you split it into any other components?

I can split 4 into 2 and 2, or 3 and 1, or 1 and 3. I cannot split 4 into any other components.

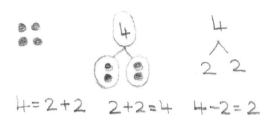

$$4 = 2 + 2 \quad 2 + 2 = 4 \quad 4 - 2 = 2$$

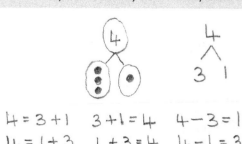

$$4 = 3 + 1 \quad 3 + 1 = 4 \quad 4 - 3 = 1$$
$$4 = 1 + 3 \quad 1 + 3 = 4 \quad 4 - 1 = 3$$

Investigate bonds of 5, 6, 7, 8 and 9

Work through the numbers 5, 6, 7, 8 and 9 in a similar way.

Remember that it is important that pupils talk about what they are doing and writing.

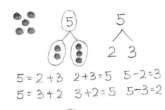

5 = 2 + 3   2+3=5   5-2=3
5 = 3 + 2   3+2=5   5-3=2

5=4+1   4+1=5   5-4=1
5=1+4   1+4=5   5-1=4

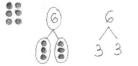

6 =3+3   3+3=6   6-3=3

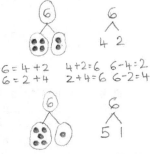

6 = 4 + 2   4+2=6   6-4=2
6 = 2 + 4   2+4=6   6-2=4

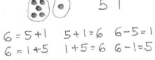

6 = 5 + 1   5+1=6   6-5=1
6 = 1 + 5   1+5=6   6-1=5

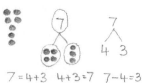

7 = 4+3   4+3=7   7-4=3
7 = 3+4   3+4=7   7-3=4

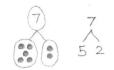

7 = 5+2   5+2=7   7-5=2
7 = 2+5   2+5=7   7-2=5

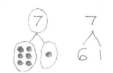

7=6+1   6+1=7   7-6=1
7=1+6   1+6=7   7-1=6

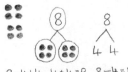

8=4+4   4+4=8   8-4=4

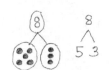

8=5+3   5+3=8   8-5=3
8=3+5   3+5=8   8-3=5

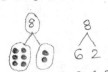

8 = 6+2   6+2=8   8-6=2
8 = 2+6   2+6=8   8-2=6

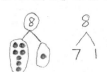

8 = 7+1   7+1=8   8-7=1
8 = 1+7   1+7=8   8-1=7

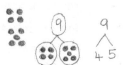

9 = 4+5   4+5=9   9-4=5
9 = 5+4   5+4=9   9-5=4

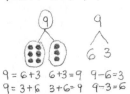

9 = 6+3   6+3=9   9-6=3
9 = 3+6   3+6=9   9-3=6

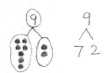

9 = 7+2   7+2=9   9-7=2
9 = 2+7   2+7=9   9-2=7

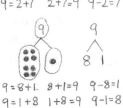

9=8+1   8+1=9   9-8=1
9=1+8   1+8=9   9-1=8

Bonds of 5, 6, 7, 8 and 9: triads and equations

Checklist - Key facts: bonds of all the numbers to 10

Pupils can:
- ☐ Model all the bonds of the numbers to 9 using counters
- ☐ Record all number bonds as triads and equations
- ☐ Recognise all the bonds of numbers to 9
- ☐ Recall all the bonds of numbers to 9
- ☐ Solve word problems (see examples p219)

Bonds of all the numbers to 10: linear model using Cuisenaire rods

Objectives

- Model bonds of all numbers from 2 to 9 using Cuisenaire rods
- Draw diagrams of Cuisenaire rod 'sandwiches'
- Write the equations that the rods represent

Pupils use Cuisenaire rods to compare bonds within a number in a linear format. Then they write all the equations represented by the rods. Pupils have already shown the bonds of 10 in this way. Use Cuisenaire rods to make number 'sandwiches' that clearly show all the possible bonds for each number. The word 'sandwich' is used because the two rods showing the number suggest pieces of bread. The bonds within the number constitute the 'filling'. Although the term 'sandwich' is not a mathematical one, it can help pupils to understand how the bonds of a number are related to it.

The concepts of odd and even are inherent in the depiction, however these terms are not taught at this stage. (See p117)

Teaching

Pupils use Cuisenaire rods to show all the bonds of the numbers from 2 to 10. They model the bonds of each number, then draw a diagram and write all the equations represented by the rods.

You can use Cuisenaire rods to show the bonds of 2.

The teacher demonstrates what is required by placing a red 2 rod horizontally and saying: *What is 2 made of?*

Teacher places 1 and 1 above the 2 rod. *1 and 1 makes 2 so now I put another 2 rod at the top.*

I call this a 'rod sandwich'. The 2 rods are like the bread and the 1 and 1 are like the filling.

Draw a diagram of the 'rod sandwich' for the bonds of 2.

Write numbers and equations alongside the diagram to show the value of the rods.

> 2 is made of 1 and 1.
>
> $$2 = 1 + 1 \qquad 1 + 1 = 2 \qquad 2 - 1 = 1$$
>
> Rod 'sandwich' showing 2 and the bonds of 2
>
> The pupil draws and colours in the diagram on squared paper (1 cm²).
>
> The pupil writes the numbers and equations on the appropriate lines on the diagram.

The pupil investigates each of the numbers from 3 to 10 showing all the possible bonds within each number. They use Cuisenaire rods to model one number at a time, draw the diagram and write the equations that the rods represent. Allow pupils plenty of time to work through these examples. They do not need to be done in one lesson. Repeat the exercise from time to time to help develop the visual image of the bonds and the relationships between them.

3 = 2 + 1	2 + 1 = 3	3 - 2 = 1
3 = 1 + 2	1 + 2 = 3	3 - 1 = 2

4 = 3 + 1	3 + 1 = 4	4 - 3 = 1
4 = 2 + 2	2 + 2 = 4	4 - 2 = 2
4 = 1 + 3	1 + 3 = 4	4 - 1 = 3

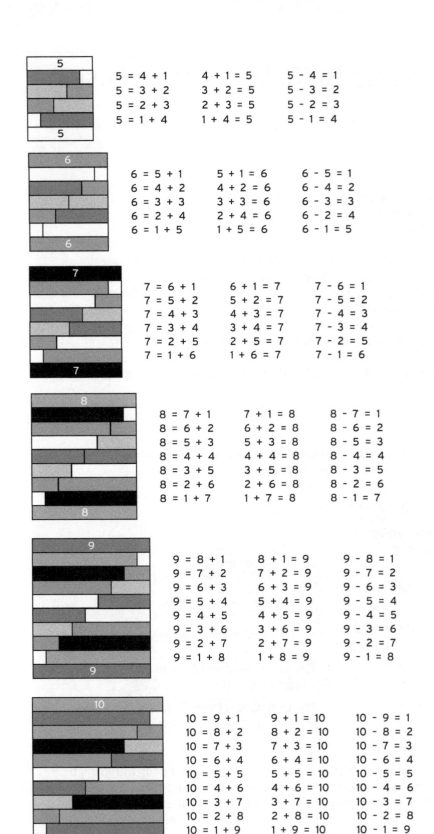

5 = 4 + 1	4 + 1 = 5	5 - 4 = 1
5 = 3 + 2	3 + 2 = 5	5 - 3 = 2
5 = 2 + 3	2 + 3 = 5	5 - 2 = 3
5 = 1 + 4	1 + 4 = 5	5 - 1 = 4

6 = 5 + 1	5 + 1 = 6	6 - 5 = 1
6 = 4 + 2	4 + 2 = 6	6 - 4 = 2
6 = 3 + 3	3 + 3 = 6	6 - 3 = 3
6 = 2 + 4	2 + 4 = 6	6 - 2 = 4
6 = 1 + 5	1 + 5 = 6	6 - 1 = 5

7 = 6 + 1	6 + 1 = 7	7 - 6 = 1
7 = 5 + 2	5 + 2 = 7	7 - 5 = 2
7 = 4 + 3	4 + 3 = 7	7 - 4 = 3
7 = 3 + 4	3 + 4 = 7	7 - 3 = 4
7 = 2 + 5	2 + 5 = 7	7 - 2 = 5
7 = 1 + 6	1 + 6 = 7	7 - 1 = 6

8 = 7 + 1	7 + 1 = 8	8 - 7 = 1
8 = 6 + 2	6 + 2 = 8	8 - 6 = 2
8 = 5 + 3	5 + 3 = 8	8 - 5 = 3
8 = 4 + 4	4 + 4 = 8	8 - 4 = 4
8 = 3 + 5	3 + 5 = 8	8 - 3 = 5
8 = 2 + 6	2 + 6 = 8	8 - 2 = 6
8 = 1 + 7	1 + 7 = 8	8 - 1 = 7

9 = 8 + 1	8 + 1 = 9	9 - 8 = 1
9 = 7 + 2	7 + 2 = 9	9 - 7 = 2
9 = 6 + 3	6 + 3 = 9	9 - 6 = 3
9 = 5 + 4	5 + 4 = 9	9 - 5 = 4
9 = 4 + 5	4 + 5 = 9	9 - 4 = 5
9 = 3 + 6	3 + 6 = 9	9 - 3 = 6
9 = 2 + 7	2 + 7 = 9	9 - 2 = 7
9 = 1 + 8	1 + 8 = 9	9 - 1 = 8

10 = 9 + 1	9 + 1 = 10	10 - 9 = 1
10 = 8 + 2	8 + 2 = 10	10 - 8 = 2
10 = 7 + 3	7 + 3 = 10	10 - 7 = 3
10 = 6 + 4	6 + 4 = 10	10 - 6 = 4
10 = 5 + 5	5 + 5 = 10	10 - 5 = 5
10 = 4 + 6	4 + 6 = 10	10 - 4 = 6
10 = 3 + 7	3 + 7 = 10	10 - 3 = 7
10 = 2 + 8	2 + 8 = 10	10 - 2 = 8
10 = 1 + 9	1 + 9 = 10	10 - 1 = 9

Checklist – Bonds of all the numbers to 10: linear model using Cuisenaire rods

Pupils can:

- ☐ Model bonds of all numbers from 2 to 9 using Cuisenaire rods
- ☐ Draw diagrams of Cuisenaire rod 'sandwiches'
- ☐ Write the equations that the rods represent

3

Numbers to 20: Counting

Teach the location of numbers in a sequence as well as number names. The ability to recall and visualise an image of the number sequence is very important for efficient calculation strategies.

Many English speaking pupils find the numbers from 11 to 20 very difficult. The English language presents particular difficulties caused by anomalies which can lead to conceptual misunderstandings. The written and spoken order of the 'teen' numbers is different. The written numbers represent ten plus some units or ones. In the spoken word the 'teen' ending indicates ten yet it comes after the unit number in the spoken and written word. For example, 14 is spoken as 'four-teen' not 'ten-four'. In other languages this is not the case. The number words from 11 to 15 are the most difficult number words: eleven (11) is unique; twelve (12) bears a passing resemblance to the number two only because both start with 'tw'; thirteen (13) has the 'th' in common with three but is more closely related to third; fourteen (14) is transparent; fifteen (15) is only loosely connected to five. The numbers from 16 to 19 are more transparent because the first syllable in each number is the same as in the words six to nine.

Further difficulties can arise from auditory confusion between the 'teen' endings and the 'ty' endings of the decade numbers. Twenty is mistakenly pronounced as 'ten teen' or 'twenteen' or even 'twelve' by pupils who are following the pattern from nineteen. At this point tell them that twenty means 2 tens, that is, 10 items and another 10 items. Help pupils remember the distinction between 'teen' and 'ty' by discussing the teenage years. Most pupils agree that they will become a teenager when they reach 'thirteen', and they will be an adult when they reach 'twenty'.

Give pupils plenty of practice reading the numbers and associating the 'teen' numbers with lines of ten objects plus 'some more' before they write them. This creates a clear visual image which will help pupils learn to write the 'teen' numbers correctly.

Equipment

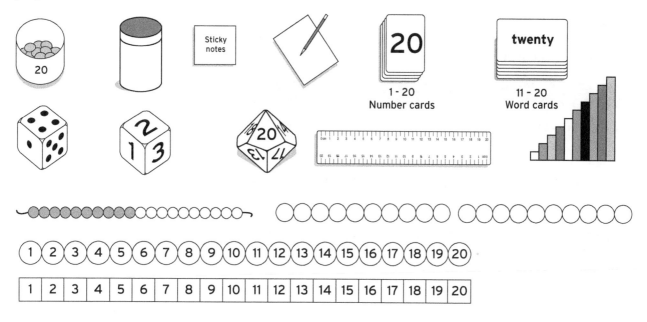

Counting to 20: number names and one-to-one correspondence

Objectives
- Recite the number names to 20 accurately and fluently without undue hesitation
- Articulate the number words correctly and pronounce the endings correctly in 'teen' and 'ty' words
- Synchronise number names with objects counted
- Order objects in a line as they are counted

Give pupils plenty of practice saying the numbers 11 to 20, and counting objects. Placing objects in a line helps pupils to count accurately. It also provides a strong visual image of the numbers as 'ten' plus 'some more'. It is important to establish this understanding before pupils are asked to write the 'teen' numbers.

Teaching

Oral counting
Teacher models the counting sequence from 11 to 20. Say each number very clearly and articulate the 'n' sound at the end of the 'teen' numbers and 'ty' at the end of 20. Do not put undue stress on the second syllable; use just sufficient emphasis to make it explicit.

The teacher says each number word, one at a time, and asks the pupil to repeat it. Continue until the pupil has said all the numbers to 20. Then the teacher and pupil recite the numbers from 11 to 20 together. Finally the pupil recites the numbers on their own. Practise counting forwards from 11 to 20 until the sequence is correct to avoid any errors developing. When the pupil can do this, they recite the whole sequence starting from number 1. If the pupil is unable to do this, the teacher and pupil count together.

Concrete counting: one-to-one correspondence
Have a container with more than 20 counters available. Give the pupil a pile of 14 counters. (Prepare these before the lesson; do not count them out in front of the pupil).

Count the counters. Leave a small space when you reach 10, then continue.

The pupil synchronises each number name with the correct counter in the sequence. Encourage them to emphasise the 'n' sound at the end of the 'teen' words.

Remove the 14 counters. Give the pupil all the counters.
Show me 17 counters. Count them into a line. Leave a small space after 10 counters.

Pupil counts aloud as they position the counters.

Ask pupil to model several other numbers from the 'teen' sequence starting from 1 each time. Also ask pupil to count 20 counters.

A line of 14 counters with a gap after the first 10 showing that 14 consists of 10 and 4 more.

Checklist – Counting to 20: number names and one-to-one correspondence
Pupils can:
- ☐ Recite the number names to 20 accurately and fluently without undue hesitation
- ☐ Articulate the number words correctly and pronounce the endings correctly in 'teen' and 'ty' words
- ☐ Synchronise number names with objects counted
- ☐ Order objects in a line as they are counted

Sequence, read and write numbers to 20

Objectives

- Read the numbers from 11 to 20
- Sequence the numbers from 11 to 20
- Place numbers in sequence from random order
- Read the words for the numbers from 11 to 20
- Match numbers and words for numbers from 11 to 20
- Write numbers from 1 to 20

Teach pupils to read the numbers to 20 before asking them to write them. Make sure that pupils see the correct formation and link it to the spoken and written word before writing the 'teen' numbers in order to help prevent errors in writing the 'teen' numbers.

Pupils order numbers and discuss the relationship between the numbers. This is the foundation of understanding number sequences. The ability to continue a sequence from arbitrary points in the sequence lays the foundations for 'counting on', the early stage of calculating.

Pupils may find it difficult to write the 'teen' numbers correctly because the 'units' number comes before the 'teen' in the number word. Some pupils write the digits in the order they hear them so that fourteen is written as 41. Watch carefully as pupils write the 'teen' numbers. Some pupils put the numerals in the correct positions but they write the unit digit first, then they write the ten digit. Although the result appears correctly as 14, they need to write the digits in the order they appear in the number, not the order they appear in the word. If pupils leave a space between each digit, as in 1 2 for 12, it indicates that they may not understand that the two digits represent a single collection of 12.

Help pupils to understand that the written number represents 'ten' plus 'some more' by using counters to model the numbers, and drawing diagrams. Do 'matching' exercises to create a visual link between the number word and the numerals as well as developing the underlying skills of tracking and matching.

Teaching

Link the written numerals from 11 to 20 with the number words using number cards and word cards.

Read and sequence numbers

Teacher puts the number cards from 11 to 20 out in order and says each number word as the card is placed. Then the pupil is asked to read the numbers.

Read the numbers. Point to each number as you say it.

When the pupil can read the sequence, ask them to identify different numbers in the sequence.
Point to 16.
Point to 13.

Shuffle the cards and give them to the pupil.
Put the cards out in order. Start with the card at the top of the pack.

If the pupil is not able to do this, the teacher and pupil read them together.

Some pupils have to start at the beginning of the sequence each time. Do not prevent them from doing this but make sure they have plenty of practice until they are able to quickly identify the numbers.

Pupil places the cards on the table starting with the card at the top of the pack. The pupil places each card in the appropriate position, relative to each other, leaving sufficient space for the missing numbers. If pupils make mistakes, allow them time to find the error before helping them to do so.

When the pupil has completed the sequence, teacher says: *Read the numbers and point to each one.*

Some pupils find it very difficult to sequence cards from a randomly ordered pack. At first the pupil may need to find the lowest card (11) and put that in position, then search the pack for 12, and so on. Allow them to do this for the first attempt.

Read and sequence 'teen' words

The teacher puts the number cards in sequence and then positions the word cards below them, saying each number word slowly and clearly.

Read the number words. Point to each word as you say it.

If the pupil is not able to do this, the teacher and pupil read them together.

When the pupil can read the words, shuffle the word cards and ask them to place them below the matching number cards.

11	12	13	14	15	16	17	18	19	20
eleven	twelve	thirteen	fourteen	fifteen	sixteen	seventeen	eighteen	nineteen	twenty

---

Where is the Number?

Aim

To locate numbers in a sequence

Equipment

- Cards from 11 to 20
- Dice 11–20

1 - 20
Number cards

Activity

Pupil puts the cards out in a line in the correct order.

Pupil rolls the dice and reads the number aloud. Pupil points to the number in the sequence and reads it aloud.

Write numbers from 11 to 20

The pupil writes the numbers from 11 to 20. First ask them to write each number on a new line. If this is correct, then they write the numbers from 11 to 20 on the same line. The numbers should be written with appropriate spacing so they can be read easily. When pupils can write the 'teen' numbers, ask them to write all the numbers from 1 to 20.

Correcting errors in written numbers

If pupils make errors, spend time helping them to construct the numbers correctly. Common errors in writing the 'teen' numbers are: reversing the digits so that they write 61 instead of 16; writing the completed number correctly but writing the unit digit prior to writing the 'ten'; leaving too much space between digits within the number.

Work with concrete materials and talk about the way that 'teen' numbers consist of one ten and some units.

Use counters to show me the number 13.

How many counters are there?

Draw a diagram of the counters. Explain what you have done.

Teacher covers up the last 3 counters on the model. *How many counters can you see?*

Write '10 counters' on the diagram.

Teacher covers up the 10 counters so only 3 are visible and says: *How many counters can you see?*

Write '3 counters' under the diagram.

There are 10 counters and 3 counters. How many counters are there altogether?

Write 10 counters and 3 counters makes 13 counters. Then read what you have written.

By this stage pupils should know to leave a small gap between 10 and the following counters.

Pupil should be able to say 13 without having to recount any of the counters.

Pupil draws the diagram and says: *I drew 13 counters.*

I can see 10 counters.

Pupil writes '10 counters' under the line of 10 counters on the diagram.

I can see 3 counters.

Pupil writes '3 counters' under the line of 3 counters on the diagram.

There are 13 counters altogether.

The pupil writes and then reads aloud: *10 counters and 3 counters makes 13 counters.* If the pupil reverses 13 and writes 31, the teacher writes the number and the pupil traces over it.

10 counters   3 counters
10 counters and 3 counters makes 13 counters.

Give pupils plenty of practice until they can write the numbers correctly with appropriate spacing. Finally ask the pupil to write the sequence of numbers to 20 starting from 1.

Checklist - Sequence, read and write numbers to 20
Pupils can:
- ☐ Read the numbers from 11 to 20
- ☐ Sequence the numbers from 11 to 20
- ☐ Place numbers in sequence from random order
- ☐ Read the words for the numbers from 11 to 20
- ☐ Match numbers and words for numbers from 11 to 20
- ☐ Write numbers from 1 to 20

Estimation to 20

Objectives
- Estimate how many counters there are in an unstructured group
- Check the estimate

It is important that pupils develop the habit of estimating quantities. The ability to estimate how many there are in a quantity of objects helps develop a 'feel' for the size of numbers. This is an important part of number sense, and essential for checking calculations. Estimation activities also give counting practise and reinforce the 10-based structure of the number system.

Teaching

Scatter between 10 and 20 counters. Let the pupil look at them for a few seconds but not for long enough to be able to count them. Cover them with a piece of paper. Continue this estimating activity until pupils can give reasonable estimates for up to 20 items. An acceptable estimate is an amount that is within five more or less than the number of counters.

How many are there?

Can you check your answer?

Pupil writes down the number they think there are.

The pupil counts the counters into a line leaving a small space after 10 counters.

The Estimating Game

How many counters are there?

Aims
- To develop the concept of the size of numbers
- To develop estimation skills

Equipment
- 20 counters in a container
- A sheet of paper to cover the objects
- Score sheet and pencil for each player (see layout opposite)

How to play

Scatter a handful of objects on the table. Allow a few seconds to look at them *but not long enough to count them*. Then cover the objects with a sheet of paper. (You will need to experiment to find a satisfactory length of time. Start by allowing five seconds and make the time shorter as players improve.)

Player A guesses how many objects there are. Everyone records this on their own score sheet. Each player gives an estimate. All are recorded.

Player A counts the actual number of objects and puts them out in a single line, counting aloud and leaving a gap between each group of ten.

Everyone records the total in the 'Actual number' column. All the counters are returned to the container and the next player has a turn.

The winner is the player whose estimate is closest to the actual number of objects. Enter the winner's name in the appropriate column.

Counters are scattered.

	Player A	Player B	Player C	Actual Number	Winner
	10	20	17		

Players write their estimates.

Player A counts counters into a line, leaving a small gap after the tenth counter. Players complete their score sheets.

Player A	Player B	Player C	Actual Number	Winner
10	20	17	13	Player A

Player A wins Game 1 because 10 is the closest number to 13 from the estimates. (This reasoning could be shown by putting the counters out on a Caterpillar track, see p64.)

Checklist - Estimation to 20

Pupils can:
- ☐ Estimate how many counters there are in an unstructured group
- ☐ Check the estimate

Locate numbers to 20 on a bead string

Objectives
- Locate the position of a number on a bead string
- Describe the position of a number on a bead string

It is essential for pupils to be able to locate the position of a number in a sequence without having to count in ones from the beginning of the sequence. Bead strings help pupils to see numbers in relation to the number 10 and multiples of 10.

Use a bead string to 20 containing 10 beads of one colour, and 10 of a second colour. This provides a clear visual image of the 10-based structure of the number system. However, the 10-based structure of the number system is not explicitly taught at this stage. Count the beads from the beginning, from left to right, preparing for later work on number lines

Teaching

Ask location questions for numbers up to 20. Concentrate on the numbers 8, 9, 10, 11, 12, 13 and 18, 19 and 20. Pay particular attention to the decade boundaries where one group of ten ends and another begins.

Show the pupil the bead string.
How many grey beads are there?
How many white beads are there?
How many beads are there altogether?

Show me where bead 8 is.

There are 10 grey beads.
There are 10 white beads.
There are 20 beads altogether.

Pupil touches the eighth bead from the left and says: *This is 8.*

Ask questions using a variety of spatial and directional language.

Pupil touches the relevant bead when answering the questions.

What is the number before 3?
What is 1 less than 10?
Which number is between 11 and 13?
Find 19. What is the next number?

2 comes before 3.
9 is 1 less than 10.
12 is between 11 and 13.
20 is the next number after 19.

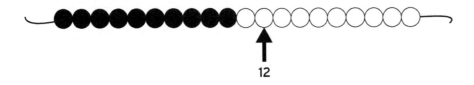

12

Pupil locates 12 and says: *12 is between 11 and 13. Also 12 is 2 more than 10.*

Checklist – Locate numbers to 20 on a bead string
Pupils can:
- ☐ Locate the position of a number on a bead string
- ☐ Describe the position of a number on a bead string

'Counting on' to 20

Objectives

- Count flexibly
- Count on from different starting points in the sequence to 20

Count forward to 20 from different starting points to build flexible counting skills. This is very important for 'counting on' to add amounts before pupils learn more efficient calculation methods. Pupils use counters and bead strings to support their thinking.

Be very careful about the language that you use. Say 'count from' or 'count on from'. Do not say 'start at' as 'count on from 12' and 'start at 12' mean different things. 'Count on' from 12 means start with the next number, which is 13; 'start at' 12 means that 12 is included in the count. If pupils are not absolutely clear about what they are being asked to do, misunderstandings can arise and these will lead to problems with calculation later. Use counters and bead strings to provide a clear visual model and remove any ambiguity. Play The Tins Game to practise 'counting on'.

A bead string consists of unnumbered beads that can be easily moved along a piece of string. This reinforces the strategy of touching or moving each item as it is counted. Use a bead string with 10 beads of one colour and 10 of another. This provides a clear visual image of the 10-based structure of the number system. The decade structure is implicit in the bead string but it is not explicitly taught at this stage.

Teaching

'Counting on' using counters

Give the pupil a pile of 15 counters. (Prepare these before the lesson; do not count them out in front of the pupil.)

Count the counters into a line. Leave a small space when you reach 10 then continue.

When the pupil has counted to 15 accurately, give them 3 more counters and ask them to 'count on' from there.
You know there are 15. Continue counting as you put out the extra counters.

Check that the pupil says the number words accurately, emphasising the 'n' sound at the end of the 'teen' words.

If pupils have to start counting all the counters from the first one, they have not reached a level of automaticity required to manage flexible counting. They need to practise 'counting on' from any number.

Repeat this exercise until the pupil can confidently count on to 20 from any number in the sequence.

Pupil counts on sixteen, seventeen, eighteen as the counters are put in position.

'Counting on' using a bead string

Pupil locates a number on the bead string and counts on from there.

Find 6. Count on from 6. Stop when you reach 13.

Give pupil plenty of practice in counting on from various starting points.

Pupil separates the beads so that 6 beads are clearly visible.

Pupil moves each bead as they count on aloud: 7, 8, 9, 10, 11, 12, 13.

Caterpillar Tracks

'Counting on' using an empty track

Aims
- To practise counting on from a number
- To introduce the idea of addition in an informal way
- To emphasise the 10s structure

Equipment
- Caterpillar track for each player (unnumbered track)
- Spinner or dice marked 1–3
- Counters (20 for each player)

20 for each player

How to play

Player A throws the dice, takes the correct number of counters and places them on the track.

Player B has a turn and places the appropriate counters on their track.

On the next turn, Player A throws the dice and takes the appropriate counters. It is important that they do not put the counters straight on the track. The counters are placed above the track as shown below. Player A says how many counters are there already and how many new ones there are. Then they count on as they move the additional counters into place.

Player B has a turn.

The winner is the first player to reach, or pass, the end of the track.

Example:
Player A rolls 2 on the third turn.

Player A: *There are 5. Now I have 2 more.*

As the counters are moved into position, Player A counts on aloud: *Six, seven.*

The Tins Game[1]

Aim
- To practise counting on from a number

Equipment
- Tin with a lid
- Pencil
- Labels or sticky notes
- 20 counters in a container
- Score sheet for each player

How to play

Activity for one player

Give the player two quantities of counters, one large and one smaller one. The player selects which quantity to count into the tin first. They count the counters, one at a time, into the empty tin and put the lid on. They write the number of counters on a label and stick it on top of the tin. They now add the second quantity of counters by counting on from the number on the tin.

Game for two players

Each player has three turns.

Player A takes a handful of at least 5 counters. They count the counters in ones into an empty tin and put the lid on. They write the number of counters on a label and stick it on top of the tin.

Player B takes at least 3 counters and counts them on the table. Player B asks Player A to add them to the counters in the tin by counting on. If the answer is correct, Player A records the total. If they are incorrect, Player B asks Player A to take the counters out of the tin and count them all. Player A writes the number on the score sheet.

Now Player B has a turn.

At the end of the game the players add up their scores. The winner is the player with the highest total. A variation is for the winner to be the player with the lowest score.

6 + 5 = 11

Checklist - 'Counting on' to 20

Pupils can:
- ☐ Count flexibly
- ☐ Count on from different starting points in the sequence to 20

[1] The Tins Game was invented by Martin Hughes, 1986

Sequence to 20: visual model using Cuisenaire rods

Objectives
- Understand the repeating pattern within the number sequence from 1 to 20
- Visualise the numbers from 11 to 20 as 10 + a single digit

The ability to recall and visualise an image of the number sequence is very important for efficient calculation strategies. Make the repeating pattern within the counting sequence explicit by building the sequence to 20 using Cuisenaire rods. This model provides a clear image of the structure of the 'teen' numbers as 10 plus a single digit. Pupils build the sequence of rods and talk about them in relative terms as they did for the numbers to 10 in Chapter 1 (p25).

Teaching
Pupil uses Cuisenaire rods to build the number sequence from 1 to 10.

Build the number that is 1 more than 10.

Pupil places a 10 and 1 in position next to the 10 rod. *1 more than 10 is 11.*

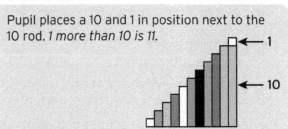

Build the number that is 1 more than 11.

1 more than 11 is 12. I need a 10 and 2 more. Pupil places a 10 and a 2 rod in position.

Can you continue building the sequence until you get to 20?

Pupil builds the sequence, discussing what they are doing.

When the pattern is completed the teacher says: *Tell me what you see.*

Pupil talks about the way the sequence of numbers from 1 to 10 is repeated in the larger numbers. They explain that the numbers from 11 to 20 are in the form 10 plus a number. They should express this idea in their own words.

The teacher helps the pupil by asking questions about the shape and composition of the model, if the pupil requires help.

Finally, ask the pupil to draw a diagram of the model on squared paper, and colour it in.

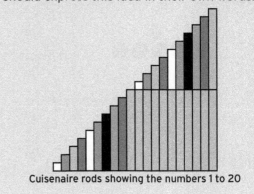

Cuisenaire rods showing the numbers 1 to 20

Checklist – Sequence to 20: visual model using Cuisenaire rods
Pupils can:
- ☐ Understand the repeating pattern within the number sequence from 1 to 20
- ☐ Visualise the numbers from 11 to 20 as 10 + a single digit

Number tracks

Objectives
- Understand the numbered track
- Count forwards from any number up to 20

Pupils should now be familiar with the unnumbered track (the caterpillar track) which emphasises the 10-based structure of the number system. Now they use a numbered track on which there is no gap between the first ten and the second group of ten.

The number track consists of consecutive, clearly defined spaces, each of which contains a number. These are often shown as squares or circles. In this book, circles are used because they make the visual distinction between the shapes clear. However pupils should also work with tracks composed of other shapes such as squares, rectangles and hexagons.

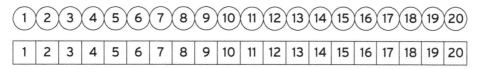

| 1 | 2 | 3 | 4 | 5 | 6 | 7 | 8 | 9 | 10 | 11 | 12 | 13 | 14 | 15 | 16 | 17 | 18 | 19 | 20 |

Number tracks

Teaching

Introduce the number track by playing the game Number Track Race, which also practises counting on. Give pupils plenty of practice in completing number sequences to 20.

Number Track Race

Aims
- To establish the structure of the counting track
- To revise the counting sequence to 20

Equipment:
- Number track for each player
- Dice (1-6)
- Counters (20 for each player)

20 for each player

How to play

Player A rolls the dice, takes the correct number of counters and places them on the track.

Then Player B has a turn.

On the next turn Player A rolls the dice, and takes the appropriate counters. It is important that they do not put the counters straight on the track.

Player A says how many counters are there already and then counts on as the additional counters are moved into place.

Player B has a turn.

The winner is the first player to reach, or pass, the end of the track.

Example showing second turn

Player A rolled 4 on the first turn, and Player B rolled 5.

Player A rolls 3 on the second turn and says: *There are 4. I have 3 more.* Player A counts on aloud *five, six, seven* as each counter is placed on the track, and then says: *There are 7 altogether.*

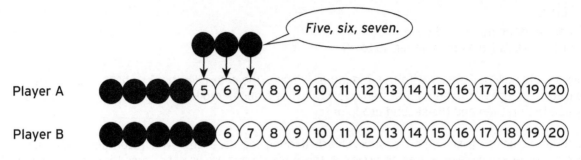

Number Tracks

Fill in the missing numbers.

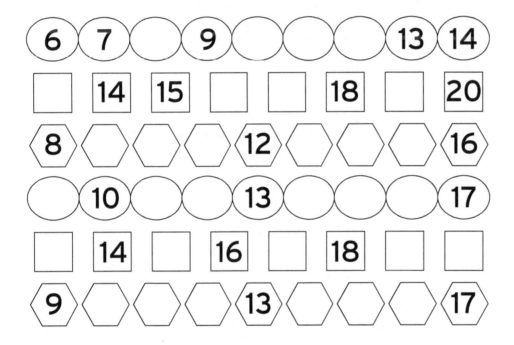

Checklist - Number tracks

Pupils can:

☐ Understand the numbered track
☐ Count forwards from any number up to 20

Counting back from 20

Objectives

- Count back from 10
- Count back from 20
- Count backwards from any number below 20

It is very important to be able to count backwards as well as forwards in order to calculate efficiently. Work on counting backwards from the decade numbers, 10 and 20, and later from any number in the sequence. Do not ask pupils to count backwards until they can count forwards fluently.

The word 'backwards' is used in two different contexts: direction and descending size. Failure to understand which meaning is required causes difficulties. Counting backwards may mean starting at the end of a written sequence and counting back to the beginning. It also describes counting from a larger number to a smaller number. Some pupils find it helpful to use the term 'count down' to help establish the idea of backwards as descending size in the number sequence.

Some pupils find counting backwards extremely difficult and so they will need to put numbered cards in a line to maintain a visual image of the counting sequence. Teachers need to use their discretion about when to ask a pupil to count backwards. All counting activities should follow the pupils' level of competence to their next stage. For those with very poor verbal memories, it is unwise to work on counting backwards too soon because it can confuse the transfer of knowledge of the forward counting sequence into the long-term memory. For those who have already found learning to count difficult, start counting back from 5.

Teaching

Count back using bead strings, counters and number cards. Then give pupils plenty of practice counting forwards and backwards by completing written number sequences.

Counting back from 10

Check that the pupil can count forwards to 10 fluently.

Can you count backwards starting at 10?

Explain that it is like counting down for a rocket launch: 10, 9, 8 and so on.

> Often pupils like to say 'blast off' at the end of the count, just as happens at a real launch.
>
> Pupils who find this too difficult can use cards or counters to help them.

Cards to help count back from 10

Teacher puts out number cards from 1 to 10. Ask pupils to say each number as they point to the card, starting with 10 and moving back through the sequence.

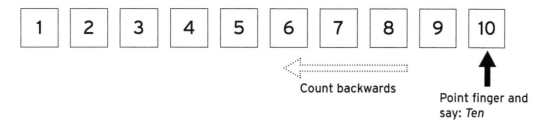

Count backwards

Point finger and say: *Ten*

Next, teacher puts out part of the sequence with the cards face down except for the cards at the beginning and the end of the sequence, which are placed face up.

Cards in order, face down between 4 and 9

Count backwards from 9. Say each number and then turn over the card to check.

Pupil says each number before turning the card over. They should be able to count reasonably quickly. If they work very slowly they may be starting at the beginning and counting forwards under their breath before finding the required number.

Counters to help count back from 10

Pupils count out 10 counters into a line. Then they point to each counter as they count backwards.

Pupil points at the relevant counter whilst saying: 10, 9, 8, 7, 6, 5, 4, 3, 2, 1.

Counting back from 20

When the pupil can count backwards from 10 confidently, do the same exercises with cards and counters to count backwards from 20.

Counting back from 20 on a bead string

Start at 1 and count to 20. Then count backwards starting at 20.

Pupil moves the beads as they count aloud.

Pupil moves the 20th bead and, while doing this, says: *Twenty*

Practise counting back from different starting points below 20. Remember that the language the teacher uses is very important. Be clear about whether the count starts from the given number, or begins with or at the given number. It may seem a small point but it is important to realise that there is a difference between beginning with the next number, or including the given number in the count.

Count back from 13 and stop at 8.

Pupil locates the 13th bead and counts back from there, starting with 12 and moving each bead as it is counted: 12, 11, 10, 9, 8.

Start with 18 and count back to 11.

Pupil locates the 18th bead and counts back, starting with 18 and moving each bead as it is counted: 18, 17, 16 , 15, 14, 13, 12, 11.

Cards to help count back from 20

Pupil puts out number cards from 1 to 20. They start at 20 and move back through the sequence. They count aloud and turn each card face down as they say the number.

Pupils can use number cards as prompts. Count back from 20 to 15. Put out the sequence and turn over the cards that are to be counted. Make sure they solve it by starting at 20 and going back from 20 rather than starting at 15 and counting up under their breath.

Checklist – Counting back from 20

Pupils can:
- ☐ Count back from 10
- ☐ Count back from 20
- ☐ Count backwards from any number below 20

The number line

Objectives
- Draw an accurate number line
- Compare a number track and a number line
- Understand the difference between a number track and a number line

A number line is a line with intervals marked at equidistant points. The number line shows the measuring numbers. All numbers, including whole numbers, fractions or decimals, positive and negative numbers, can be represented by a point on the line.

The number line is one of the most powerful tools that pupils can use as a calculation aid. Understanding the number line is essential for measurement and for interpreting and representing data on charts and graphs.

The number line is a simple representation of number. Or is it? Some people find the number line confusing because they do not realise that the number track and the number line are different representations of number. Understanding the difference between the counting numbers (the number track) and the measuring numbers (the number line) is a crucial point in developing number sense. Do not introduce the number line too early as it is a very difficult concept for young children.

Make sure that the pupil is able to count flexibly, and accurately locate numbers on a number track. Teach pupils to use a ruler to draw clear number lines with accurate marks to show important points, including at the beginning and end of the number line. At this stage pupils only mark whole numbers on the number line.

The difference between a number track and a number line
The distinction between counting numbers (discrete numbers) and measuring numbers (continuous numbers) is very important and needs to be explicitly taught. Counting numbers are represented on a number track; measuring numbers are represented on a number line. Pupils explore the relationship between the number track and the number line by playing games.

Number track
A number track shows the counting numbers. Each number occupies a defined space on the track. The numbers are written in the middle of each space. The number track does not include a space for zero.

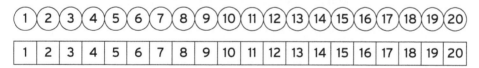

Number line
A number line shows the measuring numbers at equidistant points on a line. The number shown at each mark, or interval, is both the point on the line, and the distance away from the start of the line at zero. Fractions, or parts of numbers, can also be shown on the number line. A number line includes a position for zero.

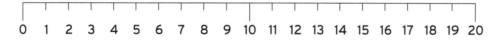

Teaching

Draw a number line

Use a ruler that is easy to read and accurate so that each number is written below the mark that shows the interval. Do not use a ruler on which the numbers are written in the spaces between the marks. If the pupil cannot manipulate a ruler, do the activity below called 'Using a ruler to draw straight lines'.

Teacher shows the ruler to the pupil and says:
This is a number line. A ruler is a number line that we use for measuring. There are small lines at equal distances. Look at the lines with numbers below them.

Point to 5 on the number line.

Ask pupil to find a few other points on the ruler.

Draw a line and mark the positions of all the numbers up to 20. Do not write the numbers yet.

Write the correct number below each mark on the number line.
Do not remind pupils that the line starts from zero. It sounds simple but even some adults get this wrong and write 1 at the beginning of the line as they do on the number track.

When the pupil has drawn the number line, ask them to use the ruler to check that their work is accurate.

The pupil uses a pencil to point exactly to the position of the number 5 on the ruler.

Pupil draws the number line. Some pupils find this very difficult. Allow them time to make errors and then to correct their own errors.

Pupil writes the numbers below each short vertical line.

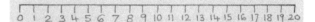

The pupil uses the ruler to check that the intervals are equidistant and the number sequence is written correctly starting with 0 (zero).

Using a ruler to draw straight lines

Pupils need to be able to draw straight lines with a ruler in order to construct a number line. However, some pupils cannot use a ruler because they cannot manipulate it. Teach them how to handle a ruler as an art lesson. Ask the pupil to draw lines at different angles. The intersecting lines will make random shapes. It does not matter if the lines are not completely straight, that will come with practice. When pupils have drawn enough lines, they can colour in the shapes to make a colourful picture. Once they can use a ruler to draw straight lines, pupils are ready to use it to draw number lines.

Hop and Jump to 20

Link the number track to the number line

Aim
- To compare a number track and a number line

Equipment
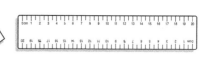
- Each player has their own number track
- Each player draws their own number line to 20
- One counter for each player
- Dice 1-6
- Ruler, pencil and paper

1 counter for each player

Preparation
Give each player a track numbered to 20. Each player draws their own number line measuring 20 cm. Players mark intervals of 1 cm with a short vertical line. Make longer marks to show the decade numbers 10 and 20. Write all the numbers to 20 below the correct marks. (If pupils have great difficulty drawing a number line correctly, provide one for this activity.)

Players can either 'hop' along the number track or 'jump' the total amount shown on the dice. Players then draw their moves on the number line. A 'hop' moves one space at a time. The player draws individual 'hops' and then shows the total distance moved on that turn by drawing an arc encompassing the hops. A 'jump' moves several spaces in one movement and is shown as a single arc.

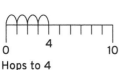

Hops to 4

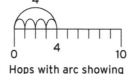

Hops with arc showing the total moved in that turn

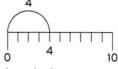

Jump to 4

How to play
Players race to reach the end of the line. Player A rolls the dice and moves the counter along the number track by hopping from one number to the next and counting each hop aloud. Players do not need to say the numbers that they land on; the important point is that they count each hop made with the counter. Do not slide the counter along the track; each hop needs to be a distinct movement.

Player A draws the hops on the number line. Draw each hop, then show the total move as an arc including all the hops in that turn. Write the total number moved on that turn above the arc. Do not write an addition sign. As players become more proficient they may show the move as one jump.

The next player has a turn on their own track and line.

The winner is the first player to reach (or pass) 20.

Example of position on the number track and recordings on the number line after 6 moves.

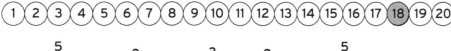

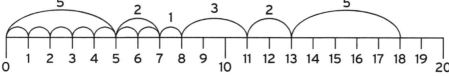

Checklist - The number line
Pupils can:
- ☐ Draw an accurate number line
- ☐ Compare a number track and a number line
- ☐ Understand the difference between a number track and a number line

The midpoint on a number line

Objectives
- Find the midpoint on an empty number line
- Reason from the midpoint to locate other points on a number line
- Sketch a number line

Pupils need to be thoroughly familiar with the number line if they are to use it effectively for calculation. The work in this section lays the foundations for later work on rounding numbers as well as fractions, although fractions are not explicitly taught at this stage.

Locating the midpoint on a number line is a key concept. Another way of saying this is that the midpoint is halfway along the line. For example, the midpoint on a line between 0 and 10 is 5 because 5 is half of 10.

When pupils can draw accurate number lines, they learn to draw partially numbered lines on which only the intervals at 5, 10, 15 and 20 are shown. Later they will work with empty number lines where only the beginning and end points are shown. They also need to learn to draw sketches of number lines so that they can use them to support their thinking for calculation with larger numbers.

Encourage pupils to discuss numbers by relating them to other points on the line and describing them in various ways such as *larger than, smaller than, before, after, between, midpoint, midway between, nearer to.*

Teaching

Find the midpoint on an empty number line
Introduce the idea of the midpoint between two numbers on a sketch of an empty number line. Pupils need to be able to identify the midpoint by eye rather than by measuring it.

Teacher sketches a number line and marks the beginning 0 and the end 10.

The midpoint of the line is in the middle of the line. It is the same distance from the beginning and the end. Where is the middle of the line?

Pupil points to the middle of the line. Encourage them to talk about why this is the midpoint using descriptions such as: *It is exactly between 0 and 10. It is halfway between 0 and 10. It is the same distance from the beginning and the end.*

Mark the midpoint. What is the number halfway between 0 and 10?

Pupil marks the midpoint. They use their own words to explain that 5 is at the midpoint.
5 is half of 10. Halfway between 0 and 10 is 5.

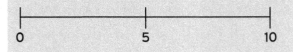

Do the same exercise with the number 20.
What is the number halfway between 0 and 20? Mark the midpoint.

Pupil marks the midpoint. They use their own words to explain that 10 is at the midpoint.
10 is half of 20. Halfway between 0 and 20 is 10.

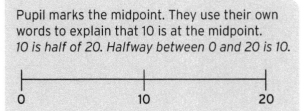

Reason to locate points on a number line

Teach pupils to reason from the midpoint to position other numbers on the number line. They use comparative language to explain their systematic thinking. This work lays the foundations for work with larger numbers on a partial number line.

Draw a number line without a ruler and mark the beginning 0 and the end 20.

I want you to find the position of 17 on the number line by reasoning. Which tens numbers is 17 between?

Where is 10 on the number line?

You know that 17 is between 10 and 20. What is the midpoint between 10 and 20?

Is 17 bigger or smaller than 15?

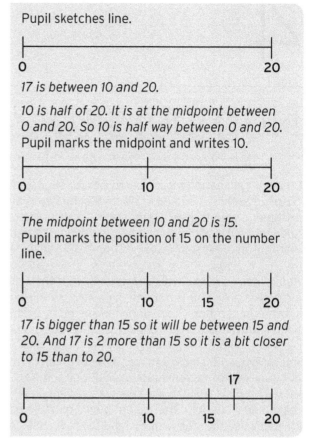

Pupil sketches line.

17 is between 10 and 20.

10 is half of 20. It is at the midpoint between 0 and 20. So 10 is half way between 0 and 20. Pupil marks the midpoint and writes 10.

The midpoint between 10 and 20 is 15. Pupil marks the position of 15 on the number line.

17 is bigger than 15 so it will be between 15 and 20. And 17 is 2 more than 15 so it is a bit closer to 15 than to 20.

Checklist - The midpoint on a number line

Pupils can:

☐ Find the midpoint on an empty number line
☐ Reason from the midpoint to locate other points on a number line
☐ Sketch a number line

4

Numbers to 20: Calculation

Efficient calculation means being able to choose the most effective method to manipulate numbers. Unfortunately the emphasis on mental maths at an early age has led some people to believe that mental arithmetic means a swift, automatic recall of facts. Pupils do need a body of core knowledge to call upon, but what is more important is 'the competent and flexible selection and application of [mental] methods in different contexts.' (DfE 2012)

Pupils learn a few universal strategies that they can adapt and apply to larger numbers. The addition strategies are: 10 plus a single digit, string addition, bridging through 10, and extending doubles. The subtraction strategies are applying key facts, bridging back through 10, and complementary addition. Solid knowledge of key facts is essential for using all these strategies effectively.

By working with small numbers and basic calculations, pupils develop the problem-solving skills required to analyse information and reason about numbers. These reasoning skills can later be transferred to more complex calculations. Teachers can guide pupils to investigate particular strategies, such as the reasoning from dot patterns, but pupils must be allowed sufficient time to consider and develop the strategies so that they understand them. If they are taught a set of procedures, they may not be able to remember the instructions correctly nor be able to apply them.

Pupils begin to use base 10 equipment to build numbers. They should be encouraged to use jottings on number lines to support their thinking. Make sure that they have plenty of experience in talking through and recording their thinking in diagrammatic as well as written form. They also need to answer and create word problems which put numbers in context. (See Chapter 10 p216)

Equipment

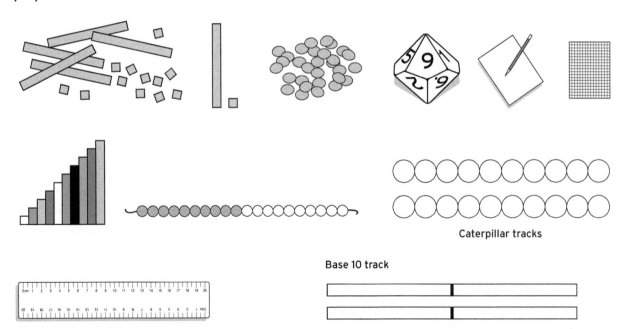

Caterpillar tracks

Base 10 track

Addition: 10 + a single digit

Objectives
- Add a single digit to 10
- Represent 10 plus a unit in linear and spatial layouts

Introduce Base 10 apparatus and the principle of exchange. The idea that several items can be represented by a single larger item was inherent in the Cuisenaire rods. Now pupils focus on the relationship between tens and ones and represent them in both linear and spatial layouts. This work begins to lay the foundations for place value work, however, do not use the place value headings 'Tens' and 'Units' at this stage. (Pupils may use the word 'ones' instead of 'units' if they prefer.)

Teaching
Use Base 10 equipment to establish that 10 units cubes (ones) have the same value as 1 ten rod.

Teacher gives pupil a ten rod and some ones:
Ones are also called units. How many units do you need to make the same length as this rod?

The rod is worth 10 units so you call it 1 ten.

Pupil puts 10 ones next to the rod and says:
The rod is the same length as 10 units.

Move the rod and cubes to one side and say:
Show me 1 ten. Add 1 unit to the ten. How many do you have altogether?

Pupil puts 1 ten and 1 unit in a line.
I have 1 ten and 1 unit. I have 11 altogether.

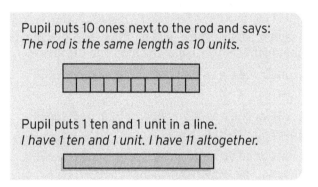

The next step is to place 1 ten in a vertical position and the unit cube to the right of the ten. This arrangement lays the foundations for later place value work, however, do not use the place value headings 'Tens' and 'Units' at this stage.

You can also show 1 ten and 1 unit in a different layout. Teacher moves the ten to the vertical position and places 1 unit next to it.
Draw a diagram and label it underneath.
Write 1 ten and 1 unit make 11. Write the equation for 10 add 1 equals 11.

Build the number 14. Tell me what you are doing. Then draw a diagram and label it. Encourage the pupil to use the pattern of 4.

The pupil practises building, describing and recording all the numbers from 11 to 19.

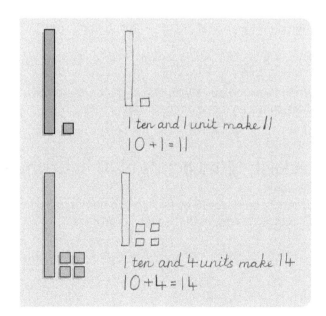

1 ten and 1 unit make 11
10 + 1 = 11

1 ten and 4 units make 14
10 + 4 = 14

Checklist - Addition: 10 + a single digit
Pupil can:
- ☐ Add a single digit to 10
- ☐ Represent 10 plus a unit in linear and spatial layouts

Find bonds of 10 in 'string addition'

Objectives
- Apply bonds of 10 by finding two numbers that make 10 in a list of numbers
- Record stages in the reasoning process

'String addition' is used to add three or more numbers. When pupils can confidently add a single digit number to 10, work on recognising bonds of 10 within the numbers to be added. Complete the addition by adding on the remaining numbers to that 10.

Pupils record their working in linear numerical form. They should use arrows rather than equal signs as this helps to emphasise the reasoning process.

Teaching

Ask the pupil to add a 'string' of 3 numbers in which 2 numbers constitute a bond of 10.

Teacher explains how to record the reasoning process in string addition. If necessary, the teacher demonstrates the use of the loop and the arrow.

Write 4 + 6 + 5. Then look for 2 numbers that make 10.

Use a loop under the numbers to connect the bonds of 10.

Now use an arrow to show that 4 and 6 make 10 and you still need to add 5.

What does 10 add 5 make? Use an arrow to complete your working.

Pupil writes 4 + 6 + 5 and says:
4 and 6 make 10.

4 + 6 + 5

4 + 6 + 5 ➔ 10 + 5

10 add 5 makes 15.

4 + 6 + 5 ➔ 10 + 5 ➔ 15

Give pupils plenty of practice finding bonds of 10 within strings of numbers.

7 + 4 + 3   5 + 9 + 1 + 2   2 + 6 + 8 + 3   3 + 5 + 4 + 5

When they can quickly and easily recognise bonds of 10 in strings of numbers and compute 10 + a single digit, they can move on to 'Bridging through 10'.

Checklist - Find bonds of 10 in 'string addition'
Pupils can:
- ☐ Apply bonds of 10 by finding two numbers that make 10 in a list of numbers
- ☐ Record stages in the reasoning process

Bridge through 10

Objectives

- Apply knowledge of key facts to make calculations easier
- Bridge through 10 to add two single digit numbers that total more than 10
- Demonstrate reasoning by using counters or Cuisenaire rods
- Record thinking using triads, number lines and equations

Bridging through 10 is the most important calculation strategy. It is used to add two single digits where the answer will be greater than 10. Ten is used as a 'bridge' in the calculation, hence the term 'bridging through 10'. In order to use this strategy pupils need to know the bonds of all the numbers to 10 and be able to compute 10 + a single digit.

Bridging is a universal strategy which can be adapted for calculations with multiples of 10. It can be used for addition, missing addend, and subtraction calculations. It is essential for working effectively with number lines.

Teaching

Use counters to demonstrate the bridging strategy by adding 8 and 5. Teacher puts out a line of 8 counters and a line of 5 counters. Place the 5 counters lower than the line of 8 as shown.

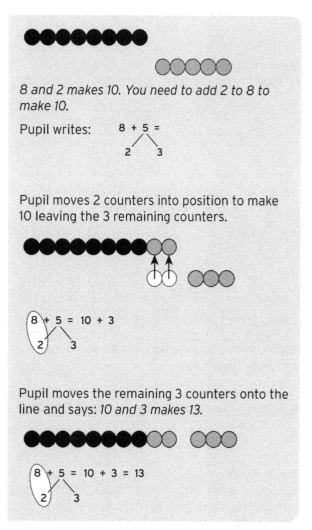

I am going to show you how you can use the bonds of 10 to make calculations easier. Look at 8 plus 5.

I use 10 as a 'bridge' to help me work out the answer. What do I need to add to 8 to make 10?

8 and 2 makes 10. You need to add 2 to 8 to make 10.

Pupil writes: 8 + 5 =

Write 8 add 5 equals .You can split the 5 into 2 and 3. Show it as a triad. If the pupil has difficulty understanding the instruction, the teacher writes it for them.

Move 2 counters to show that 8 and 2 makes 10.

Pupil moves 2 counters into position to make 10 leaving the 3 remaining counters.

Teacher demonstrates how to use a loop to link the bonds of 10.
Use a loop to show that 8 and 2 make 10. Now complete the equation to show that there are 10 plus 3 more. The teacher points to the relevant numbers whilst speaking.

There are 10 counters and 3 more. Move the counters to show 10 + 3. Show the total amount on your working.

Pupil moves the remaining 3 counters onto the line and says: *10 and 3 makes 13.*

Ask pupil to work out 7 + 6 and 4 + 8 and explain what they are doing. They demonstrate with equipment and record their thinking using triads and equations. Give them plenty of practice with other numbers.

Make sure that the bridging concept is secure before bridging from 9. Particular recording problems arise which can cause confusion because the way that the addend (the number being added on) is split, resembles the answer. In this example the pupil may read 1 and 6 as 16.

9 + 7 = 10 + 6 = 16

   1   6

This problem does not arise when pupils apply this strategy to add a single digit to larger numbers.

29 + 7 = 30 + 6 = 36

   1   6

Bridging through 10 using Cuisenaire rods and recording on a number line

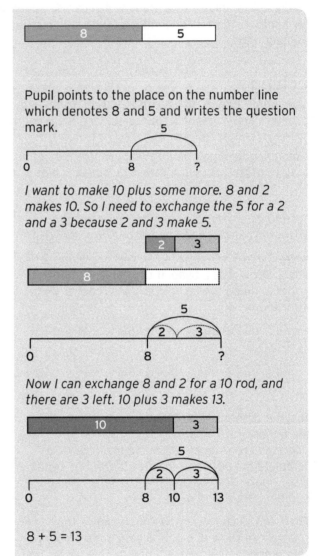

Use Cuisenaire rods to show 8 plus 5.

Draw a number line. Write 0 (zero) and 8 on the line. Use an arc to show that you add 5.

Where will you write the answer to 8 and 5 on the number line? Write a question mark to show where the answer will be.

Pupil points to the place on the number line which denotes 8 and 5 and writes the question mark.

Show me how you make 10 and some more. Change the rods and explain what you are doing.

I want to make 10 plus some more. 8 and 2 makes 10. So I need to exchange the 5 for a 2 and a 3 because 2 and 3 make 5.

Record what you have done on the number line. Use arcs to show numbers 2 and 3.

Now I can exchange 8 and 2 for a 10 rod, and there are 3 left. 10 plus 3 makes 13.

Record what you have done on the number line and write the answer.

Write the answer to 8 plus 5 as an equation.

8 + 5 = 13

Weaker pupils
Introduce bridging through 10 in stages if the pupils' number bonds are weak. Do this by adding the same number each time to reduce the number of bonds required. For example, revise the bonds of 5 and then apply them to bridging. The examples are not presented in order; pupils need to do the calculations, not merely follow the pattern of the answers. Ask the pupil to work out 8 + 5, 6 + 5 and 7 + 5.

First Past the Post
(Two or more players)

Aims:
- To practise bridging through 10
- To practise exchanging 10 ones for 1 ten

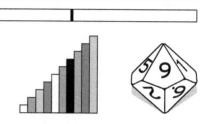

Equipment
- Cuisenaire rods
- 0-9 dice
- Board with one 'track' for each player

How to play

The track is marked in 10 cm sections. Players may not place a rod across the mark. If the numbers add up to more than 10 they must be exchanged for a ten rod and the correct units' rod.

Player A throws the dice. Player A takes the rod that corresponds to the number thrown and places it on their track.

Second player has a turn.

On the next turn, Player A throws the dice and takes another rod. Player A places it adjacent to the rod on their track. If the rod crosses the marker that shows 10, the player puts the rod slightly above the track. Then the player exchanges the single rod for its components to complete the 10 and have the appropriate amount to add on. (See diagram below.)

The winner is the first person to cross the finish line.

Example: Shows two turns played by Player A
First throw of dice is 8.

Second throw of dice is 5.

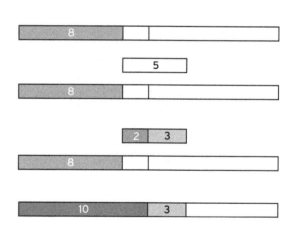

Player cannot place 5 because it will cross the line. They need to make 10 and must explain what they are doing. Player says: *8 + 2 = 10. First I need to exchange the 5 for a 2 and a 3.*

Then Player A says: *Now I can exchange 8 + 2 for 10, and put the 3 rod on the track. 10 + 3 = 13. So now I have 13.*

Checklist - Bridge through 10

Pupils can:
- ☐ Apply knowledge of key facts to make calculations easier
- ☐ Bridge through 10 to add two single digit numbers that total more than 10
- ☐ Demonstrate reasoning by using counters or Cuisenaire rods
- ☐ Record thinking using triads, number lines and equations

Extend doubles to 10 + 10

Objectives
- Use Cuisenaire rods to demonstrate the doubles facts to 10 + 10
- Recall the doubles facts to 10 + 10
- Discuss the relationship between the doubles facts
- Use the language of double and half

The ability to double and halve numbers is a useful tool for calculation which can be generalised for larger numbers. Understanding these relationships is important for working with number lines, one of the most useful tools for supporting thinking.

Pupils explored the doubles patterns to 5 + 5. Now they learn the doubles to 10 + 10. Cuisenaire rods provide a clear visual image of what it means to double or halve something.

Teaching

Doubles to 20
Give the pupil a box of Cuisenaire rods.

Build the doubles pyramid from double 1 to double 5.

Pupil puts out the rods to double 5.

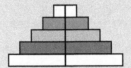

Can you use some more rods to build some bigger doubles?

The pupil takes two 6 rods and places them below 5 + 5. Pupil says: *6 and 6 is 2 more than 5 and 5, so double 6 makes 12.*

If the pupils do not continue the pattern in order of increasing size, do not intervene. When the construction is finished ask them to put them in the correct place so that it shows the doubles in order to double 10 equals 20.

The pupil continues to build the doubles numbers to 10 + 10.

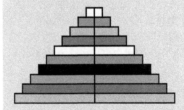

Slide the rods so that they all line up on the left hand side of the page. Tell me what you see.

Pupil moves the rods and says: *I can see a 'staircase'. Each step is 2 longer than the line above it.*

Discuss the relationships between the numbers. For example, if double 6 is 12, then double 7 will be 2 more than 12. Double 7 is 14.

Pupil describes each double in the sequence in terms of the number that is '2 more', or '2 less'.

Draw a diagram of the doubles 'staircase' and colour it in. Write the equation next to each doubles fact.

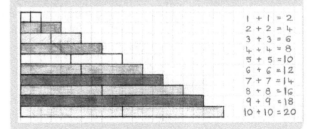

1 + 1 = 2
2 + 2 = 4
3 + 3 = 6
4 + 4 = 8
5 + 5 = 10
6 + 6 = 12
7 + 7 = 14
8 + 8 = 16
9 + 9 = 18
10 + 10 = 20

Demonstrating half

Teacher uses Cuisenaire rods to build the doubles 'pyramid' to 10 + 10. *Look at the pattern. Can you split the pattern in half?*

Pupil moves the rods apart along the mid line. They may use a pencil if they want to. *I have split the pattern in half.*

Ask the pupil to investigate each double number in turn using the Cuisenaire rods to demonstrate half of each number. The pupil investigated the doubles to 5 + 5 in Chapter 2 (p38) so they can start with double 6.

Pupil puts out double 6 and says: *I can see 12.*

Pupil moves the rods apart and says: *6 is half of 12. Half of 12 is 6.*

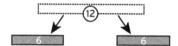

Pupil puts out double 7 and says: *I can see 14.*

Pupil moves the rods apart as they say: *7 is half of 14. Half of 14 is 7.*

Pupil puts out double 8 and says: *I can see 16.*

Pupil moves rods apart as they say: *8 is half of 16. Half of 16 is 8.*

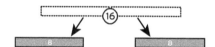

Pupil puts out double 9 and says: *I can see 18.*

Pupil moves rods apart as they say: *9 is half of 18. Half of 18 is 9.*

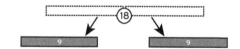

Pupil puts out double 10 and says: *I can see 20.*

Pupil moves rods apart as they say: *10 is half of 20. Half of 20 is 10.*

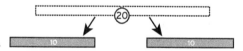

Checklist - Extend doubles to 10 + 10

Pupils can:
- ☐ Use Cuisenaire rods to demonstrate the doubles facts to 10 + 10
- ☐ Recall the doubles facts to 10 + 10
- ☐ Discuss the relationship between the doubles facts
- ☐ Use the language of double and half

Subtraction: the concept

Objectives
- Understand subtraction as taking away a portion of one quantity
- Understand subtraction as finding how much more is required to make two quantities equal
- Understand subtraction as finding the difference between two quantities
- Use a variety of language for subtraction
- Understand subtraction as a missing addend
- Understand subtraction as the inverse of addition

Establish the concept and language of subtraction using small numbers before teaching calculation strategies for subtraction. The vocabulary of subtraction is varied and includes: subtract, take away, minus, less than, remove, reduce, decrease, left over, how many more, difference. Pupils need to do plenty of examples both answering questions using different wording and constructing their own word problems (p220). It is essential to teach the concept of subtraction in context because the operation of subtraction is used in different and distinct contexts: separation (take away) and comparison which may involve either equalising or difference.

Pupils may find subtraction difficult because they do not realise that the operation is used for different concepts, and some find the actual computation difficult. These difficulties can be overcome if pupils work with small numbers while they explore the concepts and practise using the varied language of subtraction, not merely the term 'take away'. It also helps to make them aware that subtraction is the inverse of addition. If pupils know that 7 = 4 + 3, then they also know that 7 - 3 = 4. This understanding means that pupils can record subtraction questions in the form of missing addends. 7 - 3 = ? can also be written as 3 + ? = 7. This idea was introduced in the work on triads in Chapter 2.

Pupils are sometimes taught the mantra 'you *always* take the smaller number from the larger number'. This advice may seem to work in the early stages when teaching young children but can lead to confusion and errors later. Pupils often remember the mantra and misapply it when using the column method to subtract multi-digit numbers.

Subtraction as *separation* is simple to demonstrate and explain. There is one quantity, some items are removed from it and the answer is the amount that is left. For example: *I have 10. I take away 3 so 7 are left. 10 - 3 = 7.*

Subtraction as *comparison* is much more difficult to grasp and explain. There are two different concepts: making two quantities *equal,* or finding the *difference* between them. Both of these involve comparing two quantities.

Teach *equalising* first as this can intuitively be solved by counting on. Equalising answers the question 'How much more is needed to make a smaller amount the same as a larger amount?' For example: *I have 8 marbles, Mary has 5 marbles. How many more marbles does Mary need so she has the same number as me?*

Difference is a much more difficult idea for pupils to grasp. Here the quantities are compared but neither quantity will be changed. This is a more abstract idea than either removing an amount, or working out how many more to add to make them equal. Further confusion may arise because the word 'difference' means both the result of subtracting one quantity from another, and the comparison of one quantity or measure with another. Do not take it for granted that pupils will understand the criterion of comparison to be size or quantity, rather than any other attribute such as colour in the case of Cuisenaire rods.

Teaching

Subtraction as separation: take away

Teacher puts 5 counters in a line.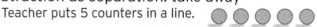

How many counters are there?	5 counters.
There are 5 counters. Take away 2. How many are left?	Pupil removes 2 counters: *I take away 2 counters so 3 counters are left.*
Draw a diagram to show 5 counters. Take away 2 counters.	Pupil draws 5 counters and crosses out 2 counters: *5 take away 2 leaves 3 counters.*
	○ ○ ○ ⊗ ⊗
Write 5 take away 2 as an equation.	Pupil writes the equation 5 - 2 = 3 and says: *5 take away 2 equals 3.*

Ask pupils to solve several examples until they can use the term 'take away' confidently and model the concept, draw diagrams and write the equations. Then introduce examples with varied language such as: *What is 5 minus 2? Find 4 less than 9. Reduce 8 by 3. Decrease 6 by 2. Take 6 away from 10.*

The wording '10 take away 3' is easy to understand as the numbers in the question appear in the order they do in the equation. The question becomes more difficult to understand if it is expressed as: 'Take 3 away from 10.' Pupils draw diagrams to show what the question means so that they realise they need to start with 10 and take 3 away and the equation is still 10 - 3 = 7.

Subtraction as comparison: equalising

Teacher puts out 8 counters in a line then makes a line with 5 counters below it, taking care to align counters as shown.

How many counters are in the top line?	8 counters.
How many counters are in the bottom line?	5 counters.
How many more counters do you need to add to 5 to make it equal to 8?	*I need 3 more counters.* Pupils who understand the number bonds should be able quickly to say '3 more'. Some pupils may have to count on from 5.
Teacher gives the pupil different coloured counters and says: *Use the counters to make the line of 5 equal the line of 8. Then draw a diagram to show what you have done.*	Pupil puts out 3 extra counters, and draws a diagram.

Write an equation to show your answer.	Pupil writes 8 - 5 = 3. The operation can also be seen as a missing addend which means answering the question '5 add what makes 8?'. In this case the equation is 5 + ? = 8 and the answer is 5 + 3 = 8.

Do several examples for equalising amounts up to 20. Vary the wording to include questions such as: *How much more is 15 than 11? How much more do you need to add to 8 to make 12?*

Put the numbers into context in word problems. (See Chapter 10 p220 for examples.)

Subtraction as comparison: difference

How much more, or less, is one quantity than another? Establish the idea of difference in quantities or measures using Cuisenaire rods and number lines to make the portions that are the same and those that are different explicit. Do not use addition or subtraction signs on the number lines. Pupils need to learn that the arc shows the distance between two points irrespective of whether you start at point A and add on to reach point B, or start at point B and subtract to reach point A.

How much more is 9 than 5? Use Cuisenaire rods to compare 9 and 5 by placing one rod below the other.

Pupil puts out the rods.

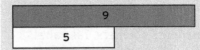

Draw two number lines to compare 9 and 5. Check that the beginnings of the lines are aligned.

Pupil draws number lines. At this early stage, pupil draws a separate number line for each quantity to emphasise the difference between them.

Draw an arc on the diagram to show the difference between 9 and 5. Explain what you are doing.

Pupil draws the arc whilst saying: *I mark 5 on the longer line. I want to find the distance from 5 to 9 so I draw an arc. I put a question mark to show where I will find the answer.*

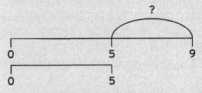

Look at the Cuisenaire rods. Exchange the 9 rod for a 5 and some more.

5 and 4 make 9 so I can exchange a 9 rod for a 5 and a 4 rod. Pupil does the exchange.

Record it on the number line and write the equation to show the difference between 9 and 5.

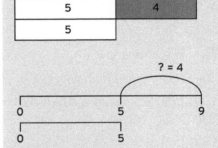

Pupil writes 9 – 5 = 4.
Pupils may also write the equation as a missing addend. The question is 5 + ? = 9 and the answer is 5 + 4 = 9. However the subtraction equation makes the concept of difference between the quantities clearer.

Give pupil further examples using a variety of language. How much less is 2 than 8? What is the difference between 13 and 17? Put the numbers into context in word problems. (See p220)

Checklist - Subtraction: the concept

Pupils can:
- ☐ Understand subtraction as taking away a portion of one quantity
- ☐ Understand subtraction as finding how much more is required to make two quantities equal
- ☐ Understand subtraction as finding the difference between two quantities
- ☐ Use a variety of language for subtraction
- ☐ Understand subtraction as missing addend
- ☐ Understand subtraction as the inverse of addition

Subtraction: applying key facts

Objectives

- Use component knowledge for subtraction with numbers up to 20
- Apply knowledge of doubles and near doubles to subtraction
- Apply knowledge of bonds of 10 to subtraction
- Talk about how the known facts are used to do the subtraction
- Use a variety of vocabulary to describe subtraction

Demonstrate how doubles and near doubles knowledge can be applied to subtraction with two-digit numbers. It is very important that pupils become competent in applying this knowledge and explaining and recording their thinking if they are to use it with larger numbers. Even if pupils are able to do the calculations easily, they must describe their thinking. Practise in reasoning about small numbers lays secure foundations for working with larger numbers later on.

Teaching

Applying doubles and near doubles knowledge

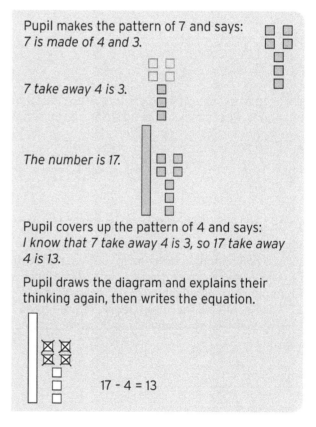

You can use doubles and near doubles facts to help you subtract. Use base 10 equipment to make the pattern of 7. What is 7 made of?

Teacher covers up the pattern of 4 and asks: *What is 7 take away 4?*

Teacher places 1 ten rod to the left of the pattern of 7 to make 17 and asks: *What is the number?*

What is 17 take away 4? Explain how you work it out.

Draw a diagram and write the equation.

Pupil makes the pattern of 7 and says: *7 is made of 4 and 3.*

7 take away 4 is 3.

The number is 17.

Pupil covers up the pattern of 4 and says: *I know that 7 take away 4 is 3, so 17 take away 4 is 13.*

Pupil draws the diagram and explains their thinking again, then writes the equation.

17 - 4 = 13

Give pupils further examples applying doubles and near doubles facts and using a variety of language such as:

18 minus 4.

I have 15. How many more do I need to make 19?

15 subtract 3.

What is the difference between 12 and 6?

Pupils need to explain which facts they are using to work out the answers. If pupils have difficulty with the explanation they may use base 10 equipment to help them.

Applying bonds of 10 knowledge

Use bead strings and Cuisenaire rods to demonstrate subtraction from 20 using bonds of 10 knowledge.

You can use the bonds of 10 to help you subtract. What is 10 take away 4?

10 take away 4 is 6.

Give pupil a bead string to 20.
You know that 10 take away 4 is 6. What is 20 take away 4? Show me on the bead string.

Pupil moves the beads and explains:
10 take away 4 is 6, so 20 take away 4 is 16.

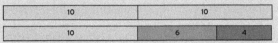

Use Cuisenaire rods to show me 20 take away 4.

Pupil puts out 2 ten rods. *I need to take away 4 so I exchange 1 ten for a 6 and a 4 because 6 and 4 make 10.*
Pupil takes away the 4 rod and says: *10 take away 4 is 6 so 20 take away 4 is 16.*

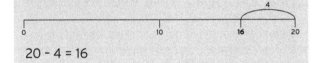

Can you show 20 subtract 4 on a number line and write the equation?

Pupil draws a number line showing 0, 10 and 20. Pupil explains as they draw the arc to show the reasoning process.
I know that 10 take away 4 is 6 so I can show 20 take away 4 equals 16.

20 - 4 = 16

Pupils need to explain which facts they are using to work out the answers. They record their thinking on number lines. Pupils may use bead strings or Cuisenaire rods if they need to.

4 + ☐ = 20   20 - 7 = ☐   20 - 9 = ☐

13 + ☐ = 16   15 + ☐ = 20   18 - 4 = ☐

Checklist – Subtraction: applying key facts

Pupils can:
- ☐ Use component knowledge for subtraction with numbers up to 20
- ☐ Apply knowledge of doubles and near doubles to subtraction
- ☐ Apply knowledge of bonds of 10 to subtraction
- ☐ Talk about how the known facts are used to do the subtraction
- ☐ Use a variety of vocabulary to describe subtraction

Subtraction: bridging back through 10

Objectives

- Subtract a unit digit from a two-digit number
- Bridge back through 10
- Record thinking on a number line
- Explain thinking

Bridging through 10 is the most important calculation strategy. It is a universal strategy which can be adapted for calculations with larger numbers. The advantage of bridging through 10 is that:
- it is rooted in the base 10 structure
- it is easy to model
- it can be used for addition, missing addend, and subtraction calculations
- it can be adapted to work with very large numbers
- it is essential for working effectively with number lines.

Pupils subtract a single digit number from a two-digit number by bridging back through 10. This strategy is the reverse of bridging forward through 10 (see p79). To use this strategy effectively, pupils need to know the bonds of 10, and be able to subtract a unit digit from a two-digit number.

Demonstrate the bridging strategy using base 10 equipment and Cuisenaire rods.

Teaching

Subtracting a unit digit.

Use base 10 equipment to show me 14. Tell me what it is made of.

Take away 4. Draw a diagram and write it as an equation.

Pupil builds 14 using base 10 equipment and says: *14 is made of 1 ten and 4 units.*

Pupil removes 4 units and says:
14 take away 4 equals 10.
Then the pupil draws the diagram and writes the equation.

$$14 - 4 = 10$$

Pupils do further examples to practise subtracting a unit digit:

$17 - 7 = \square$

$13 - \square = 10$

$\square - 4 = 10$

$12 - 2 = \square$

$16 - \square = 10$

$\square - 9 = 10$

Bridging back through 10

Subtract a single digit from a two-digit number where the answer involves crossing the decade boundary. Pupils use number lines to show their reasoning.

You can use the bonds of 10 to make taking away easier. Write '14 take away 6 equals what?' Use counters to show me 14 take away 6.

Pupil writes 14 - 6 = ?
Pupil puts out a line of 14 counters leaving a slight space between the 10 and the 4.

14 take away 4 leaves 10.
Pupil takes away 4 counters and moves them below the line so that they remain visible.

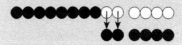

Use 10 as a 'bridge' to help work out the answer. What do you need to take away from 14 to make 10?

6 take away 4 makes 2 so I need to take away 2 more counters. 10 take away 2 is 8 .
Pupil moves 2 counters down.

You have taken away 4 counters. You need to take away 6 counters altogether. How many more counters do you need to take away? Explain your thinking.

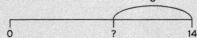

Pupil writes 14 - 6 = 8 and says:
14 take away 6 makes 8.

Pupil explains their reasoning as they draw the stages on the number line.

Record 14 subtract 6 on a number line. Show your reasoning and explain it.

Note that the pupil does not use subtraction signs on the number line diagram. The arc marks the distance between points. A question mark shows the point at which the answer will be found.

14 take away 6. I mark 0 and 14. The answer will be less than 14 so I put a question mark between 0 and 14. I am taking away 6 so I draw an arc showing 6.

It is important that pupils say where the answer will be on the number line; some pupils find this difficult.

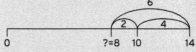

The pupil completes the diagram and explains:
14 take away 4 leaves 10. I can split 6 into 4 and 2. Then 10 take away 2 is 8, so 14 take away 6 is 8.

14 - 6 = 8

Give pupils plenty of practice in bridging back through 10 and set them word problems. They should also make up their own word problems.

15 - 8 = ☐   13 - 7 = ☐   17 - 9 = ☐   14 - 5 = ☐

Checklist - Subtraction: bridging back through 10
Pupils can:
- ☐ Subtract a unit digit from a two-digit number
- ☐ Bridge back through 10
- ☐ Record thinking on a number line
- ☐ Explain thinking

Subtraction: complementary addition (the shopkeeper's method)

Objectives

- Subtract by complementary addition, also known as the shopkeeper's method
- Understand subtraction as the inverse operation to addition
- Write a subtraction question as a missing addend question
- Record and explain thinking using a number line

Most people associate the operation of subtraction with 'counting back'. You start with an initial quantity and work back from it. Some pupils find working backwards very difficult. It may be easier for them to use complementary addition. This method involves 'adding on' to find the answer to a subtraction problem. It is often called the 'shopkeeper's method' as it was used in shops to give change. The shopkeeper said the amount that had been paid and counted forward to calculate the change that was due.

Pupils have already used 'adding on' in the work on the concept of 'equalising' two amounts. Now they learn that the method of 'adding on' can be used to find the answer to any subtraction calculation. To use this method pupils need to be able to 'count on' from any number and to use a number line.

It is important that pupils work with missing addends before learning complementary addition so that they are clear that subtraction is the inverse operation to addition. Start with questions which do not require pupils to bridge through 10. Then show how the technique they used for bridging forward through 10 (p79) can be applied to subtraction.

Teaching

Demonstrate that it does not matter whether a quantity is removed from the beginning or the end of a line of counters; the result will be the same.

Give pupil counters and 2 caterpillar tracks to 10. *Put out 2 rows of counters on the caterpillar tracks. How many counters are there in each row?*

Take 2 counters away from the end of the top row. How many counters are left?

Take away 2 counters from the beginning of the bottom row. How many are left?

Show 10 take away 2 on number lines. Show 2 removed from the end of the line, then show 2 removed from the beginning of the line. Explain what you are thinking.

Ask pupil to demonstrate and record more examples: 16 – 3 =   and 19 – 5 =

Pupil puts out counters and says: *There are 10 counters in each row.*

Pupil removes 2 counters from the top row and says: *There are 8 counters.*

Pupil removes 2 counters from the bottom row and says: *There are 8 counters.*

Pupil draws number lines. Make it clear which portion has been removed by 'scribbling out' as shown below.

10 – 2 = 8

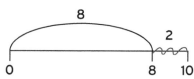

Number line showing 2 subtracted from the end of the line.

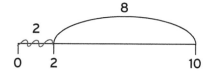

Number line showing 2 subtracted from the beginning of the line.

Use Cuisenaire rods to demonstrate removing a quantity from the beginning or end of a line.

Show me 9 subtract 5 using Cuisenaire rods. Record your thinking on a number line.	Pupil places a 9 rod and talks about what they are doing. *I have 9. I need to subtract 5. I exchange 9 for a 4 and a 5. Now I take away 5 and I am left with 4, so 9 take away 5 is 4.* 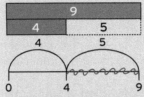
Show me how you subtract 5 from the beginning of the line.	Pupil puts out a 9 rod and reverses the order of the 5 and the 4 rods as shown below. *I have 9. I need to take away 5. I exchange 9 for a 5 and a 4. I subtract 5 and I am left with 4, so 9 subtract 5 is 4.* 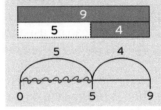

Revise missing addend

Use Cuisenaire rods to demonstrate the missing addend.

Draw a triad to show '6 subtract 2 equals what?' Use a question mark to show what you need to find. Triads were introduced in Chapter 2. (See p31)	Pupil records the triad and explains: *I can split 6 into 2 and some more.*
Write the equations that the triad represents.	Pupil writes the equations: $6 = 2 + ?$ $2 + ? = 6$ $6 - 2 = ?$
Use Cuisenaire rods to demonstrate the question. Explain your thinking.	Pupil puts out the rods as shown below. Note that the pupil does not put out the 4 rod initially. *I have 6. I want to take away 2 so I exchange 6 for 2 and some more.* Pupil writes $2 + ? = 6$.
Write the equation to show '2 add what makes 6?' This is called a missing addend question. You can also call it a mystery number question.	
Show the missing addend question on a number line. *Write the answer as an equation.*	Pupil draws the number line. The pupil does not need to draw an arc to show 2 but may do so if they prefer to. 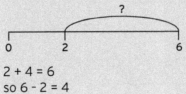 $2 + 4 = 6$ so $6 - 2 = 4$

Pupils work out questions using Cuisenaire rods and record their thinking. They need to write the subtraction question as a missing addend before they start. Example: $9 - 3 = ?$ becomes $3 + ? = 9$.

$8 - 5 =$	$17 - 11 =$	$20 - 14 =$
$10 - 3 =$	$16 - 3 =$	$19 - 5 =$

Complementary addition and bridging through 10

You can bridge forward through 10 to work out subtraction. First write the subtraction as a missing addend question then do the calculation.

Write 13 subtract 8 equals what? Then write it as a missing addend.

Use Cuisenaire rods to model the question. Explain your thinking and record it on a number line.

Pupil writes 13 - 8 = ? and then writes 8 + ? = 13

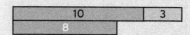

They may draw a triad to help if necessary.

Pupil shows 13 as 10 and 3, then puts an 8 rod below and says: *8 add what makes 13?*

Pupil adjusts the rods (see below) and says: *I can use 10 as a 'bridge' to help me work out the answer. What do I need to add to 8 to make 10? 8 and 2 make 10 so I add a 2 rod. I need to add 3 more to make 13. Now I can exchange 2 and 3 for a 5 rod. So 8 and 5 makes 13.*

Pupil constructs a number line to show the reasoning process and the solution to the missing addend question 8 + ? = 13

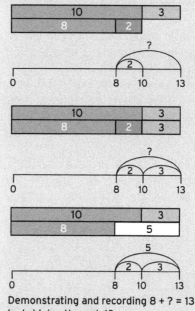

Demonstrating and recording 8 + ? = 13 by bridging through 10

Further examples for the pupil to work through:

15 - 9 =   14 - 8 =   12 - 7 =

Checklist - Subtraction: complementary addition (the shopkeeper's method)

Pupils can:
- ☐ Subtract by complementary addition, also known as the shopkeeper's method
- ☐ Understand subtraction as the inverse operation to addition
- ☐ Write a subtraction question as a missing addend question
- ☐ Record and explain thinking using a number line
- ☐ Explain thinking

5

Numbers to 100: Counting

Pupils need to count accurately and fluently to 100. However being able to recite the number names in order is not sufficient. They need to understand what the numbers represent and that it is more efficient to organise items into 'tens' to count them. Each group of ten constitutes a decade. The 'crossover' points are the positions in the sequence where one decade ends and the next begins.

In the number system the digits 0 to 9 can represent any number. The value of a digit in a number depends on its position, or place, in the number. Formal place value will be taught in Chapter 8. (See p175) It is crucial that pupils understand the principle of exchange: several items can be represented by a single item of greater value. Pupils learnt to exchange 1 ten for 10 ones in Chapter 4. (See p76)

Understanding that a two-digit number represents one total quantity, the set of the number, is a difficult concept to grasp. Concrete materials help pupils investigate the structure of the counting system and develop reasoning skills by talking about what they see and do. They record their thinking in diagrams, on number lines and as equations. Number lines are a calculation aid, especially useful for work with very large numbers. They are essential for understanding rounding in order to approximate numbers to make calculations easier. The number line is the basis for measurement of all kinds. Pupils need to be able to construct and interpret partial number lines In order to work with charts and graphs.

The 100 square is introduced to provide a spatial image of the structure of the first 100 numbers. It also shows clearly where one decade ends and the next begins. For example 20 is at the end of the 'teens' decade. The next decade starts with the number 21.

Equipment

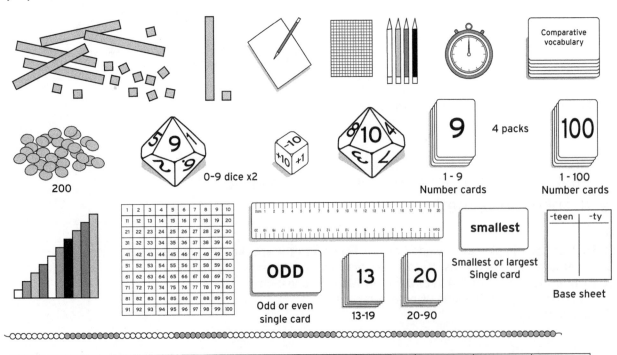

Counting in ones to 100

Objectives

- Say number names for all numbers to 100
- Articulate the sounds clearly, especially the 'teen' and 'ty' endings
- Synchronise number names with objects counted
- Locate any number from 1 to 100 on a bead string

The two-digit numbers consist of a tens number and a quantity of units, or ones. The numbers above 20 are easier to learn than the 'teen' numbers because the numbers are spoken in the order that they are written. For example, *'sixty five'* is written as 65. It means there are 60 items and another 5 items.

Pupils need a sense of the relative size of numbers, and to see numbers in relation to the decade structure. Develop this sense by using counters and a bead string and discussing the relationships between the numbers. Pay particular attention to the decade numbers. These are the numbers ending in 0. Pupils need to develop a memorable visual image of what the decades look like in a linear formation.

The decade boundaries are the most difficult positions to understand. Failure to understand where one decade ends and the next begins causes much of the confusion with working on two-digit numbers. A decade ends with a tens number and the next decade begins with a number ending in 1.

Teach the counting sequence above 20 orally using counters and a bead string to 100. Pupils learn to say the number names fluently and rhythmically and use counters to count quantities. First work on the sequence to 30. When the pupil is confident counting to 30, work on the numbers to 40. Gradually work through the decades to 100 in the same way. It is important that pupils have sufficient practice modelling the larger numbers. Plenty of space is required to lay out lines of counters to 100 so work on a long table or the floor.

Teaching

Concrete counting

Provide a container with at least 100 counters.

Count 20 counters in a line. Leave a small space when you reach 10 then continue.

The pupil puts out 20 counters and synchronises each number name with the correct counter in the sequence.

Add 1 more counter to the line. How many counters are there?
It is important to give the pupil time to find any error and correct it. If they struggle, then count with the pupil.

Pupil puts out 1 more counter and says:
There are 21.

Pupil leaves a space after 20. If they do not, ask them to count from the beginning and leave a space after each group of 10.

There are 21 counters. Add 1 more counter. How many counters are there?

Pupil puts out another counter and says:
There are 22 counters.

Ask pupils to continue to build up the sequence in this way until they reach 29.

Pupil continues to build the sequence to 29.

Add 1 more counter. How many counters are there altogether?

Pupil adds 1 more counter and says:
There are 30 counters.

Can you count in tens. Point to each tens number as you say it.

Pupil says and points to each tens number.

Ask pupil to point to other numbers in the sequence between 20 and 30. It is important that pupils can quickly identify 21, 22, 28 and 29.

Pupil says: 10   20   30

Read and write numbers to 30

Give pupil number cards with numbers 21 to 30.

Put the cards in order starting with 21. Say each number as you place the card.

Pupil puts out cards and reads the number.

Pupil says each number aloud and copies it. It is important that the spacing between numbers is appropriate so that they are easy to read.

Write the numbers from 21 to 30.

When the pupil has written the numbers, remove the cards and ask them to write the numbers from 21 to 30 from memory.

If the pupil has difficulty, they practice using the Look, Say, Cover, Write method. (Chapter 1, p18)

Give pupil A3 paper. *Use a ruler to draw a number line from 0 to 30. Mark 10 and 20 then show all the numbers between 20 and 30.*

When pupils are comfortable counting to 30, then work up through the decades to 100 in the same way.

The 100 Counter Dash

Aim
- Counting to 100

Equipment
- Dice 1-10
- Counters

 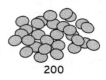

200

How to play

Players take turns to throw the dice and take the correct number of counters. They put counters out in a line, leaving a small gap between each group of 10 counters. Players say the total number of counters they have after each turn.

Note players do not need to be able to add. They 'read' the number of counters by counting the tens numbers and then counting the rest of the counters. For example to reach 53 they count 10, 20, 30, 40, 50 and 3.

Player A says: 53 ◌◌◌◌◌◌◌◌◌◌ ◌◌◌◌◌◌◌◌◌◌ ◌◌◌◌◌◌◌◌◌◌ ◌◌◌◌◌◌◌◌◌◌ ◌◌◌◌◌◌◌◌◌◌ ◌◌◌

Player B says: 44 ◌◌◌◌◌◌◌◌◌◌ ◌◌◌◌◌◌◌◌◌◌ ◌◌◌◌◌◌◌◌◌◌ ◌◌◌◌◌◌◌◌◌◌ ◌◌◌◌

The winner is the first person to reach 100.

Locate numbers up to 100 on a bead string

Use a bead string to 100 with two colours clearly showing alternating groups of 10. Ask location questions for numbers up to 100 paying particular attention to the decade boundaries - the change from one group of 10 to the next.

How many beads are there?

There are 100 beads.

Count in tens. Point to the number on the bead string as you say it.

Pupil must touch the relevant bead as they say each decade number - 10, 20, 30, 40, 50, 60, 70, 80, 90, 100.

Show me where 50 is.
It is important that the pupil counts from the left.

Pupil counts in tens from the left and points to 50: *This is 50.*

Show me 53.

Pupil points to 53 and says: *This is 53.*

When pupils can find specific numbers reasonably quickly, consolidate their use of comparative language. Encourage pupils to talk about the position of each number in relation to other numbers. Pupils touch the beads as they answer questions. Answers should be given in full sentences.

What is the number after 38?

> *39 is the number after 38. 39 is between 38 and 40. 39 is one less than 40.*

The number before 21 is 20. What is the number before 72?

> *71 is before 72. 72 is between 71 and 73.*

Ask questions using a variety of spatial and directional language as well as relative size.

What is 1 less than 60?
Which number is between 79 and 81?

What is 2 more than 49?
Find 39. What is the next number?

Find My Number

Aim
- To use comparative vocabulary to describe numbers
- To give clear instructions
- To locate numbers on a bead string

Equipment
- Bead string to 100
- Comparative word cards (between, more than, less than, before, after, next) (four sets of words)
- Timer (decide on time allowed at start of game. Use sufficient time for players to formulate a few questions)
- Score sheet and pencil

How to play
Shuffle the word cards and place them face down.

Player B starts the timer. Player A takes the top card from the pile. Player A uses the comparative word on the card to describe the position of a number.

Player B says the number and finds the correct position on the bead string.

Play continues until the time is finished.

Count the number of cards used in that round.

Player B has a turn.

The aim of the activity is to use as many cards as possible in each round.

Checklist – Counting in ones to 100
Pupils can:
- ☐ Say number names for all numbers to 100
- ☐ Articulate the sounds clearly, especially the 'teen' and 'ty' endings
- ☐ Synchronise number names with objects counted
- ☐ Locate any number up to 100 on a bead string

Counting in tens to 100

Objectives
- Say decade number names (10, 20, 30, 40, 50, 60, 70, 80, 90, 100)
- Read decade numbers 10 to 100
- Put decade numbers in order 10 to 100
- Write decade numbers 10 to 100
- Distinguish between spoken 'teen' and 'ty' numbers

Teach pupils to say, read and write the decade numbers from 10 to 100. It is essential to include 100 in the count as it is the final number in the tenth decade.

Many pupils find counting in tens fairly easy. However some may falter over 20, 30 and 50 because the number names change slightly. In 20 the 'two' changes to 'twen', in 30 the 'three' changes to 'thir' and in 50 the 'five' changes to 'fif'. Pupils may not realise that the word ending 'ty' is a compressed way of saying 'tens'. It is important that they can articulate the endings of 'teen' and 'ty' numbers and understand that the words represent very different positions in the number sequence. Sometimes pupils will count to 90 correctly then say 20 instead of 100 because they have confused 90 with 19. This indicates that they do not realise there is a difference between the 'teen' and the 'ty' numbers. It may be due to auditory confusion in learning the number names, or because they have little concept of what the words mean. The use of bead strings helps to overcome this problem.

Teaching

Count in tens
Count in tens to 100.
If the pupils has difficulty, the pupil and teacher say the numbers together, then ask the pupil to repeat the sequence.

> Pupil recites the decade numbers: *10, 20, 30, 40, 50, 60, 70, 80, 90, 100*
>
> Ensure the pupil says the words for the decade numbers clearly, emphasising the 'ty' ending.

Read decade numbers to 100
Use a set of cards showing the numbers from 10 to 100.

Teacher lays out the cards in order and says the number names *slowly and clearly*, pointing to each card to make the link between the word and the symbol explicit.

Read the numbers. Point to each number as you say it.

Shuffle the cards and give them to the pupil.
Put the cards out in order. Then read the numbers.

> The pupil should say the 'ty' endings clearly.
>
> The pupil should be able to place the cards in their relative positions from the random order. If they have to find 10, then each succeeding number in the sequence, they will need plenty of practice in sequencing the tens numbers.

Write tens numbers to 100

Put the cards in order, then write the tens numbers from 10 to 100.

When the pupil has written the numbers, remove the cards and ask them to write the numbers from 10 to 100 from memory.

Give pupil A3 paper. *Use a ruler to draw a number line from 0 to 100. Mark all the tens numbers on it.*

Pupil puts out the cards, reads each number aloud and copies it. It is important that the spacing between numbers is appropriate so that they are easy to read.

If the pupil has difficulty, they practice writing each number using the Look, Say, Cover, Write method. (Chapter 1, p18)

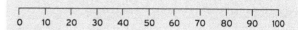

Untangling '-teen' and '-ty'

Auditory discrimination

Aim
- To distinguish between the word endings 'teen' and 'ty'

Equipment
- Pencil and paper
- Base sheet with two columns headed -teen and -ty
- Number cards: 13 to 19 and 20 to 90.
  The 'teen' cards have the ending –teen on the back, the 'ty' cards have the ending -ty on the back

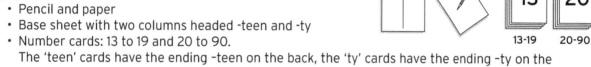

How to play
Shuffle the number cards. Player holds the cards with the number side up. Read each number, emphasising the ending. Place the card under the correct ending on the base sheet. When all the cards have been played the player turns the cards over and checks that they are correct.

Cards in play

-teen	-ty
13	30

Checklist - Counting in tens to 100

Pupils can:
- ☐ Say decade number names (20, 30, 40, 50, 60, 70, 80, 90, 100)
- ☐ Read decade numbers 10 to 100
- ☐ Put decade numbers in order 10 to 100
- ☐ Write decade numbers 10 to 100
- ☐ Distinguish between spoken 'teen' and 'ty' numbers

Estimate up to 100

Objectives
- Make a reasonable estimate for up to 100 objects
- Check the estimate by counting systematically

The ability to estimate quantities helps develop a 'feel' for the size of numbers, which is an important part of number sense. The importance of estimation was discussed in Chapter 3. (See p60) Now pupils estimate quantities up to 100. This game also provides practise in counting numbers to 100.

Teaching

The Estimating Game

Aims
- To develop estimation skills
- To practise counting to 100

Equipment
- Approximately 100 counters in a bowl
- Sheet of paper to cover counters
- Score sheet
- Pencil

How to play

Player A takes a quantity of counters and scatters them on the table. All players look at them for a few seconds before they are covered with a piece of paper.

Each player estimates how many counters they think there are. All the estimates are written down. Player A counts the counters into a line, leaving a small gap between each 10.

The winner is the person whose estimate is the closest to the actual number.

All the counters are returned to the container and the next player has a turn.

Game 1

	Player A	Player B	Player C	Actual Number	Winner
Game 1	35	47	64	52	Player B

Checklist - Estimate up to 100
Pupils can:
- ☐ Make a reasonable estimate for up to 100 objects
- ☐ Check the estimate by counting systematically

Base 10 and the principle of exchange

Objectives

- Exchange 10 ones for 1 ten
- Exchange ones for tens and tens for ones
- Use the language of exchange

The numbers from 1 to 9 and 0 (zero) are also called digits. All numbers, however large or small, are written using these digits. The value of a digit depends on its position in a number.

Numbers are structured into a base 10 system in which the values, or groups, have special names: the single item is called a unit and the larger values are tens and hundreds. Later pupils will learn the formal structure of this system, which is called the place value system (see p175). Pupils need to understand the principle of exchange, that several items can be represented by a single item of greater value so that 10 ones are equivalent to 1 ten.

Two-digit numbers are composed of tens and units. The transition from seeing 10 as an entity rather than as a 'collection of ones' is a crucial stage in developing number sense. Failure to make this transition is one of the features of dyscalculia. Pupils cannot understand multi-digit calculations until they grasp this notion.

Base 10 apparatus encapsulates the principle of exchange and makes the relationship between the quantities explicit because the size of the pieces is proportional to their value. The unit cube represents 1, the ten stick or 'long' is equivalent to 10 ones, and the 100 square, or 'flat', is equivalent to 100 ones, or 10 tens. A 1,000 cube is equivalent to 1,000 ones or 100 tens or 10 hundred squares.

Teaching

Use base 10 equipment, tens and unit cubes, to revise the idea that 10 ones has the same value as 1 ten. There is an informal convention that the ten in Base 10 apparatus is referred to as a 10 'stick' to distinguish it from the Cuisenaire 10 'rod'. If pupils prefer to use the word 'rod' to refer to both the base 10 and the Cuisenaire 10, allow them to do so.

Unit cube (1 cm²)

Ten stick (10 cm long)

Teacher holds up 1 ten and says: *Find out how many ones you need to make the same length as this stick.*

The long stick is worth 10 ones so you call it 1 ten.

Pupil puts 10 ones next to the stick and says: *I need 10 ones to be the same length as the stick.*

Pupil repeats: *1 ten equals 10 ones.*

Race to 100

Aims
- To understand the principle of exchange
- To show that numbers are composed of tens and units

Equipment

- Base 10 unit cubes (ones) and tens
- Dice 0 to 9
- Metre track for each player with 10 cm intervals
  clearly marked (alternatively use a metre rule marked in tens only)

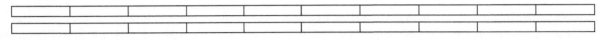

How to play
Players take turns to roll the dice and place unit cubes on their track. When a player reaches the 10 cm mark they exchange 10 ones for 1 ten stick. Players must explain the exchange in their own words as they make the exchange.

The winner is the first person to cross the finish line.

Example of play showing the moves made by Player A:
Player A rolls 5 on the dice and takes the correct number of ones (unit cubes) and puts them on the track.

100 cm

Player B has a turn.

Player A has another turn and rolls a 7. Player takes the 7 ones (unit cubes) and places them slightly above the track as shown below.

The units reach the 10 cm mark.

100 cm

Add 5 of the counters onto the track to make 10. Leave the remaining 2 counters in place above the track.

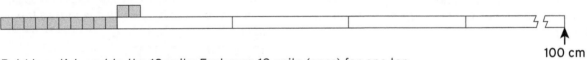

100 cm

Put 1 ten stick next to the 10 units. Exchange 10 units (ones) for one ten.

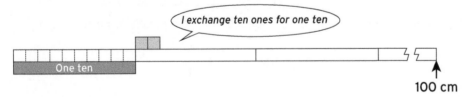

I exchange ten ones for one ten

One ten

100 cm

Place the remaining 2 counters on the track. The total now is 12. 7 add 5 is 12.

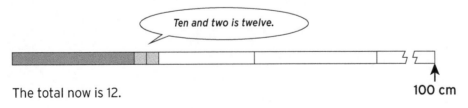

Ten and two is twelve.

100 cm

The total now is 12.

Back Track

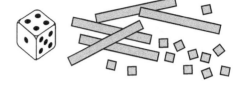

Aim
- To exchange 1 ten for 10 ones

Equipment
- Base 10 (5 tens and 15 ones for each player)
- Dice

How to play
Players take turns to throw the dice and subtract the number from the line.

They talk about what they do.

Each player places 5 tens in a line.

Player A rolls the dice. Player cannot subtract any units (ones) until 1 ten is exchanged for 10 units (ones).

Player A puts 10 units above 1 ten, then exchanges them. Now player can subtract the correct number of ones.

Player B has a turn.

The winner is the first player to have no pieces left.

Example of play:
Player A rolls a 4.

I exchange one ten for ten ones

I take away 4. There are 46 left.

Checklist - Base 10 and the principle of exchange
Pupils can:
- ☐ Establish that 10 ones has the same value as 1 ten
- ☐ Exchange ones for tens and tens for ones
- ☐ Use the language of exchange

The value of digits in two-digit numbers

Objectives
- Build and describe two-digit numbers using tens and ones
- Demonstrate numbers in linear and spatial format
- Investigate the value of each digit in a two-digit number
- Draw diagrams to show tens and units
- Compare the size of two-digit numbers
- Write equations to make the tens and units structure explicit
- Understand that the value of a digit depends on its position in the number

Pupils build numbers and describe them in terms of tens and units. They build linear models and then display them in a spatial format which makes the distinction between the tens and the units more explicit and lays the foundation for formal place value work and partitioning numbers into tens and units. It is important that pupils can work with both representations.

The position of a digit in a number determines its value in the number. Consolidate this idea by comparing numbers made with the same digits placed in different positions. For example, the digits 2 and 5 are used in both the numbers 25 and 52.

Introduce the words horizontal and vertical as these terms are used when distinguishing between informal and formal written methods. Note that the instructions are starting to get longer, but the language is kept simple.

Teaching

Build two-digit numbers
Pupils build numbers and use the terms 'tens and units'. Do not use numbers containing a 0 (zero) at this stage.

Teacher demonstrates a linear model of 23 using 2 tens and 3 units, and says: *Tell me what you see. What is the number?*

Teacher moves the sticks into a vertical position and says: *Tell me what you see. What is the number?*

Build a number using 4 tens and 5 units in a line. What is the number?

Can you move the sticks to a vertical position to show the number? What is the number?

Do plenty of examples asking the pupil to build numbers with base 10 equipment in both linear and spatial arrangements.

74   57   86

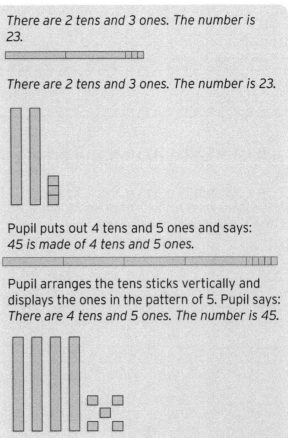

There are 2 tens and 3 ones. The number is 23.

There are 2 tens and 3 ones. The number is 23.

Pupil puts out 4 tens and 5 ones and says: *45 is made of 4 tens and 5 ones.*

Pupil arranges the tens sticks vertically and displays the ones in the pattern of 5. Pupil says: *There are 4 tens and 5 ones. The number is 45.*

Read and write two-digit numbers

Give pupil a 3 and a 5 card. *Put the cards next to each other to make a number.*

What is the number? Build it using tens and units. Sometimes pupils say 35 but put out 3 units followed by 5 tens. In this case ask them to count out a line of 35 in unit cubes (ones), then do the exchange to establish the correct representation.

Draw a diagram of the model. Write out 35 equals 3 tens and 5 units. Then write the equations 35 equals 30 add 5, and 30 add 5 equals 35.

It may seem unnecessary to ask pupils to write 35 = 30 + 5 and then write 30 + 5 = 35. However, some pupils write 35 = 30 + 5 correctly and then write 30 + 5 = 305. This shows they do not fully understand what the tens and units represent. Give them plenty of practice explaining what they are doing and what it means, whilst making, drawing and writing the two-digit numbers.

The number is 35. It is 3 tens and 5 units.

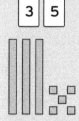

Pupil draws the diagram and writes the equations. Pupils may write the equations on one line, however it is preferable to write the different equations underneath each other.

> 35 = 3 tens and 5 units
> 35 = 30 + 5
> 30 + 5 = 35

Comparing two-digit numbers

Use two sets of digit cards 1 to 9. (Note that 0 is not included; it will be introduced in the later work on formal place value, p181.)

Give pupil a 2 and a 5 card. *Put the cards next to each other to make a number.*

What is the number? Build it using tens and units. Note that it does not matter whether the pupil demonstrates 52 before demonstrating 25.

Draw a diagram of the model. Write the equations to show 25 equals 2 tens and 5 units.

The number is 25. It is 2 tens and 5 units.

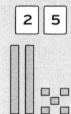

Pupil draws the diagram and writes the equations underneath each other.

> 25 = 2 tens and 5 units
> 25 = 20 + 5
> 20 + 5 = 25

Take two more cards with the digits 2 and 5. *Can you make a different number with the digits 2 and 5?*

Use base 10 equipment to make 52 and then draw a diagram and write the equations.

Ask pupils to lay out their written work as shown:

Pupil changes the order of the digits to make 52 and says: *5 tens and 2 units makes 52.*

Pupil makes 52. They lay it out alongside to make the visual comparison clear.

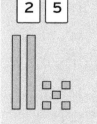

25

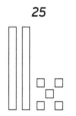

25 = 2 tens and 5 units
25 = 20 + 5
20 + 5 = 25

52

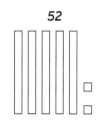

52 = 5 tens and 2 units
52 = 50 + 2
50 + 2 = 52

Look at 25 and 52. Tell me what you see.

Pupils need to practise comparing the size of numbers by making them, drawing them, writing them and talking about them.

> *25 is smaller than 52.*
> *25 is made of 2 tens and 5 units, while 52 is made of 5 tens and 2 units.*

Card Wars

Comparing two-digit numbers

Aim
- To compare the size of numbers
- To use manipulatives to show the relative size of numbers

Equipment
- Four sets of cards with one digit on each card (1 to 9) (do not use a zero at this stage)
- Tens and units (nine of each for each player)
- Size card – words 'smallest' and 'largest' on alternate sides
- Pencil and paper

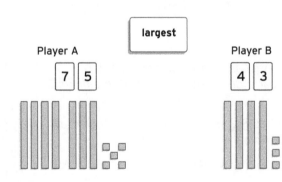

How to play

Shuffle the cards. Deal two cards, face down, to each player.

Players look at their cards but do not show anyone else.

The dealer decides whether the smallest or the largest number will win. Dealer turns the size card to show the appropriate word.

Players order their digit cards to make either the smallest or largest possible number. They make the number using tens and units.

Players take it in turns to read their number, starting with the dealer.

Dealer reads the size card and says: *The (largest or smallest) number wins.*

The person with the appropriate number says: *I have the (largest/smallest) number.*

At the end of each round, the winning player collects all the cards.

The winner is the player with the most cards when they have all been played.

Example:

| largest |

Player A
[7][5]

Player B
[4][3]

Size card shows largest number will win.
Player A has the largest number.

Checklist – The value of digits in two-digit numbers

Pupils can:
- ☐ Build and describe two-digit numbers using tens and ones
- ☐ Demonstrate numbers in linear and spatial format
- ☐ Investigate the value of each digit in a two-digit number
- ☐ Draw diagrams to show tens and units
- ☐ Compare the size of two-digit numbers
- ☐ Write equations to make the tens and units structure explicit
- ☐ Understand that the value of a digit depends on its position in the number

Number lines to 100

Objectives

- Locate numbers on a bead string
- Position numbers on a number line
- Understand that not all the numbers or marks need to be shown on a number line
- Reason to position numbers on an empty number line
- Locate numbers on a partial number line

Number lines are one of the most powerful tools that people can use to help with calculation. They make the relationships between numbers clear. Understood and used properly, they support mental methods and develop reasoning skills. Pupils need to be able to read information from a number line if they are to work effectively with measurement and later with graphs. They also help with later work on fractions and percentages.

Pupils need to be able to draw number lines free hand with confidence and to understand that it is not always necessary to draw the whole number line starting at zero. They need to use the language of double and half to support their working. The point that is midway between two relevant numbers helps to locate positions on a number line. It is important to be able to use partial number lines which show only the section needed for the calculation. This will be essential for recording calculations involving larger numbers where it is impractical to show the whole number line on one page.

Teaching

Use a bead string and a number line to 50 with all the intervals marked and the decade numbers written.

Find 39 on the bead string. Mark 39 on the number line. Say the number as you point to the bead and mark it on the number line.

Pupil points to 39 on the bead string and marks the position clearly with an arrow on the number line.

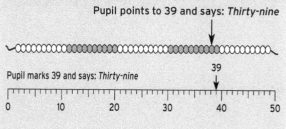

Ask pupils to do several examples; they find the position of the number on the bead string and mark it on the number line.

| 25 | 46 | 12 | 38 |

Locate numbers on a number line

What are the numbers shown on the number line? Write the numbers above the arrows and point to them on the bead string.

Pupil says and writes each number on the number line and then points to it on the bead string: *5, 17, 31, 48.*

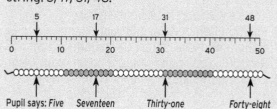

Reason to position numbers on a number line

Pupils learnt to apply their knowledge of double and half to locate points on a number line up to 20 with reasonable accuracy. Now they use this reasoning method to locate numbers up to 100.

Draw a number line from 0 to 40. Mark the following numbers on it: 10, 15. Explain your reasoning.

If pupils have difficulty, the teacher helps them with the reasoning process as explained in Chapter 3. (See p74)

Pupils need to do plenty of examples of reasoning to positioning numbers on an empty number line. They need to draw a new line for each number.

Draw a line from 0 to 50. Find 25.
Draw a line from 0 to 80. Find 20.
Draw a line from 0 to 100. Find 70.

The pupil draws a line and marks 0 at the beginning and 40 at the end.

Pupil reasons in the following manner: *I mark the midpoint. This is half way along the line. I know that half of 4 is 2, so half of 40 will be 20. I know that 10 is between zero and 20. I know that 10 is half of 20, so 10 is the midpoint between 0 and 20.*

15 is more than 10 and less than 20. The distance from 10 to 20 is 10. 5 is half of 10 so 15 will be at the point that is halfway between 10 and 20.

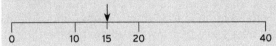

The partial number line

Give pupil a printed number line showing the decade numbers from 0 to 100 and a pair of scissors. Teacher explains: *It is not necessary to draw the whole of the number line. Sometimes it is easier to use only a portion of the line. This is called a partial number line.*

I want you to find 65. What numbers does 65 lie between?

Teacher gives pupil scissors and says:
Cut the number line so you can see the section from 60 to 70. Draw a line to show that section.

Where is 65 on the line?

65 is between 60 and 70.

Pupil cuts before 60 and after 70 and draws a line with 60 at the beginning and 70 at the end of the line.

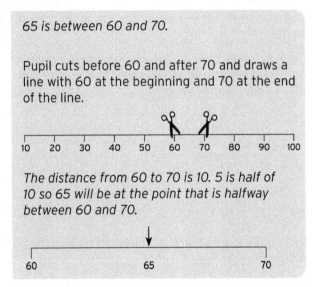

The distance from 60 to 70 is 10. 5 is half of 10 so 65 will be at the point that is halfway between 60 and 70.

Pupils can find numbers on an interactive number line at 'Numberline' on the website www.number-sense.co.uk. This activity was developed at the London Knowledge Lab, London University. The range of numbers to investigate can be set by the teacher or the pupil.

Checklist - Number lines to 100

Pupils can:
- ☐ Locate numbers on a bead string
- ☐ Position numbers on a number line
- ☐ Understand that not all the numbers or marks need to be shown on a number line
- ☐ Reason to position numbers on an empty number line
- ☐ Locate numbers on a partial number line

Flexible counting forwards and backwards

Objectives
- Count forwards in ones from arbitrary starting points
- Count forwards in tens from arbitrary starting points
- Count back in ones from arbitrary starting points
- Count back in tens from arbitrary starting points

Counting on, or back, from different starting points develops flexible counting skills. Some pupils find counting back very difficult. It is particularly important to practise crossing the decade boundaries. A decade boundary is the place in the sequence where the tens number name changes.

It is difficult for some pupils to grasp which decade the number word at the end of the decade belongs to. For example, 30 comes at the end of the third group of ten in the number system but pupils often think it 'belongs' with the numbers in the thirties. 31 is the first number in the fourth decade. Trying to explain it verbally to a pupil is not recommended as this is likely to lead to greater confusion. Give pupils plenty of opportunity to use bead strings to locate and discuss the numbers around the decade boundaries in the counting sequence until they understand how the number names relate to the structure.

Remember to use precise language: 'count from' or 'count on' requires the pupil to start with the number following the given number so that if the pupil 'counts from 4' they will say five, six, and so on. It may seem a small point but any misunderstanding will lead to calculation errors later. The same distinctions apply when pupils are asked to count backwards. If a pupil counts back from 8 they will say 'seven, six' and so on.

Teaching
Pupils use a bead string to 100 to identify the numbers as they count. Some pupils may need to use number cards to help them count backwards initially.

Counting forwards in ones
Give pupils plenty of practice counting from different starting points In ones.

Show me 28. Count on from there. Move the beads as you count. Stop at 43.	Pupil finds 28, then synchronises the number words with the movement of the beads as they are counted: *29, 30, 31, 32, 33, 34, 35, 36, 37, 38, 39, 40, 41, 42, 43.*
Count on from 47. *Find 56 and count on.* *Count on from 39.* *Count on from 60.*	When pupils can count on confidently using the bead string, they practice oral counting without the concrete support.

Counting forwards in tens
Give pupils plenty of practice counting in tens from different starting points.

Show me 8. What is 8 and 10? Find it on the bead string.	Pupil points to 18 and says: *8 and 10 is 18.*
Count in tens from 18. Move the beads as you count.	Pupils moves groups of 10 beads as they count: *28, 38, 48...*
Count in tens from 67. *Find 26 and count on in tens.* *Count in tens from 39.* *Count on from 53 in tens.*	When pupils can count on in tens confidently using the bead string, practice oral counting without the concrete support.

'Fast and slow' counting

Practise switching between counting in tens and counting in ones.

Count from 28. Count in ones. When I clap switch to counting in tens. Teacher claps when the pupil says 32. *When I clap again switch to counting in ones.* Teacher claps when the pupil says 62.

Teacher claps when the pupil says 68.

Stop the pupil when they reach 98.

Pupil counts: *29, 30, 31, 32,* *(clap)*
Pupil switches to counting in tens: *42, 52, 62,* *(clap)*
Pupil switches to counting in ones: *63, 64, 65, 66, 67, 68 (clap)*. Pupil switches to counting in tens; *78, 88, 98 (clap)*

Counting back in ones

Use numbered cards from 1 to 30 to revise counting backwards. If pupils have great difficulty, do the counting back exercises described in Chapter 3. (See p69)

1	2	3	4	5	6	7	8	9	10	11	12	13	14	15	16	17	18	19	20	21	22	23	24	25	26	27	28	29	30

Shuffle the number cards and give them to the pupil. *Put the cards out in order from 1 to 30.*

When the pupil has arranged the sequence, the teacher says: *Start with 30 and count back. Point to each card as you say the number.* If the pupil has difficulty, use cards to practise counting back for the larger two-digit numbers before working with bead strings.

Give pupils a bead string to 100.

Pupil puts the cards out in order. They should be able to do this without starting from 1 to find the position of each card.

Pupil points to each number as they say the word.

Find 30. Count back from there. Move the beads as you count.

Ask pupils to count back from different points in the sequence to 100. Target the areas around the decade boundaries.
Count back from 40.
Count back from 74.
Find 63 and count back.
Count back from 93.

Pupil finds 30, then synchronises words and movement of the beads as they are counted: *29, 28, 27, 26, 25.*

When pupils can count back in ones confidently using the bead string, practise oral counting without the concrete support.

Counting back in tens

Give pupils a bead string to 100.
Show me 53. Find 10 less than 53.

Count back in tens from 43. Move the beads as you count.
Count back in tens from 50.
Count back in tens from 67.
Find 24 and count back in tens.
Count back in tens from 93.
Count back from 61 in tens.

Pupil points to 53 and says: *10 less than 53 is 43.*
Pupil moves groups of 10 beads whilst counting: *43, 33, 23, 13, 3.*

When pupils can count back in tens confidently using the bead string, practice oral counting without the concrete support.

Checklist – Flexible counting forwards and backwards

Pupils can:
- ☐ Count forwards in ones from arbitrary starting points
- ☐ Count forwards in tens from arbitrary starting points
- ☐ Count back in ones from arbitrary starting points
- ☐ Count back in tens from arbitrary starting points

Rounding numbers

Objectives
- Say which decade numbers a number lies between
- Round a number to the nearest tens number
- Explain the terms 'rounding up' and 'rounding down'
- Know that 5 or more rounds up in a two-digit number
- Know that numbers less than 5 round down in a two-digit number

Rounding is used to adjust a number to make it easier to work with. Rounding a number gives an approximate value that enables pupils to quickly work out an estimate for a calculation. The final calculation is checked against the estimate. A large discrepancy between the estimate and the calculation indicates a calculation error.

Use number lines to teach pupils to round two-digit numbers to the nearest ten. The terms 'rounding up' and 'rounding down' need to be carefully taught. They refer to the size of a number. A number is rounded 'up' to a bigger number; a number is rounded 'down' to a smaller number. In order to understand whether a number rounds up or down, it is essential to know that the number at the midpoint between two tens numbers ends in 5. Numbers that end in 1,2,3 or 4 round down to the nearest 10. Numbers that end in 5,6,7,8 or 9 round up to the next 10. Explain that although 5 is exactly in the middle, the convention is that 5 rounds up.

Establish a sound understanding of rounding to a multiple of 10 so that pupils can generalise the concept to rounding to hundreds, thousands and larger quantities.

Teaching
Teacher explains: *Rounding is used to make numbers easier to work with. To 'round' a number to 10, you express it as the nearest tens number.*

Rounding down
Show the pupil a number line with the point 33 marked on it.

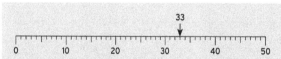

Which tens numbers does 33 lie between?

Is 33 closer to 30 or closer to 40?

33 rounds to 30 because it is closer to 30. We say 33 rounds down to 30 because 30 is less than 33. What does 33 round to?

Complete these questions. Show the numbers on a number line.

42 lies between ___ and ___. 42 rounds down to ___.

31 lies between ___ and ___. 31 rounds ___ to ___.

13 lies between ___ and ___. 13 rounds ___ to ___.

54 lies between ___ and ___. 54 rounds ___ to ___.

33 is between 30 and 40.

33 is closer to 30.

33 rounds down to 30.

Pupil marks the numbers on the number line and explains their thinking as they complete each question.

Pupils may use partial number lines if they want to.

Rounding up

Show the pupil a number line with the point 47 marked on it.

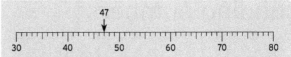

47 is between 40 and 50.

Which tens numbers does 47 lie between?

47 is closer to 50.

Is 47 closer to 40 or closer to 50?

47 rounds to 50 because it is closer to 50. We say 47 rounds up to 50 because 50 is more than 47. What does 47 round to?

47 rounds up to 50.

Complete these questions. Show the numbers on a number line.

Pupil marks the numbers on the number line and explains their thinking as they complete each question.

18 lies between ___ and ___ . 18 rounds <u>up</u> to 20.

37 lies between ___ and ___. 37 rounds ___ to ___.

Pupils may use partial number lines if they want to.

56 lies between ___ and ___. 56 rounds ___ to ___.

49 lies between ___ and ___. 49 rounds ___ to ___.

5 rounds up

Show the pupil a number line with the midpoint between 20 and 30 marked on it.

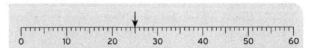

The arrow marks the midpoint between two tens numbers. Which tens numbers does the midpoint lie between? What is the number at the midpoint?

The midpoint lies between 20 and 30. The number is 25.

25 is exactly the same distance from 20 and 30. The rule is that 5 rounds up to the next 10. What does 25 round to?

25 rounds up to 30.

Complete these questions. Show the numbers on a number line.

Pupil marks the numbers on the number line and explains their thinking as they complete each question.

15 lies between <u>10</u> and <u>20</u>. It rounds <u>up</u> to 20.

35 lies between ___ and ___. 35 rounds ___ to ___.

Pupils may use partial number lines if they want to.

55 lies between ___ and ___. 55 rounds ___ to ___.

45 lies between ___ and ___. 45 rounds ___ to ___.

Checklist – Rounding numbers

Pupils can:

☐ Say which decade numbers a number lies between
☐ Round a number to the nearest tens number
☐ Explain the terms 'rounding up' and 'rounding down'
☐ Know that 5 or more rounds up in a two-digit number
☐ Know that numbers less than 5 round down in a two-digit number

Sequences and step counting

Objectives
- Step count in tens and record on number line
- Step count in fives and record on number line
- Step count in twos and record on number line

A sequence is a list of numbers organised according to a rule. If you apply the rule you can find other numbers in the sequence. Pupils need to be able to find the rule governing a sequence in order to read scales and interpret graphs.

Introduce sequences by teaching pupils to step count. Step counting means counting in equal sized groups. The ability to step count in tens, fives and twos helps consolidate understanding of the linear number system, and is a useful prelude to thinking about repeated addition of groups, or sets, that will be encountered in multiplication.

Start step counting in tens because it is easier to step count in tens than in fives or twos. Initially limit step counting to starting at points that correspond to multiples of the 'step number'. For example, counting in tens, start from any decade number, counting in fives count from any number ending in 5 or 0, and counting in twos only start with even numbers to begin with.

Pupils need to be very comfortable and confident with numbers before they will be able to step count from any number. It is best to wait until they have learnt the times tables and understood the concept of multiplication.

Teaching

Step counting in tens
Give pupils a line with all the numbers marked to 50. Ask them to count in tens and show the jumps as they count.

Start at zero and count in tens. This is called step counting. Show each step as an arc on the number line. Write 10 above each arc.

Pupil counts in tens and draws arcs on the number line. The pupil writes 10 above each arc. It is not necessary to use a + sign as the arc represents the distance between two points.

Each step is 10. I add 10 each time.

You counted in tens. How big is each step? How much do you add each time?

Practise step counting from other decade numbers in the sequence up to 100.

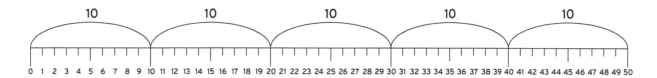

Step counting in fives

Once pupils can count to 10 through the decades, they usually find it relatively straightforward to count in fives up to 100. For practical purposes start with a number line to 50 as shown below.

Start at zero and count in fives. Show each 5 as an arc on the number line. Write 5 above each arc.

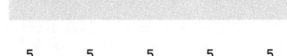

Pupil counts in fives and draws arcs on the number line. The pupil writes 5 above each arc. It is not necessary to use a + sign as the arc represents the distance between two points.

I add 5 each time.

You counted in fives. How much do you add each time?

Start at 25 and count in fives.

Practise step counting from other numbers ending in 0 or 5 in the sequence up to 100.

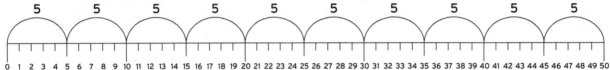

Step counting in twos

Many pupils have great difficulty counting in twos and tend to count in ones under their breath. Only ask pupils to step count in twos starting with an even numbers. Wait until pupils know all the multiplication tables before asking them to step count in twos from an odd number.

Give pupils a number line to 30 and ask them to count in twos and show the steps as they count.

Start at zero and count in twos. Show each step as an arc on the number line. Write 2 above each arc.

Pupil counts in twos and draws arcs on the number line. The pupil writes 2 above each arc. It is not necessary to use a + sign as the arc represents the distance between two points.

I add 2 each time.

You counted in twos. How much do you add each time?

Practise step counting from other even points in the sequence.

Start at 8 and count in twos.

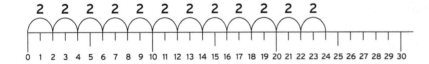

Checklist - Sequences and step counting

Pupils can:
- ☐ Step count in tens and record on number line
- ☐ Step count in fives and record on number line
- ☐ Step count in twos and record on number line

Find the rule, continue the sequence

Objectives

- Work out the rule for a sequence
- Find the next number in a sequence
- Write the rule that governs the sequence as N + 10, N + 5, or N + 2 or N - 10, N - 5, N - 2

Pupils find the rule that governs a sequence and then apply it to continue the sequence. They need to show the sequence on a number line and record the rule in written and symbolic form where N represents any term in the sequence. For example in the sequence 2, 4, 6, the rule is add 2, which can be written as N + 2.

Work on sequences that involve step counting forwards until pupils can confidently complete them, then work on sequences in which the numbers decrease in size.

Teaching

Sequencing forwards in twos, fives and tens

Give pupil a written sequence with numbers followed by three blank spaces.

Look at the sequence of numbers 0, 2, 4, 6,_, _, _.
Show them on a number line.

Draw an arc to show each step. How big is each step?

What is the rule?

Each number in the sequence is called a term.
If N is any term in the sequence, the rule can be written as N + 2. Write 'the rule is N +2'.

Find the next 3 numbers in the sequence.

Pupil draws a number line and marks the numbers.

Pupil draws the arcs and says:
Each step is 2.

The rule is add 2.

Pupils repeats the words whilst writing:
The rule is add 2. The rule is N + 2.

Pupil draws arcs to continue the sequence and works out the next 3 numbers by applying the rule add 2.

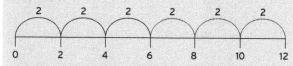

Pupil draws a number line showing the numbers and works out the distance between them. Then they write:

> The rule is add [quantity]

> The rule is N + [quantity]

The pupil finds the next 3 terms in the sequence.

Show each sequence on a number line. Find the rule. Write the rule. Complete the sequence.

30, 40, 50, ___, ___, ___

10, 15, 20, ___, ___, ___

Sequencing backwards in tens, fives and twos

Sequencing backwards involves step counting backwards, or subtracting a quantity, to find the next term in a sequence.

Give pupil a written sequence with numbers followed by 3 blank spaces.

Look at the sequence of numbers 80, 70, 60. Show them on a number line.

Pupil draws a number line and marks the numbers.

Draw an arc to show each step. How big is each step?

Pupil draws the arcs and says:
Each step is 10.

What is the rule?

The rule is take away 10.

Each number in the sequence is called a term. If N is any term in the sequence, the rule can be written as N - 10. Write 'the rule is N - 10'.

Pupil repeats the words whilst writing:
The rule is subtract 10. The rule is N − 10.

Find the next 3 numbers in the sequence.

Pupil draws arcs to continue the sequence and works out the next 3 numbers by applying the rule 'subtract 10'.

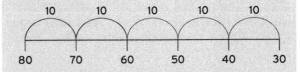

Show each sequence on a number line.
Find the rule.
Write the rue.
Complete the sentence.

16, 14, 12, _, _, _.

45, 40, 35, _, _, _

Pupil draws a number line showing the numbers and works out the distance between them. Then they write:

The rule is take away [quantity]
The rule is N - [quantity]

Checklist – Find the rule, continue the sequence

Pupils can:
- ☐ Work out the rule for a sequence
- ☐ Find the next number in a sequence
- ☐ Write the rule that governs the sequence as N + 10, N + 5, N + 2 or N - 10, N - 5, N - 2

Odd and even numbers

Objectives

- Demonstrate the meaning of even and odd numbers
- Define the terms even and odd numbers
- Identify odd and even numbers from the final digit

Pupils need to understand the concept of odd and even as well as being able to recognise odd numbers and even numbers. An even number is a multiple of 2; an odd number is not a multiple of 2. However this definition does not make the concept clear.

Allow pupils to derive a definition of odd and even by putting out counters in twos and describing what they see in their own words. For example they might say, 'I put the counters in twos. There are none left over so the number is even.' And then 'I put the counters into twos. There is 1 left over so the number is odd'.

It does not matter which words the pupils use, as long as they represent the idea that an even number is 'exactly divisible by 2'; and an odd number will have 'remainder one' when it is divided by 2.

Try and avoid the word 'pair' as it emphasises the idea of 'belonging together' rather than a multiple of 2, or dividing a quantity by 2. It is a subtle distinction so do not prevent a pupil using the word 'pair' if they choose to do so, but do not suggest it.

Pupils need to be clear that the final digit in a number determines whether it is odd or even: all even numbers end in 0, 2, 4, 6 or 8 while all odd numbers end in 1, 3, 5, 7 or 9.

An even number is a multiple of 2.
An even number is exactly divisible by 2.

An odd number is not a multiple of 2
When an odd number is divided by 2 there will be a remainder 1.

Teaching

Investigate, define and identify odd numbers and even numbers through the *Odd and Even Game*.

Odd and Even Game

Aim
- To understand the meaning of odd or even numbers
- To create a visual image of odd and even numbers
- To establish that the final digit in a number determines whether it is odd or even
- To learn that all even numbers end in 0, 2, 4, 6, 8 and all odd numbers end in 1, 3, 5, 7, 9

Equipment
- Counters
- Card marked odd on one side, even on back
- Pencil and score sheet for each player

100

ODD

Odd or even
single card

How to play
Players take turns. Each turn consists of the following procedure.

Player A scatters counters and guesses whether there is an odd or even quantity of counters. Player A turns the odd/even card to their chosen word.

To establish whether the quantity is odd or even, Player A moves counters into twos. They do not count the counters yet.

Encourage pupils to place the counters in an orderly fashion.

Say whether there is an odd or even number of counters.

If the guess was correct, record one tally point on score sheet.

Count counters. Write number under appropriate column - odd or even. (Pupils may initially count in ones. Allow them to do so, then ask them to recount in twos.)

Player B has a turn. The winner is the first player to record five tally points.

Record of Numbers

Odd	Even
9	

Checklist – Odd and even numbers
Pupils can:
- ☐ Demonstrate the meaning of even and odd numbers
- ☐ Define the terms even numbers and odd numbers
- ☐ Identify odd and even numbers from the final digit

Understanding the 100 square

Objectives
- Understand the relationship between a number track and a 100 square
- Write the number sequence to 100
- Construct a 100 square
- Locate numbers on the 100 square
- Model two-digit numbers as tens and units

The 100 square represents the numbers from 1 to 100 as a 10 x 10 grid where each space represents one number. There are 10 numbers in each row and there are 10 rows. The 100 square makes it clear that the decade numbers (10, 20, 30, etc.) come at the end of each group of 10 in the counting sequence.

The 100 square is a useful aid for addition and subtraction, for multiplication and later for understanding percentages. In order to use a 100 square as a calculation aid, pupils need to see the patterns inherent in it. Many pupils do not understand what the 100 square means; they do not realise that it is a number track displayed in a different way.

Pupils 'discover' the 100 square by constructing it from a number track to 100. Give pupils a strip of paper with more than 100 squares in which to write numbers. The numbers above 100 will not be required, however they provide useful information about how pupils think about numbers larger than 100. Instead of 101, 102, 103, some pupils may write 200, 300 or 1001, 1002, 1003.

Note that the 100 square should not be confused with the 99 square. It is best not to show pupils a 99 square as it can cause confusion. The 99 square has 100 spaces but the first number is 0 and the final number is 99. The resulting layout gives a false impression of the position of the tens numbers at the decade boundaries.

Teaching

Make a 100 square
Give the pupil a strip of paper with more than 100 squares (about 106 squares). Each square should be at least 1 cm². Do not tell pupil how many squares there are.

Write one number in each square starting with the number 1.

Once they have written all the numbers, they cut the strip into tens.
Cut the number track into tens.

If the pupil cuts in the wrong place, the teacher intervenes. *Start at the beginning and count to 10. Point to each number as you say it.*
When pupil has done this, teacher says:
Cut between 10 and 11.
Guide the pupil to count each group of 10 and then to cut the strip in the appropriate place.

The next stage is to paste the strips of tens on a sheet of blank paper.
Start with the strip with the number 1 on it. Stick it on the paper. Then put the next strip underneath. Make sure that the columns are lined up correctly when they are stuck down. All the tens numbers need to be underneath each other.

If pupils make errors do not correct them; they will be able to find the errors for themselves and correct them later in the activity.

The pupil should cut the strip at the point after each decade number. If pupil starts cutting the numbers between the ninth and tenth squares, this indicates they have not grasped the tens structure and the teacher will need to help them.

How the pupil does this task reveals much about their understanding of the number sequence. Are they methodical, or do they work by trial and error? If they have cut the strips in the wrong place, or made errors in writing the numbers, it will soon become evident as an incorrect piece will be too long or too short.

If necessary the teacher can tell pupils that the first two rows will look like this:

1	2	3	4	5	6	7	8	9	10
11	12	13	14	15	16	17	18	19	20

When the 100 square is complete, the teacher asks: *What shape have you made?*

How many numbers are there altogether?

You have made a 100 square.

1	2	3	4	5	6	7	8	9	10
11	12	13	14	15	16	17	18	19	20
21	22	23	24	25	26	27	28	29	30
31	32	33	34	35	36	37	38	39	40
41	42	43	44	45	46	47	48	49	50
51	52	53	54	55	56	57	58	59	60
61	62	63	64	65	66	67	68	69	70
71	72	73	74	75	76	77	78	79	80
81	82	83	84	85	86	87	88	89	90
91	92	93	94	95	96	97	98	99	100

It is important that pupils find their own errors. However the teacher can show them how to make adjustments by cutting out a duplicated number, or cutting the strip and leaving a space if a number has been left out. The missing number can then be written into the space.

I made a square.

There are 100.

Pupils are often quite surprised to realise that the 100 square is related to the number track.

Number location on the 100 square

Give pupils a printed 100 square. Ask them to find specific numbers and cross them out.

Find some numbers on the 100 square. Cross out each number as you find it. 10, 15, 41, 69, 82.

Ask questions relating numbers to the tens numbers.
What is the nearest tens number to 38?
What is the nearest tens number to 12?
Round 75 to the nearest 10.
Round 64 to the nearest 10

The pupil's approach to the task may give information about how they think about numbers. Do they look for each number in a systematic way? Can they use the order of the rows to find the tens digit and the columns to find the units digit?

Demon Dice

Aim
- Locate numbers on a 100 square
- Demonstrate the value of two-digit number using base 10 equipment

Equipment
- 100 square
- Two 0-9 dice
- Different colour pen for each player
- Base 10 equipment
- Pencil and paper

0-9 dice x2

How to play
The aim of the game is to get three numbers in a row - horizontally, vertically or diagonally.

Player A rolls the dice and places them next to each other to form a two-digit number. The number is written down and the player uses tens and units to model the number. Then Player A reverses the dice to make another two-digit number, writes the number and models it.

Player A chooses one of the numbers and puts a cross over that number on the 100 square.

Only one player may occupy each square. A player misses a turn if both possible squares are already taken.

The first player to get three crosses in a row – horizontally, vertically or diagonally – is the winner.

Example:
Player rolls 3 and 7 and says:
37 is made of 3 tens and 7 units. I can also make 73 which is made of 7 tens and 3 units. I choose 37.

1	2	3	4	5	6	7	8	9	10
11	12	13	14	15	16	17	18	19	20
21	22	23	24	25	26	27	28	29	30
31	32	33	34	35	36	X	38	39	40
41	42	43	44	45	46	47	48	49	50
51	52	53	54	55	56	57	58	59	60
61	62	63	64	65	66	67	68	69	70
71	72	73	74	75	76	77	78	79	80
81	82	83	84	85	86	87	88	89	90
91	92	93	94	95	96	97	98	99	100

Numbers
3 tens + 7 units = 37
7 tens + 3 units = 73

37 is 3 tens and 7 units

Checklist – Understanding the 100 square
Pupils can:
- ☐ Understand the relationship between a number track and a 100 square
- ☐ Write the number sequence to 100
- ☐ Construct a 100 square
- ☐ Locate numbers on the 100 square
- ☐ Model two-digit numbers as tens and units

1 or 10 more or less than a given number on the 100 square

Objectives
- Locate 1 more or less than any number on the 100 square
- Locate 10 more or less than any number on the 100 square

Pupils apply their flexible counting skills to find more or less than a given number on a 100 square. For weaker pupils only work with 1 more or 1 less and 10 more or 10 less.

Teaching

Give pupils a printed 100 square. Ask them to find particular numbers and then cross out the number that is 1 more.

Cross out the number that is 1 more than 15.

Pupil says: *16 is one more than 15.*
Then they cross out 16.
Some pupils may have to find 15 on the 100 square and then count on to 16. They will need to revise counting on from any number.

Ask the pupil to find further numbers:
What is 1 more than 43?
What is 1 less than 87?
What is 1 less than 52?
What is 1 more than 30?
What is 1 less than 61?

Repeat the activity asking pupils to find numbers that are 10 more or less than a given number.

Cross out the number that is 10 more than 70.

Pupil says: *80 is ten more than 70.*
Then pupil finds 80 on the 100 square and crosses it out. If they have to find 70 and then count on 10, revise flexible counting in tens.

Give the pupil further examples:

What is 10 more than 41?
What is 10 more than 90?

What is 10 less than 85?
What is 10 less than 64?

Flibbertigibbet

Aim
- Locate numbers on the 100 square
- To calculate 1 or 10 more or less than a given number

Equipment
- 100 square
- Two 0-9 dice
- Flibbertigibbet dice marked +1, - 1, +10, - 10, +10, - 10
- Different colour pen for each player
- Base 10 material

0-9 dice x2

How to play

Flibbertigibbet is an extension of Demon Dice. The aim of the game is to get three numbers in a row - horizontally, vertically or diagonally.

Player A rolls the 0-9 dice and makes two numbers as they did in Demon Dice. (See p120)

Then Player A rolls the Flibbertigibbet dice and adds or subtracts the quantity shown and writes the equations. Player A crosses out one of the new numbers.

The next player has a turn.

Only one player may occupy each square. A player misses a turn if they are unable to place a cross because both possible squares are occupied.

The winner is the first player to have 3 crosses in a row.

Example:

Player has thrown 3 and 5 so can make either 35 or 53. Player writes both numbers down and builds them using tens and units.

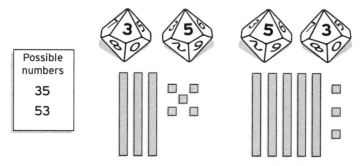

Player rolls -10 on the Flibbertigibbet dice. Player adjusts the models and records the new numbers.

35 - 10 = 25
53 - 10 = 43

Player chooses to cross out 43.

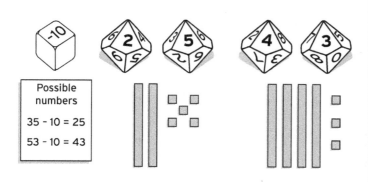

1	2	3	4	5	6	7	8	9	10
11	12	13	14	15	16	17	18	19	20
21	22	23	24	25	26	27	28	29	30
31	32	33	34	35	36	37	38	39	40
41	42	X	44	45	46	47	48	49	50
51	52	53	54	55	56	57	58	59	60
61	62	63	64	65	66	67	68	69	70
71	72	73	74	75	76	77	78	79	80
81	82	83	84	85	86	87	88	89	90
91	92	93	94	95	96	97	98	99	100

Checklist - 1 or 10 more or less than a given number on the 100 square

Pupils can:

☐ Locate 1 more or less than any number on the 100 square
☐ Locate 10 more or less than any number on the 100 square

6

Numbers to 100: Calculation

Pupils use the key facts and problem solving strategies that they have already learnt to calculate with two-digit numbers. They need to learn to choose and apply the most appropriate strategy in different contexts, and to use approximation and estimation to help check their calculations. The calculation strategies are: applying knowledge of doubles and near doubles, and bonds of 10, extending bridging through 10, complementary addition, partitioning and sequencing, and compensation methods. All these strategies can be generalised to multi-digit numbers.

It is important to be able to assess numbers and partition them into components that make it easier to carry out mental calculations. Allow pupils sufficient time and practice to become confident with rearranging and recombining numbers. This is a skill which can later be transferred to more complex calculations with larger numbers.

Doing mental calculations involving two-digit numbers places a significant load on memory. Pupils should use jottings and informal recording methods to support their thinking; they do not need to do all the calculations in their head. They also need to use numbers in context by solving word problems and making up their own questions. Refer to the section on Numbers to 100 in Chapter 10 (see p223). Using numbers in context develops conceptual understanding and prevents pupils developing the idea that computational questions and contextual questions are unrelated. Pupils continue to use equipment to model their thinking.

All the work in this section builds on prior knowledge. It is most important that pupils can apply their knowledge and skills with confidence. If they become hesitant about a strategy, revise it with smaller numbers to reassure them that they can do it, it is now merely a question of using bigger numbers.

Equipment

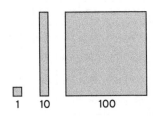

1   10   100

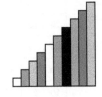

Apply doubles and near doubles facts to calculations with two-digit numbers

Objectives
- Apply doubles and near doubles facts to add tens numbers
- Apply doubles and near doubles facts to subtract tens numbers
- Apply doubles and near doubles facts to add a single digit to a two-digit number (e.g. 54 + 4 = 58)
- Apply doubles and near doubles facts to subtract a single digit from a two-digit number (e.g. 69 - 4 = 65)
- Explain the reasoning process used to apply doubles and near doubles knowledge
- Record thinking as triads, number lines and equations

The dot patterns provided clear, memorable images for the numbers to 10 and emphasised the doubles and near doubles. Pupils generalise this knowledge to calculate with two-digit numbers. First they work with calculations involving tens numbers to derive answers by reasoning from the key facts. For example, if 4 and 4 makes 8, then 4 tens and 4 tens makes 8 tens so that 40 add 40 equals 80. The doubles and near doubles facts can be used to do addition or subtraction of a single digit. Here they apply their knowledge to the units portion of the number. For example, 7 take away 3 is 4, so 37 take away 3 equals 34.

It is essential that pupils talk about what they are doing and explain their thinking in order to develop their reasoning skills. Even if pupils are able to do the calculations easily, they must demonstrate using concrete materials, describe their thinking and record it in order to develop reasoning skills. Practice in reasoning about small numbers lays secure foundations for working with larger numbers later on. This approach also helps develop a strong visual image which relates to future work on formal place value.

Teaching
Pupils use tens and units to model numbers. They explain which double or near double facts they use to derive their answers.

Add decade numbers using doubles and near doubles facts
Use 2 + 2 to derive the answer to 20 + 20.

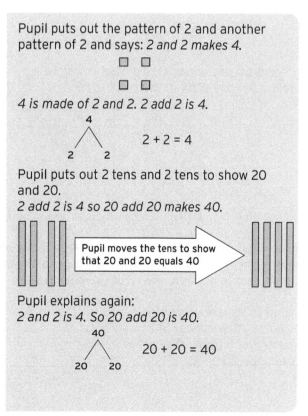

What is 2 and 2? Make the pattern to show what it means.

Pupil puts out the pattern of 2 and another pattern of 2 and says: *2 and 2 makes 4.*

4 is made of 2 and 2. 2 add 2 is 4.

Record 2 and 2 as a triad and write the equation.

2 + 2 = 4

What is 20 add 20? Use equipment to model the question. Explain how the doubles fact helps you.

Pupil puts out 2 tens and 2 tens to show 20 and 20.
2 add 2 is 4 so 20 add 20 makes 40.

Pupil moves the tens to show that 20 and 20 equals 40

Record 20 and 20 as a triad, and then write the equation.

Pupil explains again:
2 and 2 is 4. So 20 add 20 is 40.

20 + 20 = 40

Show 20 add 20 on a number line.

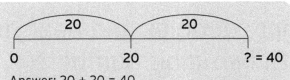

Answer: 20 + 20 = 40

Give pupils plenty of practice. In each case they explain which double or near double fact they use to derive their answers. They demonstrate, explain and record their thinking.

What is 30 and 30?
Add 20 and 30.
What is 40 and 30?
Find double 40.
Increase 50 by 40.

Encourage pupils to express their ideas in different ways. For example, calculating 30 + 30 they might say: *If double 3 is 6 then double 30 is 60.*

Subtracting decade numbers using doubles and near doubles facts

Use 6 – 3 to derive the answer to 60 – 30.

What is 6 take away 3? Make the pattern to show what it means.

Pupil puts out the pattern of 6 and takes away 3 cubes and says:
6 is made of 3 and 3. So 6 take away 3 is 3.

☐ ☒
☐ ☒
☐ ☒

6 is made of 3 and 3. So 6 take away 3 is 3.

Record 6 take away 3 as a triad and an equation.

6
/ \
3   3   6 – 3 = 3

What is 60 take away 30? Use equipment to model the question.

Pupil puts out 6 tens and says:
60 is made of 3 tens and 3 tens.

Then the pupil takes away 3 tens and says:
So 60 take away 30 makes 30.

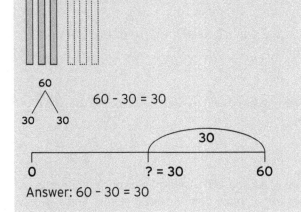

Record 60 take away 30 as a triad, write the equation, then show it on a number line.

60
/ \
30   30   60 – 30 = 30

Answer: 60 – 30 = 30

Give pupils plenty of practice. In each case they explain which double or near double fact they use to derive their answers. They demonstrate, explain and record their thinking. Encourage pupils to express their ideas in different ways. For example, *The key fact is 8 equals 4 plus 4. So 80 take away 40 is 40.*

What is 80 take away 40?
What is 70 take away 30?
Subtract 20 from 50.
Decrease 30 by 10.

Find half of 80.
How much do you need to add to 40 to make 90?
What is the difference between 50 and 100?

Add a single digit using doubles and near doubles facts

Use 4 + 4 to derive the answer to 24 + 4.

What is 4 and 4? Make the pattern to show what it means.

Pupil puts out 4 units and another 4 units to make the pattern of 8 and says:
4 and 4 makes 8.

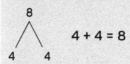

Record 4 and 4 as a triad and an equation.

Pupil explains:
8 is made of 4 and 4. So 4 add 4 equals 8

$$4 + 4 = 8$$

Build 24.

Pupil builds 24 and says: *24 is 2 tens and 4 units. Or 2 tens and 4 units makes 24.*

What is 24 add 4? Use a doubles fact to help you.

Pupil puts out another 4 units and says:
4 and 4 is 8. So 24 and 4 is 28.

4 and 4 is 8. So 24 add 4 equals 28.

Record 24 and 4 as a triad and an equation. Then show it on a number line.
Encourage pupils to draw a loop to show the connection between the known doubles fact and the new fact they have derived.

Note that the number line is an illustration of the concept. The proportions do not need to be exact as long as the idea is clear. A pupil who is confident with the use of number lines can use a partial number line.

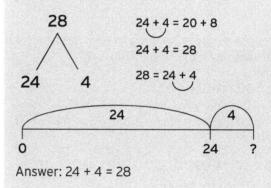

$$24 + 4 = 20 + 8$$
$$24 + 4 = 28$$
$$28 = 24 + 4$$

Answer: 24 + 4 = 28

Give pupils plenty of practice. In each case they explain which key fact can help. They demonstrate, explain and record their thinking.

What is 64 and 5?   Add 3 to 74.   Increase 32 by 3.

Subtracting a single digit using doubles and near doubles facts

Use 7 – 3 to derive the answer to 87 – 3.

What is 7 take away 3? Make the pattern to show what it means.

Pupil puts out the pattern of 7 and then takes away three units and says:
7 is made of 4 and 3. So 7 take away 3 is 4.

What is 87 take away 3? Model it using the equipment.

Pupil builds 87 and says:
87 is 8 tens and 7 units.

Then the pupil removes 3 units and says:
7 take away 3 is 4. So 87 take away 3 is 84.

Record 87 take away 3 as a triad and write the equation. Draw a loop to show the key fact that you are using. Then show 87 subtract 3 on a number line.

Pupil explains again:
7 take away 3 is 4. So 87 take away 3 is 84.

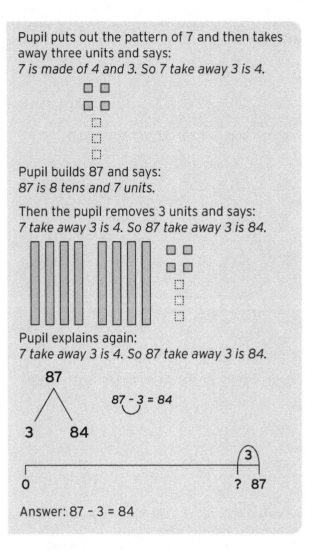

Answer: 87 – 3 = 84

Give pupils plenty of practice. In each case they explain which key fact can help. They demonstrate, explain and record their thinking.

What is 75 take away 3?   Subtract 5 from 79.
What is the difference between 58 and 54?   Decrease 46 by 3.
How much do you need to add to 85 to make 89?   97 minus 3.

Checklist – Apply doubles and near doubles facts to calculations with two-digit numbers

Pupils can:
- ☐ Apply doubles and near doubles facts to add tens numbers
- ☐ Apply doubles and near doubles facts to subtract tens numbers
- ☐ Apply doubles and near doubles facts to add a single digit to a two-digit number (e.g. 54 + 4 = 58)
- ☐ Apply doubles and near doubles facts to subtract a single digit from a two-digit number (e.g. 69 – 4 = 65)
- ☐ Explain the reasoning process used to apply doubles and near doubles knowledge
- ☐ Record thinking as triads and number lines, and equations

Apply bonds of 10 to add or subtract decade numbers to 100

Objectives

- Apply bonds of 10 facts to add tens numbers
- Apply bonds of 10 facts to subtract tens numbers
- Use bonds of 10 facts for addition to the next decade number
- Use bonds of 10 facts for subtraction from a decade number
- Model addition and subtraction in relation to the 100 square
- Explain the reasoning process used to apply bonds of 10 knowledge
- Record thinking as triads, number lines and equations

Pupils use the bonds of 10 facts to derive facts for addition and subtraction of multiples of 10. Pupils relate concrete materials to the 100 square. The relationship between the bonds of 10 and their use in larger numbers can be clearly demonstrated using base 10 equipment or Cuisenaire rods on the 100 square. It is important not to rush this work as understanding the relationship between the linear and spatial representation of the number 100 is essential for working with place value.

Pupils need to be comfortable generalising bonds of 10 knowledge to two-digit numbers if they are to use the bridging through 10 strategy efficiently. Even if pupils are able to do the calculations easily, they must describe their thinking and use number lines and equations in order to develop the reasoning skills which will be transferred later to multi-digit calculations. Practice in reasoning about small numbers and using varied language lays secure foundations for working with larger numbers later on.

Teaching

Pupils use base 10 equipment to model numbers. They explain which bond of 10 fact they use to derive their answers.

Adding decade numbers using bonds of 10 facts

Use 3 + 7 to derive the answer to 30 + 70.

What does 3 and 7 make?	*3 and 7 is 10*
Can you use the key fact 3 and 7 to work out what 30 add 70 is? Use equipment to model the question.	Pupil puts out 3 tens and 7 tens. Then the pupil moves the tens together and says: *30 add 70 makes 100.*

You have 10 tens. Exchange 10 tens for 1 hundred square.

Pupil exchanges 10 tens for 1 hundred square and says: *10 tens equals 100.*

Record 30 and 70 as a triad and write the equation. Show it on a number line.

Pupil explains:
3 and 7 is 10. So 30 add 70 equals 100.

$$30 + 70 = 100$$

Demonstrate 30 plus 70 on the hundred square. First use tens to model 30 and put them on the 100 square. Count in tens as you place each ten.

Pupil aligns each ten horizontally on the 100 square whilst counting: *Ten, twenty, thirty.*

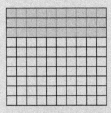

You have 30. Now add 70. Count on as you place each ten.

Pupil adds on 7 tens whilst counting: *Forty, fifty, sixty, seventy, eighty, ninety, one hundred.*

Give pupils plenty of practice. In each case they explain which key fact can help. They demonstrate, explain and record their thinking.

Add 40 and 60.
What is 20 and 80?
What is 30 more than 70?

Double 50.
Increase 90 by 10.

Subtracting decade numbers using bonds of 10 facts

Use 10 – 4 to derive the answer to 100 – 40.

What is 10 take away 4?

Can you use the key fact 10 take away 4 is 6 to work out what 100 take away 40 makes? Use equipment to model the question.

Encourage the pupil to align the tens horizontally as this is the order in which the numbers are on the 100 square. However it is also correct to place them vertically.

10 take away 4 is 6.

Pupil puts out 10 tens then removes 4 tens whilst saying: *10 tens take away 4 tens is 6 tens. So 100 take away 40 is 60.*

Record 100 take away 40 as a triad and write the equation. Show it on a number line.

10 take away 4 is 6. So 100 take away 40 is 60.

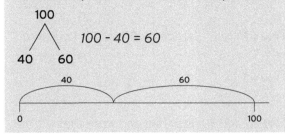

Give pupils plenty of practice. In each case they explain which key fact can help. They demonstrate, explain and record their thinking.

Subtract 30 from 100.
What is 100 minus 80?
What is 70 less than 100?

Halve 100.
Decrease 100 by 90.

Use the bonds of 10 to calculate to the next decade number

Use 4 + 6 = 10 to derive the answer to 24 + 6.

What is 4 add 6?

What is 24 add 6? Use a bond of 10 to help you. Use equipment to model the question.

Pupils may align the rods vertically or horizontally. Both are correct. The linear model represents the number line. The spatial (vertical) arrangement shows the place value positions. Pupils need to understand both representations.

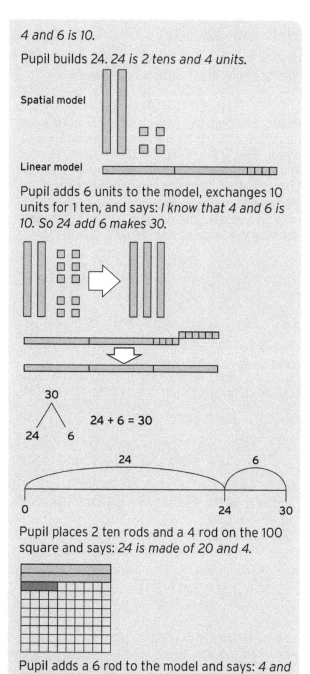

4 and 6 is 10.

Pupil builds 24. *24 is 2 tens and 4 units.*

Spatial model

Linear model

Pupil adds 6 units to the model, exchanges 10 units for 1 ten, and says: *I know that 4 and 6 is 10. So 24 add 6 makes 30.*

24 + 6 = 30

Record 24 and 6 as a triad and an equation. Then show it on a number line.

Demonstrate 24 add 6 on the 100 square. Use Cuisenaire rods.
Pupil aligns the rods horizontally as this is the order in which the numbers are on the 100 square.

Pupil places 2 ten rods and a 4 rod on the 100 square and says: *24 is made of 20 and 4.*

Pupil adds a 6 rod to the model and says: *4 and 6 makes 10, so 24 and 6 makes 30.*

Give pupils plenty of practice adding a digit to make the next decade number. In each case they explain which key fact can help. They demonstrate, explain and record their thinking.

next 10

32 + ☐ = ☐

47 + ☐ = ☐

54 + ☐ = ☐

next 10

91 + ☐ = ☐

83 + ☐ = ☐

68 + ☐ = ☐

Use the bonds of 10 to subtract a single digit from a decade number
Use 10 – 7 = 3 to derive the answer to 30 – 7.

What is 10 take away 7?

What is 30 take away 7? Use a bond of 10 to help you. Use equipment to model the question.

Pupils may align the rods vertically or horizontally. Allow them to choose the representation they prefer. Both are correct.
The linear model represents the number line.
The spatial (vertical) arrangement shows the place value positions. Pupils need to understand both representations. It is important to show and describe the exchange of 1 ten for 10 units.

Record 30 subtract 7 as a triad and an equation. Then show it on a number line.
Pupils explain their thinking in their own words as they do the recordings.

Demonstrate 30 subtract 7 on the 100 square. Use Cuisenaire rods.
Pupil aligns the rods horizontally as this is the order in which the numbers are on the 100 square.

10 take away 7 is 3.

Pupil builds 30 and says: *30 is made of 3 tens. I want to take away 7 so I need to exchange 1 ten for 10 units. Now I can take away 7. I know that 10 take 7 is 3, so 30 take away 7 is 23.*

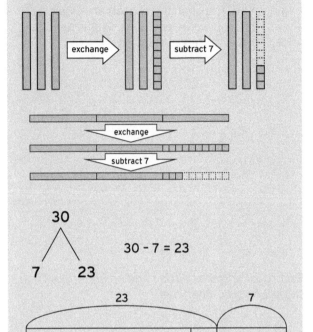

Pupil places 3 tens rods on the 100 square. *30 is made of 3 tens. I want to take away 7 so I need to exchange 1 ten for 10 units. Now I can take away 7. I know that 10 take 7 is 3, so 30 take away 7 is 23.*

Give pupils plenty of practice subtracting a single digit from a decade number. In each case they explain which key fact can help. They demonstrate, explain and record their thinking.

60 – ☐ = 52   100 – ☐ = 95   80 – ☐ = 71

40 – ☐ = 34   90 – ☐ = 83   70 – ☐ = 67

Checklist – Apply bonds of 10 to add or subtract decade numbers to 100
Pupils can:
- ☐ Apply bonds of 10 facts to add tens numbers
- ☐ Apply bonds of 10 facts to subtract tens numbers
- ☐ Use bonds of 10 facts for addition to the next decade number
- ☐ Use bonds of 10 facts for subtraction from a decade number
- ☐ Model addition and subtraction in relation to the 100 square
- ☐ Explain the reasoning process used to apply bonds of 10 knowledge
- ☐ Record thinking as triads, number lines and equations

Extend bridging through 10 to two-digit numbers

Objectives
- Add a single digit to a two-digit number by bridging through 10
- Subtract a single digit from a two-digit number by bridging back through 10
- Subtract using complementary addition to bridge through 10
- Model thinking using base 10 equipment and Cuisenaire rods
- Explain the reasoning process used to apply bonds of 10 knowledge
- Use number lines and equations to record the reasoning process

Bridging through 10 is used to make addition calculations easier by using 10 as a 'bridge'. The strategy can be adapted for subtraction by bridging back through 10. Pupils learnt this method in Chapter 4, now they apply it to multiples of 10. Make sure that pupils have plenty of practice bridging through decade numbers. Pupils need to understand this strategy and be confident using it. This is one of the most useful strategies. It can be generalised to calculations with hundreds, thousands and higher numbers.

Subtraction by complementary addition, the shopkeeper's method, is based on the concept of subtraction by equalising. This idea was explored extensively in basic number work with numbers to 10 (see p91). Provided that pupils understand this concept, it is easiest to re-phrase the subtraction question as a mystery number question. Thus 10 - 6 = ? becomes 6 + ? = 10. (The correct term is 'missing addend' but this language is too opaque for some pupils and it is not necessary to use it.)

Some pupils find bridging back very difficult so they should use complementary addition as their preferred method. However all students need to be able to use complementary addition as it can be the more efficient method in some cases.

Teaching
Pupils use Cuisenaire rods to model numbers. They explain their thinking and record it on a number line, or partial number line, and as an equation.

Addition by bridging
Bridge through 10 to calculate 35 + 7.

What is 35 add 7? Use Cuisenaire rods to model the question.
Pupils may model the question as either a linear or spatial arrangement. The linear model shown here relates directly to the number line. The spatial (vertical) arrangement (p180) shows the place value positions. Pupils need to understand both representations.

Show the question on a number line, and write the question as an equation.
Suggest pupils use a question mark to show where the answer will be. The question marks denotes the unknown quantity.

Reason to find the answer. Record your thinking on the number line and write the equation.

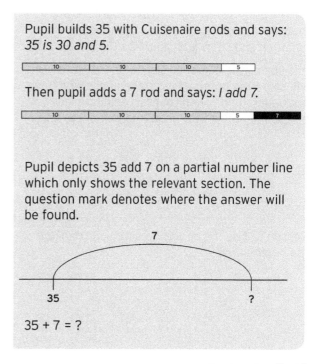

Pupil builds 35 with Cuisenaire rods and says: *35 is 30 and 5.*

| 10 | 10 | 10 | 5 |

Then pupil adds a 7 rod and says: *I add 7.*

| 10 | 10 | 10 | 5 | 7 |

Pupil depicts 35 add 7 on a partial number line which only shows the relevant section. The question mark denotes where the answer will be found.

35 + 7 = ?

Some pupils may find it easier to say: *5 needs 5 to make 10, so 35 needs 5 to make 40.* Allow them to use this wording if they wish.

Pupil adjusts the model and explains:
5 and 5 makes 10, so 35 and 5 makes 40.
I bridge through 40. I change 7 into 5 and 2.
Then I exchange 5 and 5 for 1 ten rod. Now I have 40 and 2 more. 40 and 2 is 42.
Then the pupil says: *35 add 7 is 42.*

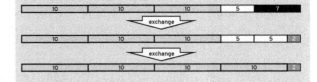

Show the pupil how to record their thinking informally on one line using arrows to emphasise the reasoning process.

Write calculations to show your reasoning on one line. Use arrows instead of equal signs.
The triad notation shows the relevant components of 7. Some pupils like to use an oval to emphasise the bond of 10. (See p79)

Some pupils find that a series of equations on one line are hard to interpret visually.
Write the equations to show your thinking.
Each step can be shown by writing the next equation on the line below.

Pupil explains each step as they write the equation.

$$35 + 7 \rightarrow 30 + 10 + 2 \rightarrow 40 + 2 \rightarrow 42$$

$$35 + 7 = (35 + 5) + 2$$
$$(35 + 5) + 2 = 40 + 2$$
$$40 + 2 = 42$$

Give pupils plenty of practice. In each case they explain which key fact can help. They demonstrate, explain and record their thinking.

57 plus 8   Increase 85 by 9   What is 8 more than 46?

Subtraction by bridging back through 10

Bridge back through 10 to calculate 32 subtract 7.

What is 32 subtract 7? Use Cuisenaire rods to model the question. Write the question as an equation and show it on a number line.

It is important that pupils say where the answer will be on the number line; some pupils who have not understood complementary addition (see below) may think they need to add the 7 to 32.

Pupil uses Cuisenaire rods to make 32 and says: *32 is 30 and 2.*

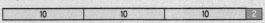

Pupil uses a question mark to denote the unknown quantity in the equation and on the partial number line. Pupil says:
I have 32. I need to subtract 7. The answer will be less than 32.

$$32 - 7 = ?$$

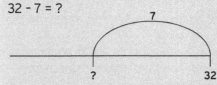

Reason to find the answer. Record your thinking on the number line.

Pupil adjusts the model and explains:
I can bridge back through 10 to help me work it out. The tens number before 32 is 30, so I am going to bridge back through 30. 32 take away 2 makes 30. 7 is made of 2 and 5 so I still need to take away 5 more. I exchange 10 for 5 and 5. 10 take away 5 is 5. If I take 5 away from 30 that leaves 25. So 32 subtract 7 is 25.

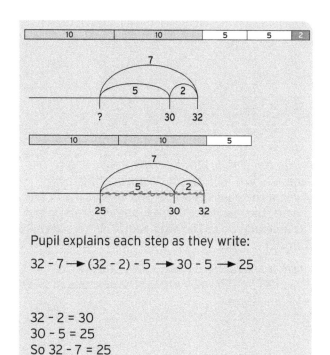

Write calculations to show your reasoning on one line. Use arrows instead of equal signs.

Some pupils find that a series of equations on one line are hard to interpret visually.

Write the equations to show your thinking. Each step can be shown by writing the next equation on the line below.

Pupil explains each step as they write:

$32 - 7 \rightarrow (32 - 2) - 5 \rightarrow 30 - 5 \rightarrow 25$

$32 - 2 = 30$
$30 - 5 = 25$
So $32 - 7 = 25$

Give pupils plenty of practice. In each case they explain which key fact can help. They demonstrate, explain and record their thinking.

$65 - 8 = ?$ $\qquad\qquad$ $93 - 7 = ?$ $\qquad\qquad$ $52 - 5 = ?$

Subtraction as complementary addition using bridging through 10

Pupils rephrase the subtraction question as a mystery number (missing addend) question. They use a number line to explain their reasoning. By this stage they may not need to use concrete materials. If they lack confidence however, allow them to use Cuisenaire rods to support their thinking initially.

Use complementary addition to calculate 35 - 8.

What is 35 take away 8? Use complementary addition to work out the answer.
Write the question as an equation and then change it to a mystery number equation. Use a question mark to show the unknown number.

Show 8 add what equals 35 on a number line. Then do the calculation and explain your thinking.

Pupil writes the equations and says:
35 take away 8 equals what? I can also write it as 8 add what makes 35?

$35 - 8 = ?$
$8 + ? = 35$

Pupil draws the number line and explains:
8 and what makes 35? I need to find how far it is from 8 to 35. They may scribble out the portion of the line between 0 and 8 to show that 8 is removed.

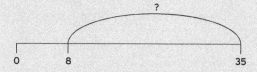

Pupil annotates the diagram whilst saying:
8 and 2 is 10. If I add 10 and 20 I get to 30. The distance from 30 to 35 is 5.

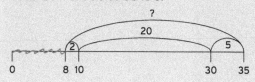

Now I can work out how far it is from 8 to 35. I add 2 and 20 and 5. So the distance from 8 to 35 is 27.

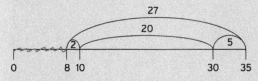

$8 + (2 + 20 + 5) \longrightarrow 8 + 27 \longrightarrow 35$
So $35 - 8 = 27$

Write calculations to show your reasoning on one line. Use arrows instead of the equal signs.
Even if the pupils can work the answer out in their heads, they need to record it both informally and as an equation so they can apply this reasoning to larger numbers.

Write the equations to show your thinking. Each step can be shown by writing the next equation on the line below.

$8 + ? = 35$
$8 + (2 + 20 + 5) = 35$
$2 + 20 + 5 = 27$
$8 + 27 = 35$
So $35 - 8 = 27$

Set a selection of questions for practising complementary addition. Pupils must show all working on number lines and record their thinking systematically as equations, both rephrasing the subtraction as a missing addend, and writing the answer to the original subtraction question.

$93 - 8 = ?$ $\qquad\qquad$ $75 - 9 = ?$ $\qquad\qquad$ $54 - 6 = ?$

Checklist – Extend bridging through 10 to two-digit numbers
Pupils can:
- ☐ Add a single digit to a two-digit number by bridging through 10
- ☐ Subtract a single digit from a two-digit number by bridging back through 10
- ☐ Subtract using complementary addition to bridge through 10
- ☐ Model thinking using base 10 equipment and Cuisenaire rods
- ☐ Explain the reasoning process used to apply bonds of 10 knowledge
- ☐ Use number lines and equations to record the reasoning process

Partitioning to add or subtract two-digit numbers

Objectives
- Partition two-digit numbers into tens and units to make calculation easier
- Think ahead before partitioning
- Partition flexibly to make the calculation easier
- Demonstrate thinking using concrete materials
- Explain the reasoning process used to partition two-digit numbers
- Record thinking as diagrams, triads, and equations

Partitioning makes it easy to add or subtract two-digit numbers. Calculation by partitioning is an essential strategy for later work with multi-digit numbers. Partitioning lays the foundations for understanding the place value structure and using formal written methods.

Partitioning is also called the 'split tens method'. When doing addition both numbers are partitioned, or split, into tens and units. The pupil calculates the total number of tens and computes the total number of units. Then they combine these totals to reach the answer. There is only one quantity in subtraction. This is partitioned into tens and units to make it easier to take away. Subtraction by complementary addition is explained in the section on sequencing. (See p141)

Pupils use base 10 equipment to model the question, and then they record their thinking as diagrams, triads and equations. Work with examples that require no exchange or decomposition before expecting pupils to do calculations that require exchange and decomposition. Pupils will continue to apply their knowledge of key facts and universal strategies within the partitioning calculations.

Pupils need to be able to partition numbers flexibly. Flexible partitioning means showing the components of a number in a variety of ways in order to find the easiest arrangement for calculation. This is particularly important for mental calculations. In primary school the term 'partitioning' is usually restricted to the place value components; initially tens and units and later hundreds and thousands.

While it is helpful to introduce the concept of partitioning numbers in this way, pupils need to develop a more flexible approach. Early work with dot patterns and the key number facts showed that there are many different ways to split, or partition, a number into its components. Now they apply this knowledge to two-digit numbers.

Make sure that pupils understand the word 'partitioning' as it is used in slightly different contexts, which can cause confusion. Partitioning describes both the act of splitting a number into components, and the process of calculating using the component parts. In the dot pattern work, the word 'split' was used to avoid confusion when the word 'partition' is used to describe tens and units components. Sometimes the word 'chunking' is used to clarify the distinction between splitting a number into tens and units (partitioning) and splitting a number into component facts (chunking). Unfortunately the change in terminology means that some pupils do not realise that both terms represent the same action. They may focus too much on whether it is a 'partitioning' question or a 'chunking' question when in reality both words describe the same underlying concept: identifying components of a number. Whatever the term used, pupils need to be able to partition, chunk or split numbers flexibly. Encourage them to use the term 'partitioning' as understanding emerges.

Number lines are not used to show the process of partitioning as it is too difficult to show the rearrangement clearly. However number lines will be essential for showing the sequencing and compensation strategies that are derived from partitioning. In partitioning both numbers are partitioned into components, while in sequencing only one number is partitioned, the other remains unchanged. The compensation method, also called rounding and adjusting, simplifies numbers by rounding. Make sure that pupils have a good grasp of partitioning before teaching sequencing and the compensation method.

Teaching

Pupils use base 10 equipment to demonstrate addition and subtraction by partitioning. They record their thinking as diagrams, triads and equations.

Add two-digit numbers (no exchange) using partitioning
Partition both numbers into tens and units to calculate 57 + 32

What is 57 and 32? Build the numbers using tens and units. Put the tens in the vertical position and make the dot pattern of the units. Then draw a small diagram. Show the triad under the diagram of each number.

By this stage diagrams should be compact and clear sketches.

Pupil builds both numbers and says: *57 is 5 tens and 7 units; 32 is 3 tens and 2 units.* The pupil draws the diagrams and completes the triads whilst explaining: *I can partition 57 into 50 and 7. I can partition 32 into 30 and 2.*

57 + 32 = 50 + 7 + 30 + 2

Write the equation to show that 57 and 32 is 50 and 7 plus 30 and 2.

Use the equipment to add the tens, then add the units. Explain what you are doing.

Make it clear that you are adding the tens together and the units together by using curved and square links.

Teacher demonstrates how to use a box bracket above the numbers to indicate the tens, and a curve below the numbers to identify the units.

Pupils should also lay out the equations in a way which emphasises the successive steps. Finally they write the answer to the original question.

Pupil combines the tens and then combines the units whilst saying:
50 add 30 is 80. 7 add 2 is 9.

57 + 32 = 50 + 7 + 30 + 2 = 80 + 9 = 89

57 + 32 = 50 + 7 + 30 + 2
50 + 7 + 30 + 2 = 80 + 9
80 + 9 = 89

Answer: 57 + 32 = 89

Add two-digit numbers (with exchange) using partitioning
Partition both numbers into tens and units to calculate 35 + 46.

What is 35 and 46? Build the numbers using tens and units. Put the tens in the vertical position and make the dot pattern of the units. Show how they are partitioned into tens and units in diagrams and triads and write the equation.

Pupil builds both numbers and says: *35 is 3 tens and 5 units; 46 is 4 tens and 6 units.* Pupil draws the diagrams and triads and says: *I can partition 35 into 30 and 5. I can partition 46 into 40 and 6.*

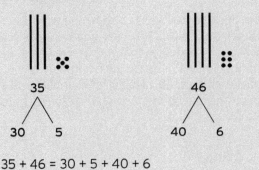

35 + 46 = 30 + 5 + 40 + 6

Use the equipment to add the tens, then add the units. Explain what you are doing.

Pupil demonstrates with the equipment whilst saying:
30 add 40 is 70. 5 add 6 is 11. I exchange 10 units for 1 ten.

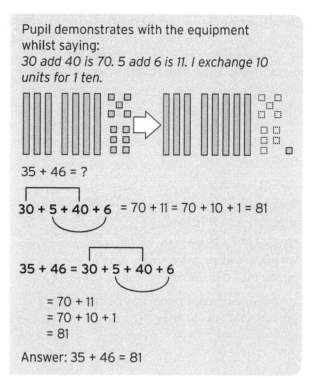

35 + 46 = ?

30 + 5 + 40 + 6 = 70 + 11 = 70 + 10 + 1 = 81

35 + 46 = 30 + 5 + 40 + 6

= 70 + 11
= 70 + 10 + 1
= 81

Answer: 35 + 46 = 81

Write the equations to show your working. Make it clear that you are adding the tens together and the units together.

Pupils should also write the equations in a way which emphasises the successive steps. Finally they write their answer to the original question.

Pupils practise partitioning to add two-digit numbers. They record their reasoning using diagrams, triads and equations. Once pupils are confident they do not need to draw the diagrams of the tens and units.

| 63 + 45 | 27 + 71 | 36 + 43 | 47 + 25 | 58 + 16 | 29 + 35 |

Subtraction back (no decomposition) using partitioning

What is 58 take away 36? Use tens and units to demonstrate. Put the tens in the vertical position and make the dot pattern of the units. Show your thinking using diagrams and triads and equations.

Pupil builds 58 and says:
I build only 58 because I am going to take away from it. I partition 58 into 50 and 8. I also draw the triad of 36 to show 36 is made of 30 and 6.

58 - 36 = ?

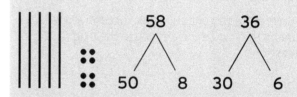

It is important that pupils realise that they need to take away 30 and take away 6.

Pupil writes the equation: *58 take away 36 is 50 plus 8 take away 30 and take away 6.*

58 - 36 = 50 + 8 - 30 - 6.

Use the equipment to take away 36. Explain what you are doing.

Pupil removes the tens and units: *50 take away 30 is 20. 8 take away 6 is 2. 20 and 2 is 22. So 58 take away 36 is 22.*

58 - 36 =
50 + 8 - 30 - 6 = 50 - 30 + 8 - 6 = 20 + 2 = 22

So 58 - 36 = 22

Write the equation to show your reasoning. Show the pupil how to rearrange the numbers to subtract the tens and the units. This is in preparation for using brackets.

Pupils should also lay out the equations in a way which emphasises the successive steps. Finally they write the answer to the original question. Show pupils how to use brackets to highlight the subtraction involving the tens and the units.

58 - 36 = 50 + 8 - 30 - 6
= (50 - 30) + (8 - 6)
= 20 + 2

Answer: 58 - 36 = 22

Subtraction back (with decomposition) using partitioning

What is 62 take away 37? Use tens and units to demonstrate. Show your thinking using diagrams and triads.

Pupil builds 62 and says: *I only build 62 because I am going to take 37 away from 62. I partition 62 into 60 and 2.*
I also draw the triad of 37 to show 37 is made of 30 and 7.

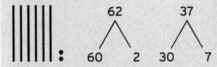

62 - 37 = ?
You can't take 7 from 2 without exchanging.

Write the question and look at the units carefully. What do you notice?

It is easier if you partition 62 into 50 and 12. Then you can work out 12 take away 7. Record it as a triad and an equation.

Use the equipment to work out 62 take away 27. Start by working out the units.

Pupil models the subtraction and says:
I partition 62 into 50 and 12. Then I exchange 1 ten for 10 units so I have 12 units. Now I can take away 37. 12 units take away 7 is 5 units. 50 take away 30 is 20. I have 25 left. So 62 take away 37 is 25.

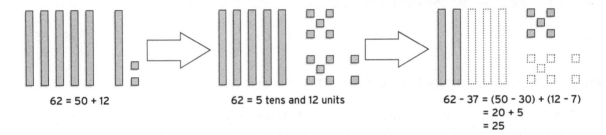

62 = 50 + 12   62 = 5 tens and 12 units   62 - 37 = (50 - 30) + (12 - 7)
= 20 + 5
= 25

Write the equation to show your reasoning. Pupils rearrange the numbers to subtract the tens and the units. Pupils may use brackets if they want to.

Pupils write the equations as successive steps. Finally they write the answer to the original question.

62 - 37 =
50 + 12 - 30 - 7 = 50 - 30 + 12 - 7 = 20+5 = 25

62 - 37 = 50 + 12 - 37
= (50 - 30) + (12 - 7)
= (50 - 30) + 5
= 20 + 5
= 25

Answer: 62 - 37 = 25

Give pupils plenty of practice using partitioning to subtract two-digit numbers. They demonstrate, explain and record their thinking.

47 - 24   96 - 43   78 - 25   64 - 29   52 - 36   83 - 57

Checklist – Partitioning to add or subtract two-digit numbers
Pupils can:
- ☐ Partition two-digit numbers into tens and units to make calculation easier.
- ☐ Think ahead before partitioning
- ☐ Partition flexibly to make the calculation easier
- ☐ Demonstrate thinking using concrete materials
- ☐ Explain the reasoning process used to partition two-digit numbers
- ☐ Record thinking as diagrams, triads, and equations

Sequencing to add or subtract two-digit numbers

Objectives
- Keep one number unchanged and partition the second number to calculate
- Use a partial number line to demonstrate understanding
- Explain the reasoning process used to partition two-digit numbers
- Record thinking on number lines and as equations

Sequencing is a simplified form of partitioning. In sequencing one number is unchanged and the second number is partitioned into tens and units. Sequencing evolves from partitioning as pupils' confidence grows and they realise that they can handle a number as a whole. Make it clear that sequencing is a refinement of partitioning rather than a separate method. Sequencing works particularly well with informal recording on a number line. It is the method used most frequently in real life situations.

The work on partitioning emphasised the base 10 structure, now the focus is on developing mental calculation strategies. Pupils use number lines to show their reasoning. By now number lines should be drawn freehand with only the relevant sections shown. The advantage of showing the calculation on a partial number line is that it draws attention to where the answer is to be found.

The subtraction methods discussed are subtraction back and complementary addition. In subtraction the number that is taken away (the subtrahend) is split into tens and units. The tens are subtracted from the initial quantity (the minuend) and then the units are subtracted. Complementary addition is used to find the difference between two numbers. The subtraction question is rephrased as a mystery number (missing addend) problem. The number line representation makes it clear that the solution is the distance from one point to another.

Teaching

Add two-digit numbers using sequencing
Pupils record their thinking on a partial number line. Allow pupils to use base 10 equipment if they lack confidence but encourage them to attempt the calculation without it.

What is 64 and 23? Write the question and show it on a partial number line.

You keep 64 as a whole . Partition 23 into tens and units. Write the equation and explain what you are doing.

Do the calculation. Show it on the number line and explain what you are doing.

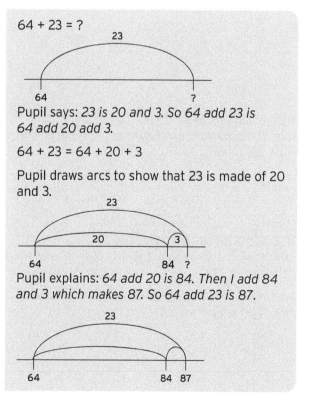

64 + 23 = ?

Pupil says: *23 is 20 and 3. So 64 add 23 is 64 add 20 add 3.*

64 + 23 = 64 + 20 + 3

Pupil draws arcs to show that 23 is made of 20 and 3.

Pupil explains: *64 add 20 is 84. Then I add 84 and 3 which makes 87. So 64 add 23 is 87.*

Write equations to show your reasoning.

Write the equations emphasising the sequence of steps.

64 + 23 = 64 + 20 + 3 = 84 + 3 = 87

64 + 23 = 64 + 20 + 3
        = 84 + 3
        = 87

Answer: 64 + 23 = 87

Subtraction back (no decomposition) using sequencing

Pupils explain their thinking and use a number line to support their reasoning. They write equations to show the steps in the calculation. Allow pupils to use base 10 equipment if they lack confidence but encourage them to attempt the calculation without it.

What is 59 subtract 24? Write the question and show it on a partial number line.

59 take away 24.
The answer will be less than 59
59 - 24 = ?

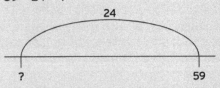

You keep 59 as a whole. Partition 24 into tens and units. Write the equation and explain what you are doing. Show it on the number line.

Pupil writes the equation, draws arcs on the number line and says: *24 is 20 and 4. So 59 take away 24 is 59 take away 20 take away 4.*

59 - 24 = 59 - 20 - 4

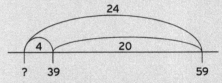

Do the calculation. Show it on the number line and explain what you are doing.

Pupil explains: *59 take away 20 is 39. Then 39 take away 4 is 35. So 59 take away 24 is 35.*

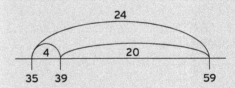

59 - 24 = 59 - 20 - 4= 39 - 4 = 35

Write equations to show your reasoning.
Write the equations emphasising the sequence of steps.

59 - 24 = 59 - 20 - 4
        = 39 - 4
        = 35

Answer: 59 - 24 = 35

Subtraction back (with decomposition) using sequencing

Subtract the appropriate quantity of tens, and then deal with the units by bridging back through 10.

What is 64 subtract 37? Write the question and show it on a number line.

64 take away 37.
The answer will be less than 64.
64 - 37 = ?

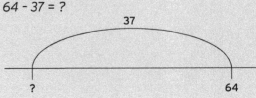

Keep 64 as a whole. Partition 37 into tens and units. Write the equation and show it on the number line. Explain what you are doing.

Pupil writes the equation, draws arcs on the number line and says: *37 is 30 and 7. So 64 take away 37 is 64 take away 30 take away 7.*

$64 - 37 = 64 - 30 - 7$

Pupil explains: *64 take away 30 is 34.*

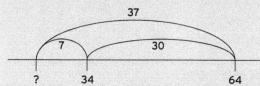

Now work out what 34 subtract 7 is. Write the equation and record it on the number line.

I can bridge back through 30. 7 is made of 4 and 3 so 34 take away 4 is 30. Then 30 take away 3 is 27.

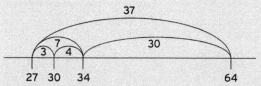

Write equations to show your reasoning.

$64 - 37 = 64 - 30 - 7 = 34 - 7 = 34 - 4 - 3$
$= 30 - 3 = 27$

Write the equations emphasising the sequence of steps.

$64 - 37 = 34 - 7$
$= 34 - 4 - 3$
$= 30 - 3$
$= 27$

Answer: $64 - 37 = 27$

Subtraction using complementary addition

Pupils rephrase the subtraction question as a mystery number (missing addend) question. They use a partial number line to explain their reasoning. See p91 for instructions on teaching subtraction by complementary addition.

What is 59 subtract 24? Use complementary addition. Write the equation and rephrase it as a mystery number question. Then show it on a partial number line.

59 take away 24 equals what?
I can rearrange it to 24 and what is 59.

$59 - 24 = ?$
$24 + ? = 59$

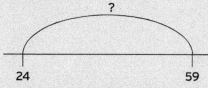

Explain how you find out how far it is from 24 to 59. Record it on the number line.

Pupil counts on 3 tens and shows the count as a single arc of 30 on the number line.
24 add 30 is 54. I need to add some more to get to 59.

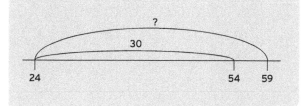

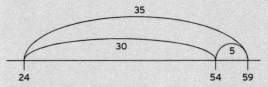

I know that 4 add 5 is 9, so 54 add 5 is 59. The distance from 24 to 59 is 30 add 5 which is 35.

What is 59 subtract 24? Write the equations and explain your thinking.

24 add 30 is 54 so I still need to add 5 more to make 59. So 24 add 35 is 59.

59 - 24 = ?
24 + ? = 59
24 + 30= 54
54 + 5 = 59
So 24 + 35 = 59

Then 59 subtract 24 is 35.

Answer: 59 - 24 = 35

Give pupils plenty of practice using sequencing to add and subtract two-digit numbers. They demonstrate, explain and record their thinking.

45 + 32	87 - 34
63 + 26	59 - 15
37 + 25	94 - 36
18 + 54	72 - 47

Give pupils word problems to solve. Pupils summarise what the question is asking, draw diagrams, use number lines, write equations and write the answer as a full sentence. (See information on word problems on p221.) Pupils should also make up their own word problems.

Checklist - Sequencing to add or subtract two-digit numbers
Pupils can:
- ☐ Keep one number unchanged and partition the second number to calculate
- ☐ Use a partial number line to demonstrate understanding
- ☐ Explain the reasoning process used to partition two-digit numbers
- ☐ Record thinking on number lines and as equations

The compensation method to add or subtract two-digit numbers

Objectives
- Round numbers to make the calculation easier
- Adjust numbers to compensate for the rounding
- Record thinking on number lines
- Record calculations as equations
- Decide whether subtraction back or complementary addition is most appropriate
- Explain reasoning

The compensation strategy is also called 'rounding and adjusting'. One number is adjusted to make the calculation easier, and a compensatory change made to the other number or the answer. Pupils require a clear understanding of the number line and the ability to round numbers to be able to use this method. They need to develop a flexible approach in order to choose the most efficient way to adapt the numbers.

Pupils often find this strategy confusing because they are not sure whether to add or subtract an amount to compensate. This problem can be overcome by recording the information on a partial number line. The number line representation also makes it clear which number it is best to round up or down.

It is not advisable to teach this method to pupils unless they can confidently handle the other strategies. However, if pupils devise this method for themselves, encourage them to use it. Pupils with a vulnerable working memory find this method particularly difficult. If they use it, they should always use a number line.

Teaching

Round the first number
You can make a calculation easier by rounding and adjusting the numbers. This is also called 'the compensation method'.

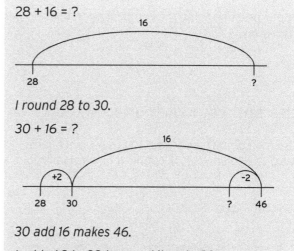

What is 28 add 16? Write the question. Show it on a number line.

$28 + 16 = ?$

Round 28 to the nearest 10.

I round 28 to 30.

Write the question 30 add 16. Explain your thinking and record it on the number line.

$30 + 16 = ?$

30 add 16 makes 46.

How much did you add to 28 to round it up to 30?

I added 2 to 28 to round it up to 30.

Now you need to adjust the answer. What do you do to compensate? Show it on the number line and write the equations.

I take away 2 from 46 to make the adjustment. 46 subtract 2 is 44, so 28 add 16 is 44.

$$(28 + 2) + 16 = 30 + 16$$
$$30 + 16 = 46$$
$$46 - 2 = 44$$

Answer: $28 + 16 = 44$

Round the second number

What is 34 add 17?
Show it on a partial number line.

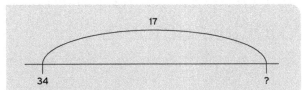

Round 17 to the nearest tens number.

What is 34 add 20? Show 20 as an arc on the number line. Explain what you do.

17 rounds up to 20.

I know that 30 and 20 is 50 so 34 add 20 is 54.

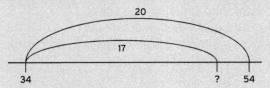

How much did you add to 17 to round it up to 20?.

Now you need to subtract 3 from 54 to compensate. Show it on the number line and write the equations. What is 34 add 17?

It is important that pupils develop their competence with these small numbers, as the compensation strategies will be the method of choice when calculating with multi-digit numbers.

I added 3 to 17 to round it to 20.

I take away 3 from 54 to make the adjustment. 54 subtract 3 is 51, 34 add 17 is 51.

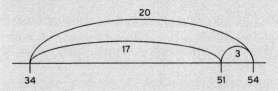

34 add 17.
I round 17 to 20 by adding 3 so I need to take away 3 to compensate.
34 add 20 is 54 then I need to subtract 3 which is 51. So 34 add 17 is 51.

$$34 + 17 = 34 + (17 + 3) - 3$$
$$= (34 + 20) - 3$$
$$= 54 - 3$$
$$= 51$$

Pupils practise using the compensation method and record their thinking on number lines and as equations.

39 + 47
56 + 28

73 + 19
18 + 64

Subtract back by rounding and adjusting

Use the compensation method to subtract back. What is 85 subtract 47? Show it on a number line.

85 take away 47. The answer will be less than 85.

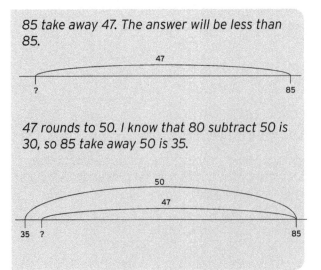

It is easier to take away a tens number.
Round 47 to the nearest 10. Show it on the number line and write the equation.

Note that the proportions shown on this number line diagram are not correct. Pupils need to understand that this is a sketch to show the relative positions of the numbers, rather than an accurate record of the relative size.

47 rounds to 50. I know that 80 subtract 50 is 30, so 85 take away 50 is 35.

You have calculated 85 subtract 50. The question was 85 take away 47. Make the adjustment to compensate for the rounding.

47 is 3 less than 50 so I need to add 3 to 35 to compensate. 35 and 3 is 38. So 85 take away 47 is 38.

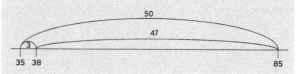

Write the equations and explain your thinking.

I round 47 to 50 then I work out 85 take away 50 is 35. I needed to take away 47 so I have taken away 3 too many. I add 3 to compensate.

$$85 - 47 = (85 - 50) + 3$$
$$= 35 + 3$$
$$= 38$$

Answer: 85 - 47 = 38

Complementary addition to add or subtract two-digit numbers

Use complementary addition to find the difference, 'how far' it is between two numbers. There is no distinction between the sequencing method and the compensation strategy when complementary addition is used. Pupils who find subtracting back difficult should use complementary addition as their preferred method of calculation. It may also be the most efficient method to use with multi-digit numbers. For example, 946 – 782 is much easier to solve by complementary addition than by subtracting back. Instructions for teaching subtraction by complementary addition are on p91.

Give pupils plenty of practice using the compensation method to subtract two-digit numbers. It is important that they become proficient in recording their thinking using number lines and equations with these small numbers, as the compensation strategies will be the method of choice when calculating with multi-digit numbers.

74 - 38

89 - 45

68 - 42

53 - 37

Checklist – The compensation method to add or subtract two-digit numbers

Pupils can:
- ☐ Round numbers to make the calculation easier
- ☐ Adjust numbers to compensate for the rounding
- ☐ Record thinking on number lines
- ☐ Record calculations as equations
- ☐ Decide whether subtraction back or complementary addition is most appropriate
- ☐ Explain reasoning

7

Multiplication and division

Pupils need to know the multiplication tables facts for all the numbers up to ten. They need to be able to quickly recall or derive a multiplication fact and be able to recognise multiples of a number. It is also important that they understand what the concepts of multiplication and division mean. Knowledge of the multiplication facts is essential for work with fractions and ratios.

Many pupils feel that learning all the times tables is an impossible task; however pupils need only learn the key facts: 10 times a number (10 x N) and 5 times a number (5 x N). Provided they understand the concept of multiplication all the other multiplication facts can be quickly derived by reasoning. They can also apply their knowledge to division. With repeated practice many of the facts may become automatic.

Learning 'times tables' has become a controversial topic. On one side are those who advocate rote learning and on the other the proponents of understanding-based learning. It seems a spurious argument about methods rather than substance. Pupils with good verbal memories can learn the times tables facts. Those pupils with weak memories keep 'forgetting' their tables so must be able to derive the answers. Knowing facts by rote is no guarantee that pupils will understand what they mean and when to use them.

Multiplication is the operation used to combine equal-sized groups. Division is the inverse of multiplication. Division is used to separate a quantity into equal-sized groups. In this sense multiplication and division are simply more efficient ways of adding or subtracting quantities. However the idea of repeated addition or subtraction is only one of the mathematical concepts represented by multiplication and division. Pupils need to understand the concept of multiplication as an array and the area model where objects, or squares, are arranged in rows and columns. It is essential to understand the division concepts of grouping and sharing, rather than as repeated subtraction.

Take great care with the language that is used: terms include 'groups of', 'lots of', 'times' and 'multiply by'. These instructions can cause confusion because they mean different things. For example 5 times 3 means there are 5 groups composed of 3 items, whereas multiply 5 by 3 means there are 5 items which are repeated 3 times. Teach the use of the term 'group' very explicitly. In everyday usage the term 'lots of' means a large, but unspecified, quantity so it is best to avoid using 'lots of' until pupils have a secure grasp of multiplication. At the beginning it is best to avoid confusion by keeping the language as simple and transparent as possible. Avoid any confusion by using the form: 'What are 5 threes?'. This makes it clear that the amount in each group is 3. There will be 5 groups.

The best way to learn times tables facts is to use a multi-sensory approach which makes the relationships between the facts explicit as well as providing plenty of opportunity for revision of facts. Teach pupils to understand the concept of multiplication by reasoning. They use step counting skills and their knowledge of number patterns to see multiplication as the structured repetition of a quantity. If pupils know the key facts of 10 x N and 5 x N for each times table, and understand the structure of multiplication, they can quickly derive other facts.

Work with concrete materials makes the concepts clear provided that the pupils talk about what they see and do. Demonstrate the concepts of multiplication and division by using counters (all the same colour and size), bowls (muffin cases provide a cheap alternative to bowls), number pattern cards, base 10 equipment and Cuisenaire rods as well as a multiplication mat. This is an empty track marked with

10 large squares. The fifth and tenth boxes are marked with a thicker (or coloured) outline to draw attention to these key positions. The half-way point is marked with a thick line. Equal groups of counters, in dot patterns, are placed in the squares to model multiplication. This provides a visual image to help develop reasoning skills by deriving multiplication facts from the key facts of 10 x N and 5 x N. This image makes the inverse relationship between multiplication and division explicit.

Teach the use of the symbol 'x' very carefully with plenty of discussion and plenty of examples. x and + are different symbols, but some pupils confuse them. This may be a visual perceptual difficulty, akin to reversing numerals or letters, or it may be a conceptual misunderstanding. (Anghileri, 1997) Any confusion becomes quickly apparent if pupils read questions aloud.

Multiplication is commutative which means that the answer is the same, irrespective of the order in which the numbers are multiplied. The commutative law means that 6 x 4 = 4 x 6. The commutative law also applies to addition so that 3 + 2 = 2 + 3. Here each number represents a specific quantity so the meaning does not change when the order is changed. However, the numbers in a multiplication question have different meanings: one number, the multiplicand, refers to the quantity within each group, the other number, the multiplier, refers to the total number of same-sized groups. Many calculation errors are rooted in failure to understand this idea. Put numbers in context to make the difference in meaning clear. Consider people in sports teams: 6 groups of 4 means there are 6 teams with 4 people in each team; 6 multiplied by 4 means that 6 is repeated 4 times so there are 6 people in each of 4 teams. Pupils need to be clear about this concept if they are to reason to derive new facts from known facts. Fortunately it is relatively easy to demonstrate the alternative scenarios by using concrete equipment.

Equipment

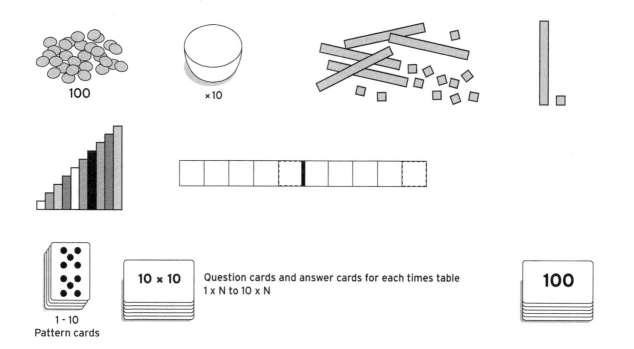

100

×10

1 - 10
Pattern cards

10 × 10   Question cards and answer cards for each times table
1 x N to 10 x N

100

Multiplication: the concept of repeated addition

Objectives
- Understand the concept of multiplication as repeated addition
- Step count forwards and backwards in twos and tens
- Understand the word ' group' to refer to a particular collection of objects which can be repeated
- Demonstrate and explain multiplication as repeated groups
- Use a multiplication mat and record repeated groups on a number line

Teach the concept of multiplication as repeated addition by step counting and putting groups of objects into containers to emphasise the idea of a group. This creates a stronger visual image of the idea of the group as an entity than simply putting them out in separate groups on a table. Start by exploring the multiples of 2. This is for practical reasons as it is quicker for pupils to put out groups of 2 counters than use larger quantities. Once the principle is established, pupils can use dot pattern cards, rather than counters, to work with groups of 10. Put numbers into context both in discussing the concrete objects and in word problems (see p224). Pupils record multiplication as step counting on a number line and learn to use the multiplication sign to write multiplication as an equation.

Introduce the terms 'group' and 'groups of' in meaningful contexts, first by putting counters into bowls and then using a multiplication mat. This emphasises the relationship between the groups. A multiplication mat is an empty track marked with 10 large squares. Pupils place same sized groups of counters into each square. Start by building 5 groups as this is easier to visualize than all 10 groups. It is very important that the image that pupils see, represents what they are saying. If pupils point to each fact as they say it, the cumulative effect of multiplication is not explicit. For example, when a pupil points to the fourth square as they say '4 twos are 8' they are actually seeing a single pattern of 2 in that square. Do not assume that they understand that all the counters in the first, second and third squares are included in the count. This is similar to the confusion that can arise in early counting. For a discussion of the important difference between cardinality and ordinality see Chapter 1 (p8). The problem can be easily overcome by using a piece of paper to cover up all the counters that are not included in the count. The pupil moves the paper as they say the tables so it is clear that the words '4 twos are 8' refer to all the counters that are visible. Some pupils find it helpful to use a finger in a circular motion to indicate all the counters that are included in a particular multiplication fact.

Teaching

Multiplication as repeated addition
Pupils step count forwards and backwards. They use the term 'group' to refer to a collection of objects, and use counters and bowls to demonstrate repeated groups. They put numbers into context whilst explaining what they are doing and draw diagrams to show their thinking. The multiplication mat is introduced.

Groups of 2: the concept of repeated addition

Step count in twos to 24.
Count back from 20 in twos.

Show me 3 bowls with 2 counters in each bowl.
Some pupils do not understand what the term 'in each' means. In this case the teacher demonstrates and explains that 'in each' means in one bowl, in the next bowl, and so on.

How many bowls are there?
How many counters are there in each bowl?
How many twos can you see?
How many counters can you see altogether?

The pupil should be able to count fluently without undue hesitation.

Pupil puts out the 3 bowls with 2 counters in each bowl.

There are 3 bowls.
There are 2 counters in each bowl.
I can see 3 twos.
I can see 6 counters altogether.
Pupils may need to step count to work out the total number of counters.

Can you draw a diagram and explain it?

Pupil draws diagram and explains, in their own words: *There are 2 counters in each bowl. There are 3 bowls, so there are 6 counters altogether.*

Write that as an equation to show that 2 add 2 add 2 equals 6.

2 + 2 + 2 = 6

Instead of writing two add two add two you can use a multiplication sign. This looks like an x.
Teacher writes 3 x 2 = 6 and says: *3 twos are six. There are 3 groups with 2 in each group.*

Write the equation to show 3 twos are 6.

3 x 2 = 6

Ask pupils to make up word problems with groups of two. They write the problem, model it using counters and bowls, draw a picture, then write the equation and write the answer as a sentence. Encourage the use of varied language to indicate the groups of two.
Example: *There are 4 cats. How many eyes do they have altogether?*

4 x 2 = 8

Answer: There are 8 eyes.

Give the pupil a multiplication mat.
This is called a multiplication mat. How many squares are there on the multiplication mat?

Pupil points to each square as they count. *There are 10 squares.*

Describe what you see on the multiplication mat. Encourage varied vocabulary, such as: *There is a dotted line around the fifth square and the tenth square.*

There is a dotted line around square 5 and square 10.
There is a black line at the halfway point. It shows that 5 is half of 10.

Build groups of 2. Put 2 counters in each square on the multiplication mat. Stop when you get to the halfway mark.
How many groups have you built? How many in each group?
The orientation of the counters does not affect the value. If pupils arrange the dots horizontally ○○ rather than vertically ⊛ it is not wrong. However encourage them to use the vertical orientation as this emphasises the pattern rather than linear counting.

Pupils use counters to put out 5 groups of 2 on the multiplication mat.

There are 5 groups. There are 2 in each group. There are 5 twos.

Continue to build groups of two to the end of the mat.

How many groups have you built? How many in each group? How many counters are there altogether?

There are 10 groups. There are 2 in each group. There are 10 twos so I have 20 counters altogether.
At this stage, allow pupils to step count form the beginning if they need to do so.

10 twos are 20. Look at the multiplication mat and say all the twos facts. Start with 1 two is 2, 2 twos are 4.

It is very important that the image that pupils see, represents what they are saying. If pupils point to each fact as they say it, the cumulative effect of multiplication is not explicit. For example, when a pupil points to the fourth square as they say '4 twos are 8' they are actually seeing a single pattern of 2 in that square. Use a piece of paper to cover up all the counters that are not included in the count. The pupil moves the paper as they say the tables so it is clear that the words '4 twos are 8' refer to all the counters that are visible.

Draw a number line to 24 to show counting in twos. Draw an arc to show each jump of 2.

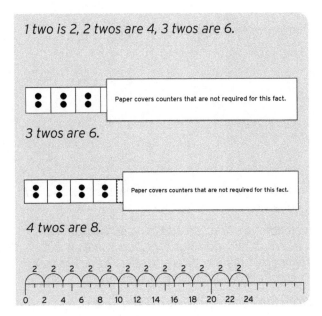

1 two is 2, 2 twos are 4, 3 twos are 6.

Paper covers counters that are not required for this fact.

3 twos are 6.

Paper covers counters that are not required for this fact.

4 twos are 8.

Groups of 10: the concept of repeated addition

Count in tens to 100.
Count back from 80 in tens.

Give the pupil a multiplication mat.
Show the pattern of 10 in the first square on the multiplication mat. Build groups of 10 in each square until you reach the fifth square.

How many groups have you built? How many in each group?

How many counters are there altogether?

Continue to build groups of 10 to the end of the mat.

How many groups have you built? How many in each group? How many counters are there altogether?

10 tens are 100. Say all the tens facts. Start with 1 ten is 10, 2 tens are 20.

The image that the pupil sees must represent what they are saying. Use a piece of paper to cover up the counters that are not included in the fact they are expressing. They move it along so that what they say matches what they see.

Draw a number line to 100 to show step counting in tens. Draw an arc to show each step of 10.

The pupil should be able to count fluently without undue hesitation.

Pupil models 5 groups of 10 to create a strong visual image.

I built 5 groups. There are 10 in each group. There are 5 tens.

There are 50 counters altogether.

I built 10 groups. There are 10 in each group. There are 10 tens. There are 100 counters altogether.

1 ten is 10, 2 tens are 20, 3 tens are 30...

Paper covers counters that are not required for this fact.

2 tens are twenty.

Paper covers counters that are not required for this fact.

3 tens are thirty.

Checklist – Multiplication: the concept of repeated addition

Pupils can:
- ☐ Understand the concept of multiplication as repeated addition
- ☐ Step count forwards and backwards in twos and tens
- ☐ Understand the word 'group' to refer to a particular collection of objects which can be repeated
- ☐ Demonstrate and explain multiplication as repeated groups
- ☐ Use a multiplication mat and record repeated groups on a number line

The 10 times table

Objectives
- Demonstrate x 10 as repeated groups of 10 on a multiplication mat
- Explain the relationship between x 10 facts by reasoning from the most convenient starting point (1 x 10, 5 x 10 or 10 x 10)
- Quickly recall any fact in the 10 times table
- Record reasoning as equations

Pupils must know the 10 times table 'off by heart'. Introduce the term 'times tables'. Check that pupils remember the x 10 facts by giving them frequent oral and written questions.

The 10 times table lays the foundation for learning all the other multiplication tables. It is essential that pupils have automatic recall of the 10 times table facts both for deriving other multiplication facts, and for estimation and approximation in calculation. Many pupils will already know the 10 times table from their work with counting and calculating. Even if they can recall them easily, they need to learn the reasoning techniques. It is particularly important to be clear about which number is the multiplier (the number of repetitions) and which number is the multiplicand (the quantity).

Pupils who cannot remember multiplication facts need to be able to derive them quickly from known facts. Use the fact that half of 10 tens is 5 tens to show that half of 10 times a quantity equals 5 times the quantity. Establishing this 'halfway' point in multiplication sequences makes it much quicker to step count if necessary as the count can start at 5 times a number instead of returning to the beginning each time.

Pupils need to understand that 10 times a quantity makes it ten times bigger. It is not helpful to mention 'add a zero': this is merely a trick that is often presented without working on the reasoning behind the process. This instruction only works with whole numbers: it will lead to confusion with decimal work. Consider 0.24 x 10 where 'adding a zero' would give the incorrect result 0.240 whereas it should be 10 times larger, which is 2.4.

Do not teach division explicitly at this stage. However, the concept of division is implicit in the model of the multiplication mat, so use the opportunity to introduce the language of division informally, as in: 'There are 50 counters. There are 10 in each group. How many groups of 10 will you need to build 50?' In this way pupils are unaware they are beginning to divide the total quantity into groups. The omission of the word division also serves to protect those who believe they do not understand 'division' from previous negative learning situations.

Teaching

Figuring out facts in the 10 times tables
The times 10 facts are known as the 10 times table. You need to know all the 10 times table facts off by heart. You can work out all the facts for all the other tables by reasoning from the x 10 facts. It also helps to know all the x 5 facts.

Give the pupil dot pattern cards showing the pattern of 10.

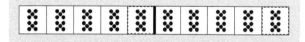

What is 10 times 10? This is another way of saying 'What are 10 tens?' Show me 10 times 10 using pattern cards on the multiplication mat.

How many dots are there in each square?
How many squares are there?
How many dots are there altogether?
What is 10 times 10?
Write the equation to show 10 times 10.

There are 10 dots in each square.
There are 10 squares.
There are 100 dots.
10 times 10 makes 100.
10 x 10 = 100

What is half of 10?

If you take half the cards off the mat, how many cards will there be?
Take half the cards off the mat.

How many squares have got cards on them now?

How many dots are there in each square?

How many dots can you see altogether?
Encourage pupils to use their own words to describe their thinking.

10 times 10 is 100. 5 tens are half of 10 tens therefore 5 tens are half of 100. 5 times 10 is 50.
Write the equation for 5 times 10.

5 is half of 10.
There will be 5 cards.

Pupil removes 5 cards.

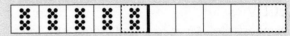

5 squares have got cards on them.

There are 10 dots in each square.

I can see 50 dots.
5 tens make 50. 5 times 10 is 50.

5 x 10 = 50

Figure out all the facts for x 10 by reasoning from the closest known fact.
- Reason from 1 ten for 2 x 10 and 3 x 10
- Reason back from 5 tens for 4 x 10
- Reason forwards from 5 tens for 6 x 10 and 7 x 10
- Reason back from 10 tens for 9 x 10 and 8 x 10.

Use pattern cards on a multiplication mat to reason forwards from 1 times 10 to derive 3 times 10.

You can work out 3 tens, or 3 times 10, by reasoning from 1 times 10.

Put 1 ten on the multiplication mat.
What is 1 times 10?

Put out another ten. How many tens are there?
What is 2 times 10?

Put out another ten. How many tens are there?
What is 3 times 10?

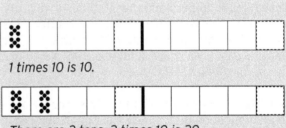

1 times 10 is 10.

There are 2 tens. 2 times 10 is 20.

There are 3 tens. 3 times 10 is 30.

Step-count to work out 3 times 10.

Write the equations to show 3 times 10 equals 10 add 10 add 10 and another equation to show that 3 x 10 = 30.

Pupil reasons forwards to calculate 6 tens.
What are 6 tens? Start at 5 tens.

Pupil says: *Ten, twenty, thirty.*

3 x 10 = 10 + 10 + 10
3 x 10 = 30

Pupil puts out 5 tens and says: *5 tens are 50. 6 is one more than 5 so I add 1 more ten.*

Pupil puts out one more group of 10, then step counts starting at 50. Pupil says: *Fifty, sixty. 6 tens are 60. 6 times 10 is 60.*

6 tens equals 5 tens plus one more ten. 6 times 10 is 50 add 10. 6 times 10 is 60.

Write the equations and explain your reasoning.

$$6 \times 10 = (5 \times 10) + 10$$
$$= 50 + 10$$
$$= 60$$

Continue to explore each fact of 10 in this way. Encourage pupils to extend their reasoning.

What is 7 times 10? Start at 5 tens.

Note that the reasoning in this example applies knowledge of the basic bond 5 + 2 = 7.
Some pupils may need to work forwards and backwards step counting to add one group at a time to avoid confusion.

5 tens are 50. 7 is 2 more than 5 so I add 2 more tens.
Encourage pupils to express their ideas in different ways. *2 tens are 20, so 7 tens will be 50 plus 20 which is 70.*

Write the equations and explain your reasoning.

7 is 2 more than 5 so 7 tens equals 5 tens plus 2 more tens. 7 times 10 is 50 add 20.
7 times 10 is 70.

$$7 \times 10 = (5 \times 10) + (2 \times 10)$$
$$= 50 + 20$$
$$= 70$$

Use pattern cards on a multiplication mat to reason backwards from 10 tens to calculate 9 times 10.

What is 9 times 10?

10 tens are 100. 9 is one less than 10, so I take away 1 ten.

9 is one less than 10 so 9 times 10 equals 10 tens take away 1 ten. 9 times 10 is 100 take away 10 so 9 times 10 is 90.

$$9 \times 10 = (10 \times 10) - (1 \times 10)$$
$$= 100 - 10$$
$$= 90$$

Pupils continue to explore and record each fact of 10 in this way. When pupils have completed this exercise ask them to recall facts of 10. Give them both oral and written questions in random order.

10 x 10	5 x 10	3 x 10
7 x 10	4 x 10	8 x 10
2 x 10	9 x 10	6 x 10

Linear comparison of 10 tens and 5 tens

Use base 10 tens and number lines to demonstrate that 5 tens are half of 10 tens.

Put out a line of 10 tens. Put a line of 5 tens underneath it. Write the equations and draw number lines to show 10 tens and 5 tens.

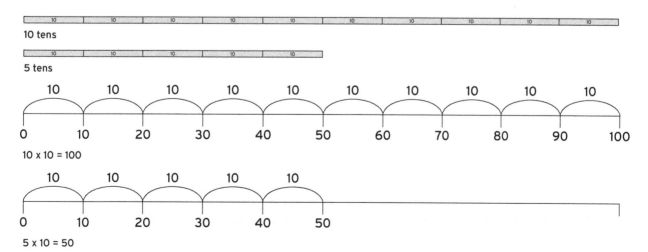

Fun Times

(A matching and memory game.)

Aim
- To practise the 10 times table
- To improve memory

10 × 10

Question cards and answer cards 1 x 10 to 10 x 10

Equipment
- Times table question cards
- Times table answer cards
  (Each set of cards should be a different colour.)

100

How to play

Spread all the cards, face down, on the table.

Player A turns up a question card. They read the table question and say what they are looking for. (Talking about the cards is an essential part of this game. The players should stop occasionally and say which cards have been turned up, what they are and who turned them up, without turning them up.)

Example: Player turns up 3 x 10. Player says: '3 tens are 30 so I am looking for 30.'

Player A turns up an answer card. If they are a matching pair, player A keeps them and has another turn.

If the player does not find a matching pair, they read the number on the answer card and say what multiplication makes that number. Example: Looking for 30 turns up 50. They say: '50 is made of 5 tens.'

If player A does not find a matching pair, they turn the cards face down. It is very important that cards always remain in the same position on the table.

The next player has a turn.

The winner is the person with the most pairs when all the cards have been collected.

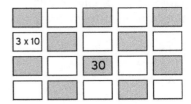

Checklist – The 10 times table

Pupils can:
- ☐ Demonstrate x 10 as repeated groups of 10 on a multiplication mat
- ☐ Explain the relationship between x 10 facts by reasoning from the most convenient starting point (1 x 10, 5 x 10 or 10 x 10)
- ☐ Quickly recall any fact in the 10 times table
- ☐ Record reasoning as equations

The 5 times table

Objectives

- Remember the key facts: 10 x 5 = 50, 5 x 5 = 25
- Demonstrate x 5 as repeated groups on the multiplication mat
- Explain the relationship between x 5 facts by reasoning from the most convenient starting point (1 x 5, 5 x 5 or 10 x 5)
- Record reasoning as equations
- Quickly recall any fact in the 5 times table

Pupils learn the facts in the 5 times table by deriving them from the x 10 facts. They use the dot patterns on the multiplication mat and Cuisenaire rods to support their reasoning and to develop memorable visual images. Pupils explain their thinking and record it in on number lines and as equations.

Knowing 5 x a number is a key fact for learning all the times tables. It is a pivotal point from which to derive other multiplication facts efficiently.

Teaching

Derive the 5 times table facts from 10 times table facts.

The x 5 facts are known as the 5 times table. It is very helpful to know all the x 5 facts off by heart. If you know the 10 times table and the 5 times table facts you can figure out the facts for all the other tables.

Revise the concept and language of groups using counters and bowls, as well as a multiplication mat.

Check that pupil can step count in fives forwards and backwards in the sequence to 50.	The pupil should be able to count fluently without undue hesitation.

Count in fives to 50.
Count back from 35 in fives.
Show me 2 bowls with 5 counters in each bowl.

Pupil puts out the bowls with five counters in each one.

There are 2 bowls.
There are 5 counters in each bowl.
5 and 5 is 10 so 2 fives are 10. So there are 10 altogether.

How many bowls are there?
How many counters are there in each bowl?
How many counters are there altogether? Explain how you work it out. Write it as an equation.

5 + 5 = 10
2 x 5 = 10

Show me 3 fives? What is 3 times 5? Write the equation.

Pupil puts out another bowl with 5 counters in it and says: *3 fives are 15. 3 times 5 is 15.*

5 + 5 + 5 = 15
3 x 5 = 15

Give pupil a multiplication mat.
Use counters to show 5 fives on the multiplication mat.
Pupils may use dot pattern cards for convenience.

How many groups did you build? How many in each group? How many counters are there altogether?

I built 5 groups with 5 in each group. There are 25 counters altogether.

Now build 5 more groups of five. How many groups of 5 do you have?

Pupil continues to add groups of 5. Encourage pupils to explain their ideas in their own words, such as: *There are 10 groups of 5 so I have 50 counters.* Or: *There are 50 counters because there are 10 groups with 5 in each group: or 10 fives are 50.*

There are 50 counters altogether. That is 10 fives. Half of 10 is 5 so half of 10 fives is 5 fives.

Pupil removes 5 fives (25 counters) and says: *Half of 50 is 25.*

Show me what half of 50 is.
Encourage pupils to describe the result in different ways, such as: *5 squares have counters on them. There are 5 counters in each square. There are 25 counters. 5 fives are 25. There are 5 fives in 25.*

This reasoning is starting to use the language of division, however, do not point out that they are talking about division yet.

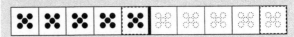

Reasoning to derive all the facts for x 5 from the closest known fact
- Reason from 1 x 5 for 2 x 5 and 3 x 5
- Reason back from 5 x 5 for 4 x 5
- Reason forwards from 5 x 5 for 6 x 5 and 7 x 5
- Reason back from 10 x 5 for 9 x 5 and 8 x 5

Use pattern cards on a multiplication mat to reason forwards from 1 times 5 to derive 3 times 5.

What are 3 fives? Reason from 1 five. Explain your thinking. Write it as an equation.

Pupil makes 3 fives on the multiplication mat and reasons from 1 five to work out what 3 fives are. They use their own words, such as: *1 five is 5. 3 is 2 more than 1 so I need to add 2 more fives. 2 fives are 10. 5 and 10 is 15 so 3 fives are 15. 3 times 5 is 15.*

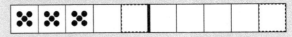

$5 + 5 + 5 = 15$
$3 \times 5 = 15$

Calculate 8 fives by reasoning back.

What are 8 fives? Reason back from 10 fives. Then write the equations.

Pupil puts out 10 fives and says: *10 fives are 50.*
At first the pupil may need to work back one step at a time saying: *9 fives are 5 less than 50 so 9 fives are 45. 8 fives are 5 less than 9 fives so 8 fives are 40. 8 times 5 is 40.*

$8 \times 5 = (10 \times 5) - 5 - 5 = 40$

$8 \times 5 = (10 \times 5) - (2 \times 5)$
$\qquad = 50 - 10$
$\qquad = 40$

As soon as pupils are confident enough, encourage them to reason back more efficiently, saying:
10 fives are 50. 8 is two less than 10. 2 fives are 10, so 8 fives are 50 take away 10. 8 fives are 40.

Pupils continue to explore and record each times 5 fact in this way. When pupils have completed this exercise ask them to recall the 5 times table facts. Give them both oral and written questions in random order.

10 x 5	7 x 5	2 x 5
5 x 5	4 x 5	9 x 5
3 x 5	8 x 5	6 x 5

Practise the 5 times table by playing the game Fun Times with the multiples of 5. (p156)

Linear comparison of 10 fives and 5 fives

Use Cuisenaire rods (yellow 5) and number lines to demonstrate that 5 fives are half of 10 fives.

Use the 5 rods and put out 10 fives in a line. Put a line of 5 fives underneath it. Tell me what you see.

Write the equations and draw number lines to show 10 fives and 5 fives

Pupil describes the rods in their own words. The explanations need to encapsulate the idea that 5 fives are half of 10 fives or 5 fives are half as long as 10 fives. Pupils may also note that 10 fives are double 5 fives.

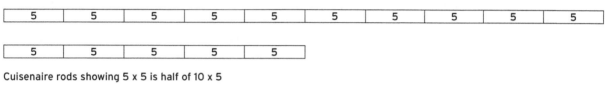

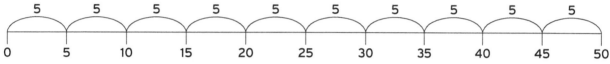

Cuisenaire rods showing 5 x 5 is half of 10 x 5

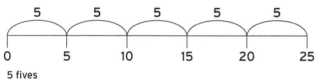

10 fives
10 x 5 = 50

5 fives
5 x 5 = 25

Checklist - The 5 times table

Pupils can:
- ☐ Remember the key facts: 10 x 5 = 50, 5 x 5 = 25
- ☐ Demonstrate x 5 as repeated groups on the multiplication mat
- ☐ Explain the relationship between x 5 facts by reasoning from the most convenient starting point (1 x 5, 5 x 5 or 10 x 5)
- ☐ Record reasoning as equations
- ☐ Quickly recall any fact in the 5 times table

Learning all the multiplication tables

Objectives
- Remember the key facts for each table: 10 x N = 10N, 5 x N = 5N
- Recall (or quickly derive) all the times tables facts for numbers up to 10
- Reason from the most convenient starting point to derive a fact
- Demonstrate any times tables fact as repeated groups on the multiplication mat and by using Cuisenaire rods
- Record multiples as repeated groups on a number line (step counting)
- Write all times tables facts as equations

When pupils know the 5 times and 10 times tables start work on the other tables. A suggested teaching order is: x 2, x 4, x 3, x 6, x 8, x 9, x 7.

Each table is taught in the same way. Pupils have already worked with the 2 times table so the instructions below are for teaching the 4 times table. The same approach is then used to teach the 3 times table and the 6 times table. Once pupils have mastered these facts, the remaining tables are x 7, x 8 and x 9 which contain relatively few new facts if the principle of commutativity is understood. The commutative property of multiplication will be explicitly taught on the work with arrays later in this section (see p163). It is not necessary for pupils to learn the word 'commutative'.

Give plenty of practice in putting out concrete quantities as well as doing oral and written work. Once the pupils have grasped the concept of the set of the number being multiplied, dot pattern cards can be used to make it quicker to demonstrate the tables.

Teaching

The 4 times table
Establish the key facts 10 x 4 = 40, 5 x 4 = 20 by relating them to the 10 times table. Explore the idea by putting Cuisenaire rods in a line and recording the result on a number line. Some pupils may already be comfortable with the idea that 10 fours (10 x 4) gives the same result as 4 tens (4 x 10). Even if they are, they should carry out this exercise in order to create a visual image which can then be generalised to larger quantities and fractions in the future.

The x 4 facts are called the 4 times table. Use the 10 rods to show me 4 tens. Put them in a line. Now use the 4 rods. Show me 10 fours. Put them in a line below the 4 tens. Write the equations for both lines.

Use a number line to show 4 tens. Show each ten with a large 'jump'.

Now show 10 fours on the same line. Use a coloured pencil to mark each 4 jump. Count in fours. Show each 4 and write the numbers under the line.

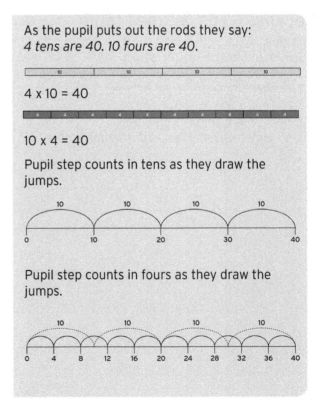

As the pupil puts out the rods they say:
4 tens are 40. 10 fours are 40.

4 x 10 = 40

10 x 4 = 40

Pupil step counts in tens as they draw the jumps.

Pupil step counts in fours as they draw the jumps.

Use counters to show 10 fours on the multiplication mat.

10 fours are 40.

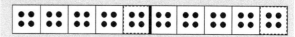

How many groups did you build? How many in each group? How many counters are there altogether?

I built 10 groups with 4 in each group. There are 40 counters altogether.

Paper covers counters that are not required for this fact.

You know 10 fours are 40. What are 5 fours? How did you work it out?
Any explanation is acceptable that conveys the idea that 5 is half of 10, therefore a multiple of 5 will be half a multiple of 10.

Possible explanations include: *5 is half of 10, so 5 fours will be half of 10 fours.*

Draw a number line with jumps to show 5 fours. Write the equation.
If pupils are unsure allow them to model it with Cuisenaire rods. They make a line of 5 fours and then measure it with 2 tens rods to prove that 5 fours make 20.

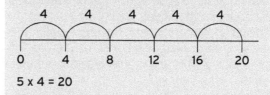

5 x 4 = 20

Reason to derive the 4 times table facts from the closest known fact.
• Reason forward from 1 x 4 for 2 x 4 and 3 x 4
• Reason back from 5 x 4 for 4 x 4
• Reason forward from 5 x 4 for 6 x 4 and 7 x 4
• Reason back from 10 x 4 for 9 x 4 and 8 x 4

What is 3 times 4? Use pattern cards on a multiplication mat to reason forward from 1 times 4. Write the equations.

1 four is 4. I need to add 2 more fours. 2 fours are 8 so I add 8 more to 1 four. 4 add 8 makes 12 so 3 fours are 12. 3 times 4 is 12.

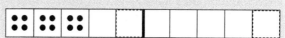

3 x 4 = (1 x 4) + (2 x 4) = 4 + 8 = 12
3 x 4 = 12.

Use Cuisenaire rods to show 3 fours. Record 3 fours on a number line and write the equation.

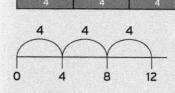

3 x 4 = 12

What is 4 times 4? Reason back from 5 fours.

5 fours are 20. 4 is one less than 5, so I take away 1 four.
20 take away 4 is 16 so 4 fours are 16.

4 x 4 = (5 x 4) - (1 x 4)
       = 20 - 4
       = 16

Pupil puts out 5 fours and then removes 1 four to demonstrate the reasoning process.

Use Cuisenaire rods to show 4 times 4. Record 4 fours on a number line and write the equation.
As they become more proficient, pupils may prefer to write the equation first, and then use the concrete materials to prove they are correct.

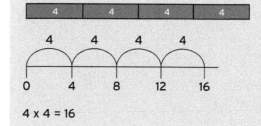

4 x 4 = 16

Pupils continue to explore and record each times 4 fact in this way. When pupils have completed this exercise ask them to recall the 4 times table facts. Give them both oral and written questions in random order.

10 x 4	5 x 4	3 x 4
7 x 4	4 x 4	8 x 4
2 x 4	9 x 4	6 x 4

Learning x 2, x 3, x 6, x 7, x 8, x 9, x 11, x 12

Once pupils have mastered the 10 times, 2 times, 4 times, and 5 times tables, they learn the 3 times table and the 6 times table using the same method. Teachers use their judgement as to whether pupils learn the 7, 8 and 9 times tables in the same way. Alternatively the number of remaining times table facts that need to be learnt can be considerably reduced by using the commutative property of multiplication. So that if you know that 7 threes make 21, you also know that 3 sevens make 21. Applying the principle of commutativity, the only totally new facts that need to be learned are 7 x 7, 8 x 7 and 9 x 7 in the 7 times table; 8 x 8 and 9 x 8 in the 8 times table; 9 x 9 in the 9 times table. Teach these remaining facts by using pattern cards on multiplication mats, Cuisenaire rods and number lines.

When pupils can confidently multiply all the numbers up to 10, they extend their knowledge to derive the 11 and 12 times table facts by reasoning from the key facts 10 x N and 5 x N.

Checklist - Learning all the multiplication tables

Pupils can:
- ☐ Remember the key facts for each table: 10 x N = 10N, 5 x N = 5N
- ☐ Recall (or quickly derive) all the times tables facts for numbers up to 10
- ☐ Reason from the most convenient starting point to derive a fact
- ☐ Demonstrate any times tables fact as repeated groups on the multiplication mat and by using Cuisenaire rods
- ☐ Record multiples as repeated groups on a number line (step counting)
- ☐ Write all times tables facts as equations

Multiplication as an array

Objectives

- Demonstrate multiplication facts as an array using counters
- Demonstrate the equivalence of a x b = b x a using counters
- Demonstrate the equivalence of a x b = b x a using Cuisenaire rods
- Investigate the commutative property of multiplication by showing equivalence: a x b = b x a

An array is a systematic arrangement of objects in rows and columns. Arrays show the commutative property of multiplication. This can be expressed in the equation a x b = b x a. This layout also provides a strong visual image of the relationship between multiplication and division. Using Cuisenaire rods to show the equivalence of a x b = b x a provides a link to the area model of multiplication.

Working with arrays is a precursor to understanding the area model of multiplication. The area model is used for calculating the area of shapes. In the early stages of teaching only use the word 'row'. Introduce the word 'column' and the associated idea at a later stage. Describe the array as a series of rows with an equal number of items in each row.

Teaching

Arrays show the equivalence of 3 x 5 and 5 x 3. Whichever way you look at it there are 15 dots. Use counters that are all the same colour. Then demonstrate using Cuisenaire rods.

Put out one row of 3 counters. How many rows do you have? How many threes do you have?

Put 3 counters in a row underneath the first row. How many rows do you have? How many threes do you have?

This layout is called an array. How many counters are there in each row?

Continue the array by adding one row at a time until you have 5 rows.

How many rows are there? How many counters in each row?

How many counters are there altogether? Check your answer.

I have 1 row.
I have 1 three. 1 three is 3.

I have 2 rows.
I have 2 threes. 2 threes are 6.

There are 3 counters in each row.

There are 5 rows with 3 counters in each row.

5 threes are 15. There are 15 counters.

Pupils check the answer by counting. They should be able to count in threes. If they count in ones, allow them to do so. This may be because they cannot count in threes confidently, or it may be because they do not believe that there really are 15 counters in the array. They need to be allowed to count in the way in which they are satisfied that the final count is the same as the calculation.

Draw a diagram of the array. Start with one row of 3. How many threes have you drawn?

Those with significant motor weaknesses may not be able to draw circles well enough to be visually clear. They can create the array with coloured circular stickers.

Write the equation.

I have drawn 1 three.
The pupil continues to draw each row of 3 until the diagram of 5 x 3 is complete.

5 x 3 = 15

5 rows of 3 equals 15. 5 threes equal 15.
5 x 3 = 15

Start another array next to the first one. This time put 5 counters in each row.

Teacher stops the pupils after they have put out 3 rows with 5 counters in each row.

Pupils explain what they are doing step-by-step as they did above.

There are 5 counters in each row.
There are 3 rows.
3 fives are 15. There are 15 counters.

How many counters are there in each row?
How many rows are there?
How many counters are there altogether? Check your answer.

Draw a diagram of the array. Start with 1 row of 5. How many fives have you drawn?

I have drawn 1 five.   ○○○○○
The pupil continues to draw each row of 5 until the diagram of 3 x 5 is complete.

○○○○○
○○○○○
○○○○○

Write the equation.

3 rows of 5 equals 15.
3 fives equal 15.
3 x 5 = 15

What have you found out?

The total number of counters is the same in both cases proving that 5 threes is the same amount as 3 fives. Write the equations.

5 threes are 15 and 3 fives are 15.

5 x 3 = 15   3 x 5 = 15

Therefore, 5 x 3 = 3 x 5

Use Cuisenaire rods to demonstrate the equivalence of 5 x 3 and 3 x 5. Build arrays and compare them by placing one array on top of the other.

Put out one 3 rod. How many rows do you have?

Put another 3 below the first 3.

Continue to put out threes until there are 5 threes. What are 5 threes?

1 row of 3.

Cuisenaire rods showing 5 x 3 = 15

Start another array. Put out a 5 rod. How many rows do you have?

Put another 5 below the first 5.

Continue to put out fives until there are 3 fives.

I have 1 row of 5.

Cuisenaire rods showing 3 x 5 = 15

What are 3 fives?

3 fives make 15.

Turn the array of 3 fives through one right angle. That means rotate the array of 3 fives through 90 degrees.
If the pupil does not understand the terms, teacher demonstrates what is required, and then asks the pupil to do it.

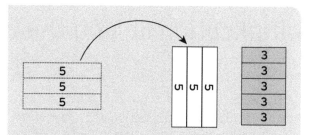

Put the 3 fives on top of the 5 threes. What do you see? Can you write the equations?

Pupil explains in their own words that they fit exactly over each other. Comments might include:
They cover exactly the same area.
It shows that 3 x 5 and 5 x 3 are the same.
3 fives and 5 threes are equivalent.

Pupil writes:

3 x 5 = 15
5 x 3 = 15
3 x 5 = 5 x 3

Give pupils plenty of practice in investigating other multiplication facts in this way.

4 x 6 = 6 x 4   3 x 7 = 7 x 3   2 x 8 = 8 x 2

Checklist – Multiplication as an array

Pupils can:
- ☐ Demonstrate multiplication facts as an array using counters
- ☐ Demonstrate the equivalence of a x b = b x a using counters
- ☐ Demonstrate the equivalence of a x b = b x a using Cuisenaire rods
- ☐ Investigate the commutative property of multiplication by showing equivalence a x b = b x a

Multiplication linking the array to the area model

Objectives
- Model multiplication facts using unit cubes
- Demonstrate the commutative property of multiplication
- Demonstrate multiplication facts as the area covering a rectangle
- Draw multiplication facts as the number of squares covering the area of a rectangle

In the area model of multiplication squares are arranged systematically to cover the surface of a rectangle. The area model is similar to the array in that the arrangement of the squares can be seen as rows and columns. This idea will be important in working with measurement where the length multiplied by the width of a rectangle will give the area of the shape.

Pupils use unit cubes to make the array and then draw it on squared paper to make the link between the array and the area model clear. Continue to use only the word 'row'. Describe the area as a series of rows with an equal number of items in each row and the area as the total number of squares within the shape.

Teaching
Use unit cubes to make arrays of 3 x 5 and 5 x 3. Pupils repeat the process of putting out 5 threes and 3 fives, using similar language to that used with the counters. Make sure that pupils explain clearly what they are doing. Draw diagrams on 1 cm² paper to show the area model for 3 x 5 and 5 x 3.

Put out one row of 3 unit cubes. How many rows do you have? How many threes do you have?

Continue to expand the array by 1 row at a time until you have 5 rows.
Give pupil 1 cm² squared paper. Draw a diagram of the array you made. Draw 1 row of 3 squares, then the next rows of 3. Write the equation.

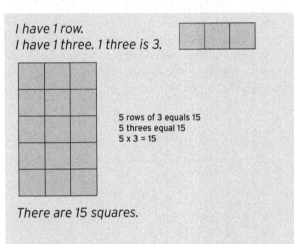

I have 1 row.
I have 1 three. 1 three is 3.

5 rows of 3 equals 15
5 threes equal 15
5 x 3 = 15

There are 15 squares.

The shape is called a rectangle.

How many squares make up the rectangle? Sometimes pupils want to count the squares to convince themselves that there really are 15 squares. Encourage them to tick each square as they count to help them count systematically.

Put the cubes out on top of the squares you have drawn. Check that the array is the same size as the rectangle.

Pupils place the array onto the rectangle to cover the rectangle exactly.

The space that the rectangle takes up is called the area. Area is measured by finding how many squares fit into a space.

Turn the array of 5 threes through one right angle. That means rotate the array of 5 threes through 90 degrees.
If the pupil does not understand the terms, teacher demonstrates what is required, and then asks the pupil to do it.

A good way to make the introduction to area multi-sensory is for the pupils to stroke the top of the cubes as they are saying the area. The teacher can also perform the movement of stroking to get the word area across as an image.

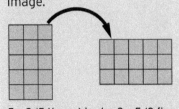

5 x 3 (5 threes) is also 3 x 5 (3 fives)

How many unit cubes are in each row?
How many rows are there?
How many fives?

Draw a diagram of the array on the squared paper to show 3 fives.
When pupils have drawn the diagram, ask them to describe what they see in terms of fives.

There are 5 unit cubes in each row.
There are 3 rows.
There are 3 fives.

Explanations will include terms such as: *There are 5 in each row. There are 3 fives. 3 rows of 5 are 15.*

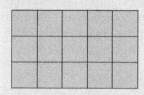

3 rows of 5 equals 15
3 fives equal 15
3 x 5 = 15

How many squares make up the rectangle?

Put the cubes onto the squares you have drawn. Check that the array is the same size as the rectangle.

Can you write the equations for both rectangles?

15 squares.

Pupils place the array onto the rectangle to cover the rectangle exactly.

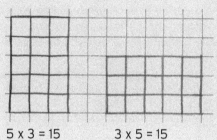

5 x 3 = 15   3 x 5 = 15

Therefore, 5 x 3 = 3 x 5

Ask pupils to make and draw the following rectangles.

2 x 6 = 6 x 2   3 x 4 = 4 x 3
4 x 5 = 5 x 4   7 x 3 = 3 x 7
8 x 3 = 3 x 8

Extension work
Ask pupils to model the following multiplication questions and draw the shapes. Ask them what all these have in common. Obviously they all make squares. This is an opportunity to briefly mention the difference between square arrays and rectangular arrays to foreshadow the work on area.

3 x 3   7 x 7
4 x 4   8 x 8
5 x 5   9 x 9
6 x 6   10 x 10

Checklist - Multiplication linking the array to the area model
Pupils can:
- ☐ Model multiplication facts using unit cubes
- ☐ Demonstrate the commutative property of multiplication
- ☐ Demonstrate multiplication facts as the area covering a rectangle
- ☐ Draw multiplication facts as the number of squares covering the area of a rectangle or a square

Division concepts: grouping and sharing

Objectives
- Investigate the inverse relationship between multiplication and division
- Demonstrate and explain the grouping concept of division
- Demonstrate and explain the sharing concept of division
- Draw a diagram to show division by grouping
- Draw a diagram to show division by sharing
- Record thinking on a number line

Division is the operation that splits a quantity into smaller, equal sized quantities. Pupils need to understand the two different concepts of division: grouping and sharing.

Grouping: The quantity in each group is known. The number of groups is unknown. (The grouping model links directly with multiplication.) The question is asking: 'How many groups will be required?'
e.g. There are 12 biscuits. Put 2 biscuits on each plate. How many plates will you need?

Sharing: The number of groups is known. The quantity of items in each group is unknown. The answer is found by sharing the items equally between the groups. The question is asking: 'How many items will there be in each group?'
e.g. There are 12 biscuits. There are 6 plates. How many biscuits will there be on each plate?

Sharing is usually the first concept of division that pupils encounter as it is used to share things out equally between people, as in sharing out sweets. It is often associated with the idea of fairness, however it is best to use the word equal rather than fair as fair is a value judgement, not a numerical concept.

Division is the only one of the four operations which is not a closed operation. Addition, subtraction and multiplication involving whole numbers will always produce an answer that is a whole number. They are closed operations. In division the answer need not be a whole number, there may be a remainder. Start teaching division by always using examples that will give an exact answer. Only introduce remainders once pupils understand, and are thoroughly comfortable with, the division facts that are the inverse of the multiplication facts.

Make a clear distinction between the concepts of division (grouping and sharing) and division calculation procedures (repeated subtraction and partitioning). The universal strategy for division is to derive division facts from multiplication. This method uses the fact that division is the inverse of multiplication. Pupils who have used a variety of language to discuss multiplication facts should be able to use this knowledge to work out division facts by reasoning. For example, if you know that 5 sevens are 35 you also know that 35 is made of 5 sevens. Pupils with a flexible approach to multiplication understand that 5 x 7 = 35 can be presented as 35 = 5 x 7.

Pupils learned that the inverse relationship between addition and subtraction meant that c = a + b could also be expressed as c - a = b or c - b = a. For example knowing that 10 = 4 + 6 means you also know that 10 - 4 = 6 and 10 - 6 = 4. They also learned to express subtraction as a missing addend (mystery number) question so that 10 - 6 = ? can be expressed as 6 + ? = 10. Pupils need to be able to apply the same reasoning to work out division facts from multiplication facts. For example, 5 x 7 = 35 so 35 ÷ 5 = 7 and 35 ÷ 7 = 5. This can be expressed in general terms: if a x b = c then c ÷ a = b and c ÷ b = a. Division can also be expressed as a mystery number question so that 35 ÷ 7 = ? can be expressed as 7 x ? = 35. Some pupils may intuitively grasp this relationship from their work on the multiplication mat: most will need to be explicitly taught.

Pupils model the question using concrete materials: counters, bowls, multiplication mats, and Cuisenaire rods. They record the information in diagrams, on number lines and as equations. Reinforce the conceptual link between multiplication and division through language. The key facts are used to guide pupils towards division answers by investigating the following kinds of questions:
'How many fours would you need to build 20? If you have 30, how many fives could you make out of the 30? If you start out with 60, how many tens could you build from the 60?'

Teaching

The grouping concept of division

Use bowls and counters to explore equal-sized groups. Provide more bowls than are required so that pupils have to work out the answer.

You can use the multiplication facts to derive the division facts.
Take 12 counters. Put 3 counters in each bowl. How many bowls do you need?

Pupil demonstrates and says:
I have 12 counters. If I put 3 counters in each bowl, I need 4 bowls.

You can also say you divided 12 into threes, or you divided 12 by 3.
Teacher draws the division sign and says:
The division sign is a horizontal line with a dot above and below it.
Can you write 12 divided by 3 equals 4 using the division sign?

Pupil writes the equation and says:
3 fours make 12, so 12 divided by 3 is 4.

$12 \div 3 = 4$

Work on the multiplication mat to divide counters into equal-sized groups. Give the pupil 15 counters.
How many counters are there?

Pupil counts the counters.
There are 15 counters.

Pupil puts 3 counters in each square.

How many threes can you make out of the 15? Show me on the multiplication mat. Tell me what you see.

I had 15 counters. I put 3 in each group so there are 5 groups. 15 divided by 3 is 5.

5 threes are 15 so 15 divided by 3 is 5. Write the equation.

$15 \div 3 = 5$

Ask pupils to explore other quantities in this way, predicting what the answer will be, and then checking it by putting counters onto the mat.

Use a number line to record your thinking. Draw a number line to 15. Draw jumps to show how many threes there are in 15. Write the multiples of 3 under the line. Write the equation.
Introduce the term 'multiples' gradually. A multiple is the result, or answer, when two numbers are multiplied.

Pupil draws a number line to 15 and shows successive jumps of 3. They do not use addition or subtraction signs. Then they count the number of jumps and answer the question:
There are 5 threes in 15 so 15 divided by 3 is 5.

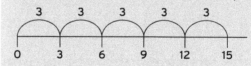

$15 \div 3 = 5$

Give pupil a word problem to show the use of the grouping concept in context. Ask pupils to make up their own word problems.

Sam has 12 crayons. He puts them into packs of 3. How many packs does he have now?
Draw a diagram, write the equation and write the answer.

4 threes are 12, so 12 divided by 3 is 4.
He has 4 packs.
$12 \div 3 = 4$

Answer: *Sam has 4 packs of pencils.*

The sharing concept of division

Give pupil 20 counters and 4 bowls.

There are 20 counters. Share them equally into the 4 bowls. How many counters will you have in each bowl?

Pupil takes 4 bowls and shares the counters, one by one, between the bowls.
There are 5 counters in each bowl.

I have divided 20 into 4 groups. There are 5 counters in each group. 20 divided by 4 is 5.

$20 \div 4 = 5$

Tell me what you have done. Draw a diagram and write the equation.

Work on the multiplication mat. Give pupils 24 counters. *There are 24 counters. Share them equally between 4 groups. How many counters will you have in each group?*
Allow pupils to cover up the squares that are not being used if they wish to do so.
Explain your reasoning and write the equation.

Pupil shares the counters, one by one, between 4 groups until all the counters have been used, then says: *There are 6 counters in each group.*

There are 4 sixes in 24, so 24 divided into 4 groups is 6.

$24 \div 4 = 6$

Pupils should explore other quantities in this way, predicting what the answer will be, then checking it by putting counters onto the multiplication mat.

Give pupil a word problem to show the use of the sharing concept in context. Ask pupils to make up their own word problems.

There are 12 tennis players. There are 4 tennis courts. How many people play on each court?
Draw a diagram, write the equation and write the answer.

4 threes are 12, so 12 divided by 4 is 3.
There are 3 players on each court.

$12 \div 4 = 3$

Answer: 3 people play on each court.

Checklist – Division concepts: grouping and sharing

Pupils can:
- ☐ Investigate the inverse relationship between multiplication and division
- ☐ Demonstrate and explain the grouping concept of division
- ☐ Demonstrate and explain the sharing concept of division
- ☐ Draw a diagram to show division by grouping
- ☐ Draw a diagram to show division by sharing
- ☐ Record thinking on a number line

Division calculation methods

Objectives
- Relate division as repeated subtraction to multiplication as repeated addition
- Record division as repeated subtraction on a number line
- Partition quantities into easily divisible components
- Demonstrate and explain division by partitioning using equipment
- Use an array to divide a quantity where there will be a remainder
- Interpret division with remainders in context
- Record thinking diagrammatically
- Write equations

The work on the concept of division emphasised the link with multiplication: division and multiplication are inverse operations. Now pupils learn calculation methods and the language of division.

- **Repeated subtraction:** Subtract equal-sized groups. The answer is found in the number of groups that are subtracted.
- **Partitioning:** Divide by partitioning numbers into components which can be easily divided, and then recombining the answers. This approach lays the foundations for the formal algorithm.
- **Remainders:** Use arrays to demonstrate division. This makes it clear that any amount that can not be included in the array will be the remainder as it is left over. It is important that pupils can use this method as it links directly to the standard written algorithm.

Division by repeated subtraction shows that division is the reverse of multiplication as repeated addition. Pupils subtract equal-sized groups from the dividend (the quantity to be divided). Some pupils are confused as the final result of these calculations will be zero (or a small number if remainders are involved). They may not realise that the answer is found in the number of groups that are subtracted. The calculation must be recorded on a number line so that pupils are clear that the initial quantity is not actually removed; it is rearranged.

Pupils should be familiar with partitioning numbers from their work with two-digit numbers (p137). The number to be divided (the dividend) is partitioned into components that make the calculation easier. Calculating by partitioning lays the foundations for formal division. Pupils should model division by chunking using concrete materials, however they should be discouraged from putting quantities out in 'clumps' of ones. Pupils need to discuss their thinking at each stage and write the calculation as equations.

Use base 10 equipment, Cuisenaire rods or counters to model the question as an array. This format serves as a concrete model of the long-division algorithm which will be discussed later. The rectangular shape of the array makes the layout of formal division explicit. The array makes it clear that the total number of counters or rods represents the dividend (the initial quantity), the number of rows represents the divisor (what it is divided by) and the number in each row gives the quotient (the answer to the question).

Introduce division with remainders when pupils can confidently handle division without remainders. They build arrays to model the question. If there are counters which cannot be included in the rectangular array, these will be 'left over'. The counters that remain outside the array are known as the remainder, which can be abbreviated to 'rem' in calculations. It is best to work with small quantities at first, to establish the concept and avoid confusion.

Pupils need to work with division in context to see how the remainder is used to solve a problem. In some cases the remainder is what is left over; in others it needs to be taken into account. For example, an egg box holds 6 eggs. There are 9 eggs. How many egg boxes are required? The answer is 2 egg boxes. Although the second box will only hold 3 eggs, it is still required.

Teaching

Division by repeated subtraction

Give pupil 30 counters.

You learnt to multiply by repeated addition.
You can divide by repeated subtraction. Here are
30 counters. Divide 30 by 5.
You can do this by subtracting fives. Record your
working on a number line as you subtract each 5.
Write the equation.

Note that the pupil does not write a subtraction
sign next to each 5. Omitting the sign reinforces
the image of the inverse relationship between the
operations.

Pupil arranges counters in a line, then
subtracts groups of 5 and records each 5 as a
step on the number line. The pupil starts at 30
and subtracts by step-counting back in fives.

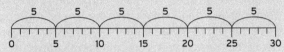

Then the pupil counts the number of jumps.
Pupil explains in their own words:
Each step is 5. There are 6 steps.
So 30 divided by 5 equals 6.

$$30 \div 5 = 6$$

Partitioning applied to division

Use base 10 equipment to demonstrate the importance of flexible partitioning. This work lays the
foundations for both the informal and formal written methods of division.

What is 78 divided by 6? Use tens and units to
show 78.

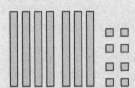

78 is 7 tens and 8 units.

You make this calculation easier if you partition 78
into numbers that are easier to divide by 6. This
is called partitioning. Use a triad to help you and
write the equation.

If the pupil wishes to experiment, allow them to
do so, otherwise guide them to find two suitable
quantities by asking questions: *What are 10 sixes?*
Partition 78 into 60 and some more. Write it as a
triad.

Pupil moves the counters and uses a triad to
support their reasoning.
I know that 6 tens are 60, so 60 divided by 6 is
10. Then I have 18 left. I can partition 78 into 60
and 18.

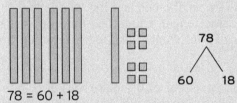

$$78 = 60 + 18$$

Divide each component by 6. Put the tens and
units in an array then demonstrate and explain the
stages in the calculation.

Pupil models the array with 6 rows.
There are 6 rows. There is 1 ten in each row.
Then I need to exchange the ten in 18 into 10
ones. I know that 6 threes are 18 so 18 divided
by 6 is 3. I put out 6 rows with 3 in each row.

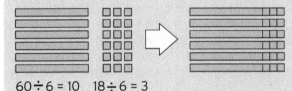

$$60 \div 6 = 10 \quad 18 \div 6 = 3$$

$$78 \div 6 = (60 \div 6) + (18 \div 6)$$
$$= 10 + 3$$
So $78 \div 6 = 13$

Write the equations and tell me what you do.
It is important that the pupil talks through the
stages again as they write the equations.

The pupil explains the reasoning. *60 divided by*
6 is 10. 18 divided by 6 is 3. I add the answers
from each chunk. 10 add 3 makes 13. So 78
divided by 6 is 13.

Division with remainders

Use arrays to demonstrate the effect of dividing a quantity which will result in a remainder. It is essential that pupils work with numbers in context as the remainder may be 'left over', or need to be taken into account in answering the question.

Give pupil 13 counters to demonstrate 13 ÷ 5.
There are 13 counters. Put the counters in an array to show 13 divided by 5.

Discuss the fact that when a quantity is divided into groups, the quantity in each group must be the same size. Some counters may be left over because there are not enough to make all the rows the same size. What is left over is called the remainder.

There are 13 counters. Look at the counters. Tell me what you see.

Write the equation and explain your thinking.

Pupil re-arranges the counters into 5 rows with 2 counters in each row.

They should put the remaining 3 counters to one side.

I can see an array with 10 counters and 3 counters left over. There are 5 rows with 2 counters in each row and 3 left over.

5 twos are 10 so 13 divided by 5 is 2 with 3 left over.

13 ÷ 5 = 2 remainder 3

Give pupils word problems to solve both where the remainder remains as a quantity 'left over' and where the remainder affects the outcome. They need to write the question, model it with equipment, draw diagrams, show their working and write the answer as a sentence. Pupils also need to make up their own questions.

Sam has 11 biscuits. She shares them equally among 3 friends. How many biscuits are left over?

5 people can fit into one car. There are 14 people. How many cars are needed to transport everybody? (Remember everyone has to be in a car.)

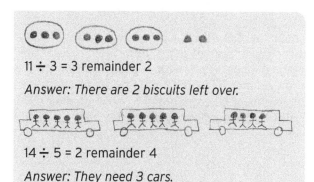

11 ÷ 3 = 3 remainder 2

Answer: There are 2 biscuits left over.

14 ÷ 5 = 2 remainder 4

Answer: They need 3 cars.

Checklist – Division calculation methods

Pupils can:

☐ Relate division as repeated subtraction to multiplication as repeated addition
☐ Record division as repeated subtraction on a number line
☐ Partition quantities into easily divisible components
☐ Demonstrate and explain division by partitioning using equipment
☐ Use an array to divide a quantity where there will be a remainder
☐ Interpret division with remainders in context
☐ Record thinking diagrammatically
☐ Write equations

Part 2:
Formal Numeracy

This section introduces the formal structures of numeracy: the place value grid and the standard written methods. The final chapter concerns word problems.

By this stage pupils should be familiar with the terms hundreds, tens and units and be able to exchange between tens and units. Now they apply this knowledge to the formal place value structure and learn that hundreds, tens and units (HTU) can be represented in a formal structure called the place value grid. The group of HTU is repeated within the larger groups of thousands, and millions. Pupils learn to exchange between higher place value positions, and explain and record their thinking. This leads on to work with standard algorithms.

Modelling questions using base 10 equipment is an important part of the transition from mental methods to formal written methods. As pupils develop confidence they will be able to discard the concrete apparatus. However they should be allowed to use it check their calculations if they wish to do so until they have complete confidence in their ability. Pupils use rounding to estimate their answers before working out formal calculations. This helps to alert them to errors if they make mistakes in exchanging between place value positions.

Finally there is a section on word problems. This chapter has been put at the end of the book because of the constraints of space. However, it is essential that pupils use numbers in contexts at every stage in learning numeracy. Too often pupils consider that word problems are a topic separate from calculation. A few examples of word problems are given for each stage of number learning; this is a starting point. Pupils should be encouraged to make up their own questions with increasingly complex scenarios so that they can confidently use numbers to solve problems.

8

The place value system

The place value system is a brilliantly efficient invention that denotes all numbers, whatever their size; however it can be a very difficult concept for pupils to learn. In any place value system, the position, or place of a digit in a number determines its value. In the decimal, or base 10 system, all numbers, from the gigantic to the miniscule, can be written using combinations of the digits 0, 1, 2, 3, 4, 5, 6, 7, 8, and 9. For example: 6 in 672 has a value of 600 whereas 6 in 261 represents 60 and the 6 in 856 is worth 6.

The structure of the place value system can be shown on a diagram with columns which is referred to as a place value grid. The value of each place is 10 times larger than the column to its right and 10 times smaller than the column to its left. Start teaching by introducing the place value grid with three columns called: hundreds, tens and units (HTU). Pupils need to fully understand this pattern of three places (HTU). This structure is repeated throughout the number system to represent larger whole numbers. Thousands, millions, billions, trillions and onwards, each contain the three HTU columns.

MILLIONS			THOUSANDS					
Hundreds	Tens	Units	Hundreds	Tens	Units	Hundreds	Tens	Units
H	T	U	H	T	U	H	T	U

Teach place value in two stages. First pupils build numbers with base 10 equipment to link the changing scale of place values with the written digits. Then teach formal place value on the place value grid. Use base 10 equipment to show the change in scale between the place value positions. Base 10 equipment is designed to make the relative size of numbers clear and can be used to model numbers up to 9,999.

Writing numbers: the international convention

It is easier to read large numbers if the clusters of three (HTU) can be easily identified. The correct way to write large numbers is to leave a space between each group of three digits (HTU). The international convention (SI convention) for writing large numbers is that 'A space should be left between groups of three digits… in four digit numbers the space may be omitted. Commas should not be used.' (www.npl.co.uk/reference/measurement-units/si-conventions/)

SI convention
123 456 789

Traditional British
123,456,789

Before the international standard was established, methods of demarcating the clusters of three differed. Traditionally people in Britain used a comma as a separator between millions, thousands, and HTU, whereas European countries used a full stop rather than the comma. In Britain the decimal marker was a decimal point; the Europeans used a comma. It was to avoid confusion that the Standard International convention stated that there should be no marks between digits and the border between whole numbers and decimal fractions can be either a comma or a point (full stop). The SI convention assumes that handwriting will be clear with consistent spacing between digits. For many pupils this is not the case. They may also fail to register the significance of the larger spaces in typed numbers.

Teach pupils with learning difficulties to use a comma to mark every HTU group within the number. This helps them focus on the relevant part of the number and reinforces the structure of the place value system. Explain that this is to help them learn numbers. They can stop using the comma when they are confident with numbers, and can write them tidily and clearly.

Another difficulty is that many pupils with poor numeracy skills have directional difficulties. They may not be sure at which 'end' of the number they start marking off the groups of three. If they cannot remember that they should start from the right it may be that they cannot recall where 'right' is. For this reason ask them to write place value headings above numbers until they feel confident they can discard them.

Equipment

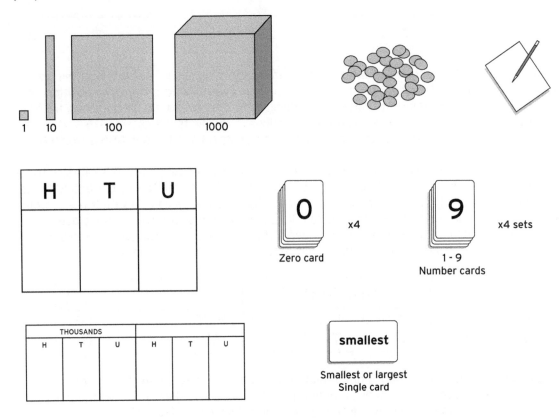

Build 3-digit numbers with hundreds, tens and units

Objectives
- Represent numbers in base 10, and partition them into hundreds, tens and units.
- Build 3-digit numbers with base 10 equipment
- Record 3-digit representations in diagrams
- Record 3-digit numbers as hundreds, tens and units
- Investigate the value of digits in 3-digit numbers

It is helpful if pupils explore the change in scale between the different place value positions before they start work on the formal place value grid. It is best to use base 10 equipment as this makes the relative size of the hundreds, tens and units (ones) clear. Pupils have already built two-digit numbers using base 10 equipment. Now they work on building three-digit numbers in a similar way. Pupils have already established that 10 ones is the same as 1 ten, now they learn that 100 ones can be exchanged for a one hundred square, and that 10 tens are the same as one hundred.

Teaching
Use base 10 equipment tens and unit cubes to establish that 100 ones have the same value as a 100 square.

How many ones do you need to have the same amount as the square? Use the square and the units to find out.

The square is a called a hundred square because it is the same size as 100 ones.

How many tens do you need to have the same amount as the square? Use the square and the tens to find out.

Pupil puts ones (unit cubes) on top of the square to find that 100 ones are required.
The square is the same size as 100 ones.

Pupil puts tens on top of the square to find that 10 tens make 100.
The square is the same size as 10 tens.

Build 3-digit numbers
Pupils explore spoken numbers using hundreds, tens and units. Do not use numbers containing a zero at this stage.

Teacher builds a number using 2 hundreds, 3 tens and 6 units, and says: *Tell me what you see. Read the number.*

Build a number using 4 hundreds, 5 tens and 3 units. What is the number?

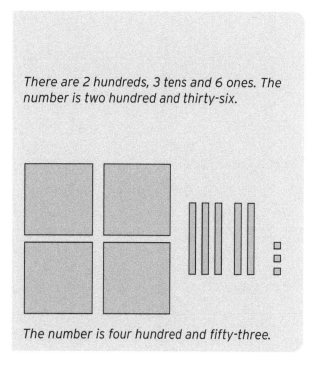

There are 2 hundreds, 3 tens and 6 ones. The number is two hundred and thirty-six.

The number is four hundred and fifty-three.

Build 574 and describe what you have done.
If necessary point out that we say 5 hundred even if it should be 5 hundreds. Pupils with language weaknesses can get confused by this counter-intuitive language convention.

Encourage pupils to put the hundred squares into the number patterns, however if space is limited, stack the hundred squares. The most important point is that pupils work systematically so the way the numbers are modelled is easy to read.

Draw a diagram of 574 and describe how it is made of hundreds, tens and units.

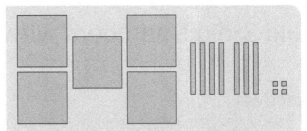

Pupil puts out the base 10 equipment and says: *Five hundred and seventy-four is made of 5 hundreds, 7 tens and 4 ones.*

Pupil draws a diagram of the concrete model.

Investigate the value of digits in a 3-digit number
Use three digits to compare how the value changes when the arrangement of the digits changes.

Give the pupil cards with the digits 1, 2 and 3. *The value of a digit depends on its position in a number. Use number cards to build different numbers. Start with one hundred and twenty-three. Use base 10 equipment to build the number.*

Describe the numbers, draw diagrams and record how the numbers are made of hundreds, tens and units.
Encourage pupils to work in a systematic way by starting with the smallest number and working through all the possibilities to the largest number. They can write down all the number permutations before starting to build and draw each one, so that they compare and order the numbers from the smallest to the largest.

The pupil describes each number as it is built.

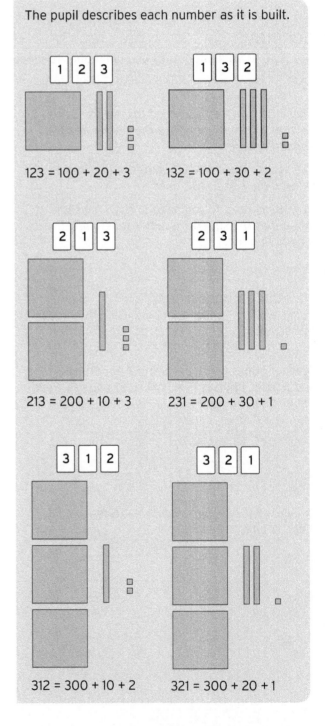

123 = 100 + 20 + 3   132 = 100 + 30 + 2

213 = 200 + 10 + 3   231 = 200 + 30 + 1

312 = 300 + 10 + 2   321 = 300 + 20 + 1

Card Wars

Aim
- To compare the size of numbers
- To use base 10 equipment to show the relative size of numbers

Equipment
- 4 sets of cards with one digit on each card (1 to 9)
- 9 hundred squares, 9 base 10 rods (tens) and 9 unit cubes (ones) for each player
- Size card - words 'smallest' and 'largest' on alternate sides

smallest

Smallest or largest
Single card

9

1 - 9
Number cards
x4 sets

x9 for each player

How to play
Shuffle the cards. Deal three cards, face down, to each player.

Players look at their cards but do not show anyone else.

The dealer decides whether the smallest or the largest number will win. Dealer turns the size card over to show the appropriate word.

Players order their digit cards to make either the smallest or largest possible number and make the numbers using base 10 equipment.

Players take it in turns to read their number, starting with the dealer.

Dealer reads the size card and says: *The (largest or smallest) number wins.*

The person with the appropriate number says: *I have the (largest/smallest) number.*

At the end of each round, the winning player collects all the cards.

The winner is the player with the most cards when they have all been played.

Example: A game in progress. Each player has made the largest number they can.

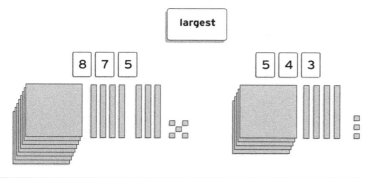

Pupils need to practise building 3-digit numbers, and recording them as diagrams.

425	659	714
362	286	538

Checklist - Build 3-digit numbers with hundreds, tens and units
Pupils can:
- ☐ Represent numbers in base 10, and partition them into hundreds, tens and units
- ☐ Build 3-digit numbers with base 10 equipment
- ☐ Record 3-digit representations in diagrams
- ☐ Record 3-digit numbers as hundreds, tens and units
- ☐ Investigate the value of digits in 3-digit numbers

Understanding the place value grid

Objectives

- Understand the place value grid
- Build 2-digit and then 3-digit numbers on the place value grid (no zeros)
- Draw a diagram of base 10 equipment on the place value grid
- Write numbers under the place value headings (HTU)

The place value grid is a diagrammatic representation of the place value positions. The basic place value grid is a diagram with three columns headed HTU for hundreds, tens and units. Introduce all three columns together, even when working on two-digit numbers, to secure the image of the repeating pattern of three places. Present the place value grid on A4 plain paper. Squared or lined paper can cause confusion because the place columns may not stand out. Encourage pupils to draw their own place value grids as this helps imprint the structure in their minds.

Use base 10 equipment to model calculations on the place value grid. Teaching must not be rushed and must be checked and revised regularly to ensure that pupils understand and retain the concept. Sometimes people think that it is helpful to weave stories around place value and use scenarios such as 'people in houses'. This is likely to confuse pupils who are finding the concept difficult.

Teaching

Pupils use base 10 equipment to model a variety of numbers on the place value grid. At this stage do not use numbers containing a zero (0).

Teacher shows pupils a place value grid on A4 paper. *This diagram is called a place value grid. How many columns can you see?*

The headings of the columns are H for hundreds, T for tens and U for units or ones.

Give the pupil a blank piece of A4 paper. Draw a large place value grid on the paper.
Build the number 256 on the place value grid.
Draw a sketch of the place value grid in your book. Write the heading HTU. Write the number 256 under the correct headings
It is best to show the pupil an example of the layout that is expected.

Write the equations under the diagrams.

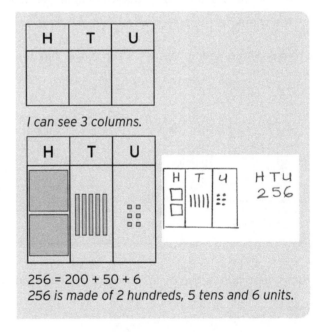

I can see 3 columns.

256 = 200 + 50 + 6
256 is made of 2 hundreds, 5 tens and 6 units.

Pupils need to practise working on the place value grid so that they are thoroughly familiar with it.

583   341   739

Checklist – Understanding the place value grid

Pupils can:

- ☐ Understand the place value grid
- ☐ Build 2-digit and 3-digit numbers on the place value grid (no zeros)
- ☐ Draw a diagram of base 10 equipment on the place value grid
- ☐ Write numbers under the place value headings (HTU)

Zero as a place holder

Objectives

- Recognise 0 as a place value holder
- Read numbers including zero
- Write numbers including zero

Teach the concept of zero as a place holder. It occupies a position in a number to ensure that the other digits in the number are in their correct places.

The concept of zero needs to be carefully taught. Some children with poor number sense have misconceptions about zero. Many think that zero means nothing, therefore it can be ignored. Pupils learn about zero by writing 2-digit and 3-digit numbers on a place value grid, then drawing diagrams and writing the numbers under HTU headings.

Teaching

Zero in the units column

Use a digit card with 0 on it to emphasise the empty place. Use two place value grids. Give oral instructions as well as using digit cards.

Build 2 on one place value grid. *Build 20 on another place value grid.*	Pupil puts 2 ones in the units column on one grid. Pupil puts 2 tens in the tens column on a second grid.
It is important that the place value grids are placed below each other to draw attention to the comparative size of the numbers.	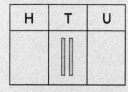
If the place value grids are placed alongside each other there is potential for visual confusion with the 6 column thousand place value grid.	
How many tens are there in 20? *How many units are there in 20?*	*20 is made of 2 tens.* *There are no units in 20.* Pupil uses the word 'no' rather than 'zero' at this stage as they are describing the lack of a physical object.
Give the pupil a digit card with 0 on it: Put a zero in the units column. The zero tells you there are no ones in the units column.	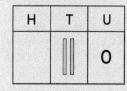
Draw a diagram to show 2 and another diagram to show 20. Write the heading HTU and write 2 under the correct heading. Then write 20 on the line below. Teacher demonstrates the layout as shown on the right.	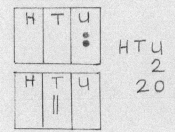

Compare 34 and 340. Build 34 on one place value grid. Build 340 on the other place value grid. Explain your thinking.
Encourage the pupil to start using the word zero. If they are unsure allow them to use 'no' as well as 'zero'.

34 is made of 3 tens and 4 units.
340 is made of 3 hundreds, 4 tens and 0 (zero) units.

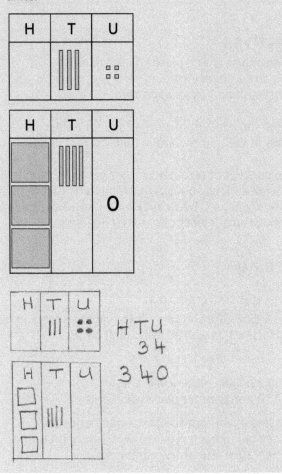

Use a number card to show zero in the unit column. The zero tells you there are no ones in the unit column.

Draw diagrams of the numbers. Write the heading HTU and write 34 under the correct heading. Then write 340 on the line below. Explain what you are doing.

Zero in the tens column

Build 304 on a place value grid. Explain your thinking.
Use a number card to show zero in the tens column. The zero tells you there are no tens in the tens column.

304 is made of 3 hundreds and 4 units.
There are no tens in 304.

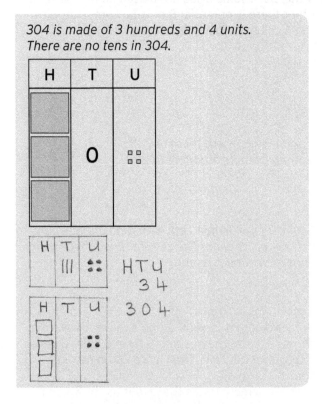

Draw a diagram to show 34 and 304. Write 34 and 304 under the HTU headings. Explain what you are doing.

Pupils need to build a variety of numbers containing zero (0) in different positions to establish the concept. Play the game, Zero Holds the Place. This is based on Card Wars but players are required to use a place value grid.

Zero Holds the Place

(3-digit numbers)

Aim

- To use zero as a place holder
- To compare the size of numbers
- To use manipulatives to show the relative size of numbers

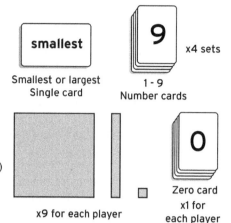

smallest

Smallest or largest
Single card

9 x4 sets

1 - 9
Number cards

0

Zero card
x1 for
each player

Equipment

- 4 sets of cards with one digit on each card (1 to 9)
- Size card - words 'smallest' and 'largest' on opposite sides
- Each player has a zero (0) digit card
- Each player has 9 hundred squares, 9 tens and 9 units (ones)
- Pencil and paper for each player

x9 for each player

How to play

Shuffle the cards. Deal 2 cards, face down, to each player.

Players use the dealt cards and the zero (0) card to make 3-digit numbers. Players look at their cards but do not show anyone else.

The dealer decides whether the smallest or the largest number will win. Dealer displays the size card to show the appropriate word.

Players order their digit cards to make either the smallest or largest possible number and make the numbers using base 10 equipment. Each player writes their own number under HTU columns.

Players take it in turns to read their number, starting with the dealer.

Dealer reads the size card and says: *The [largest/smallest] number wins.*

The person with the appropriate number says: *I have the [largest/smallest] number.*

At the end of each round, the winning player collects all the cards except the zeros.

The winner is the player with the most cards when they have all been played.

Example:

Size card shows largest number will win.

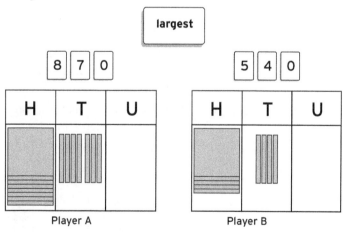

largest

| 8 | 7 | 0 |

| H | T | U |

Player A

| 5 | 4 | 0 |

| H | T | U |

Player B

Checklist - Zero as a place holder

Pupils can:

- ☐ Recognise 0 as a place value holder
- ☐ Read numbers including the zero digit
- ☐ Write numbers including the zero digit

Exchange on the place value grid

Objectives
- Exchange from units to tens on the place value grid
- Exchange from tens to hundreds on the place value grid
- Explain the effect of adding 1 to a multi-digit number ending in 99

The ability to exchange and decompose is essential for developing understanding of the place value structure and enabling pupils to work out calculations from first principles. It is a necessary foundation for recording calculations using the standard algorithms. Do not underestimate how hard this will be for some pupils.

Pupils practise exchanging on the place value grid, concentrating on the exchanges at the decade boundaries and the hundreds boundaries. They describe what they are doing in their own words. The base 10 equipment makes the logic of the steps in the exchanges explicit and helps pupils self-correct errors. It is important that the pupils place 10 ones next to 1 ten (or 10 tens next to 1 hundred) as they carry out the exchange. It is the conjunction of the words and the image that develops the essential visual image as a memory.

This process is sometimes referred to as 'exchanging up' and 'exchanging down'. This may cause confusion as 'up' and 'down' indicate vertical directions whereas the terms are being used to describe a change in value. Further confusion may arise because the movement is horizontal to the left or to the right on the place value grid. In this book the term exchange is used to refer to several items being represented by one item of greater value. The term decompose refers to breaking a single item into several of lower value. Use the words hundreds, tens and units rather than directional language.

Teaching
Give the pupil a place value grid, base 10 equipment and digit cards 0 to 9.

Exchange units to tens: Add 1 to a number ending in 9

Build the dot pattern of 9 on the place value grid. Put the correct number card below the pattern.

Pupil puts 9 in the units column.

Add 1 more unit to 9. How many ones do you have in the units column?

9 and 1 is 10 so I have 10 ones in the units column.

Use the digit cards to show how many there are. What is the number?

Pupil removes the 9 card and replaces it with digit cards to show 10 and says:
The number is 10.

You are only allowed to put 1 digit in each column.

Pupil puts the cards for 10 on the place value grid to show 1 ten and 0 units.

The numbers show 1 ten and no units. Can you do the exchange and show the correct model for 10?

I exchange 10 ones for 1 ten.

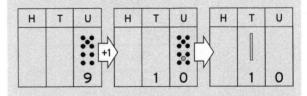

Ask pupil to build 29 on the place value grid. They use digit cards to show the number. Then they add 1 more unit to 29. *How many tens and units do you have?*

The pupil builds 29 on the place value grid and adds 1. Then the pupil makes the adjustments and explains why 29 add 1 is 30.

Do several more examples adding 1 to a 2-digit number ending in 9.

Exchange tens to hundreds: Add 10 to a number ending in 90

Build 90 on the place value grid.

Use digit cards to show the number.

Add 1 more ten to 90.

Pupil counts out 9 tens and puts them in the tens column.

90 is made of 9 tens and 0 units.

Pupil puts another 10 in the tens column.
9 tens and 1 ten makes 10 tens. 10 tens are 100.

Pupil removes the 9 card replaces it with 1 and 0 cards so the number now reads 100.
I can only have 1 digit in each HTU column. I need to exchange 10 tens for 1 hundred square.

Use the cards to show how many there are. What is the number?

90 add 10 is 100.

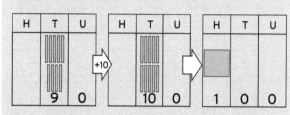

Write an equation to show your thinking.

90 + 10 = 100

Build 190 on the place value grid. Use digit cards to show the number.

Add 1 more ten to 190. How many tens do you have?

Pupil puts 1 hundred square and 9 tens on the place value grid. *190 is made of 1 hundred, 9 tens and 0 units.*

Pupil puts another 10 in the tens column.
I have 10 tens. 9 tens and 1 ten makes 10 tens. 10 tens are 100.

I can only have 1 digit in each HTU column. I need to exchange 10 tens for 1 hundred square.

Use the cards to show how many there are. What is the number?

There are 2 hundred squares in the hundred column. The number is 200. There are 0 tens and 0 units.

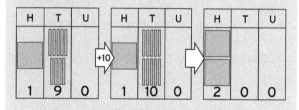

Write equations to show your thinking.

190 + 10   = 100 + 90 + 10
            = 100 + 100
            = 200
So 190 + 10 = 200

Pupils practise exchanging by adding 10 to numbers up to 900. Ask pupils to build the number and then add 10. They explain their working and write the equations.

390   590   890

Exchange units to tens to hundreds: add 1 to a number ending in 99

Build 99 on the place value grid. Show that in numbers using the digit cards.

Pupil puts out 9 tens and 9 units and places the cards in the correct columns.

Add 1 more unit to 9. How many units do you have?

9 and 1 is 10 so I have 10 in the units column.

Use the digit cards to show how many there are now. What is the number that you see?

Pupil puts the digit cards for 10 under the units. *There are 9 tens and 10 units. I must exchange 10 ones for 1 ten and put it in the tens column.*

How many tens can you see?

I can see 10 tens in the tens column. I must exchange 10 tens for one 1 hundred.

Pupil adjusts the digit cards so they are in the correct columns.

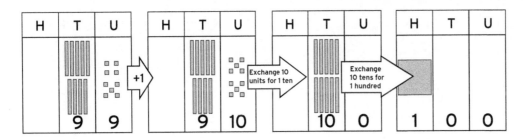

Write equations to show your thinking.

$$99 + 1 = 90 + 9 + 1$$
$$= 90 + 10$$
$$= 100$$
$$\text{So } 99 + 1 = 100$$

Pupils practise adding 1 to 3-digit numbers ending in 99 and doing the exchanges. They build the number, add 1 more and discuss their thinking as they make the necessary exchanges. Then they write the equations.

399   499   799

Checklist – Exchange on the place value grid

Pupils can:
- ☐ Exchange from units to tens on the place value grid
- ☐ Exchange from tens to hundreds on the place value grid
- ☐ Explain the effect of adding 1 to a multi-digit number ending in 99

Decomposition on the place value grid

Objectives
- Subtract from 2-digit numbers involving decomposition from tens to units
- Subtract from 3-digit numbers involving decomposition from hundred to tens
- Record reasoning steps to show the decomposition

Decomposition is the process of separating a number into the smaller quantities it represents. The process can be clearly shown using base 10 materials where 1 ten rod can be exchanged for 10 ones and 1 hundred is changed for 10 tens, or 100 unit cubes. Teach decomposition as 'change'; do not use the word 'carry'. Use the word 'decompose', or 'change', rather than 'exchange' in order to make a distinction between exchanging 'up' and decomposing 'down'.

Demonstrating decomposition by subtracting a quantity gives a clear model of the standard written method of subtraction. In this section pupils record their thinking under HTU headings. The workings are those of the standard written method, however it is not yet necessary to draw pupils' attention to the fact that this is the standard algorithm unless they ask. They work with the concrete equipment at all times.

Encourage the pupil to talk about what the question is asking. If they need prompting, the teacher asks questions to guide the pupil to consider each part of the question.

Teaching

Decomposition of 2-digit numbers (tens to units)
Use base 10 equipment on a place value grid. Pupils record their working under HTU headings. The teacher demonstrates decomposition before asking pupils to decompose numbers and record their thinking both diagrammatically and in written form.

What is 32 take away 5? Write the question under HTU headings.
Show the pupil how to lay out the question with the subtraction sign on the right.

Build 32 on the place value grid.

Can you take away 5?
You need to change 1 ten for 10 ones. This is also called decomposition.

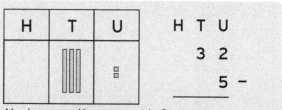

No, because there are only 2 ones.

Pupil puts 1 tens stick against the line and places 10 ones next to it. Then pupil removes the tens stick.
I change 1 ten for 10 units.

Now there are 2 tens in the tens column and 12 ones in the units column.

You need to record this to show what you have done. Write a small 1 next to the 2 to show 12 ones.
Teacher demonstrates how to make it clear that the 1 depicts 10 units rather than 1 ten.

The recording shows what has happened on the concrete model. How many tens are there now?

Cross out the 3 in the tens column. Write 2 in the tens column to show there are 2 tens in the tens column.

There are 2 tens.

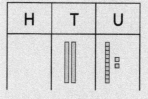

You want to work out 32 subtract 5. Can you subtract 5 on the place value grid now?

How much is left altogether?

Show that on your recording.
How many units are in the unit column?

How many tens are there in the tens column?

Pupil removes 5 ones from the units column and says: *12 take away 5 is 7.*

There are 27 altogether.

There are 7 units left in the units column. I write 7.
There are 2 tens in the tens column so I write 2 in the tens column. That makes 27.

```
H  T  U
   ²3̸ ¹2
      5  -
   _____
   2  7
```

32 take away 5 is 27.

What is 32 – 5?

Pupils practise subtracting a single digit from a 2-digit number where decomposition is required.

43 - 8   36 - 7   54 - 6

Decomposition of 3-digit numbers (hundreds to tens)

Pupils decompose a number in the 100 position on the place value grid. Encourage the pupils to generalise from what they have learnt by working with 2-digit numbers. At this stage the number should not contain any zeros. Wait until pupils can confidently work out and demonstrate subtraction with numbers containing the digits 1 to 9 before introducing numbers containing an empty HTU place.

What is 345 take away 62? Build the number on the place value grid. Write the question under the place value headings (HTU).

```
H  T  U
3  4  5
   6  2  -
_____
```

You need to take away 62. Start with the units.

5 take away 2 is 3. Pupil removes 2 units and records 5 subtract 2 is 3.

```
H  T  U
3  4  5
   6  2  -
_____
      3
```

What do you need to do next?

I need to take away 6 tens.
There are only 4 tens in the tens column.
I need to change 1 hundred square for 10 tens.

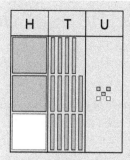

Record what you have done. Explain what you are doing.

The pupil lays 10 tens on top of the 100 square to develop the visual image. Then the 100 square is removed and the 10 tens are placed in the tens column.

Now there are 2 hundreds, 14 tens and 5 ones.

I cross out 3 in the hundreds column and write 2. The hundred was changed for 10 tens, so I show 10 tens in the tens column. There are 14 tens in the tens column.

$$\begin{array}{ccc} H & T & U \\ {}^2\cancel{3} & {}^1\!4 & 5 \\ & 6 & 2 \quad - \\ \hline & & 3 \end{array}$$

Now I can take away 6 tens. 140 subtract 60 is 80. There are 8 tens left.

Pupil completes the written calculation and says: *There are no hundreds to take away, so 345 take away 62 is 283.*

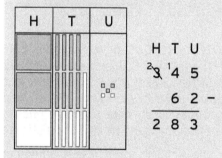

$$\begin{array}{ccc} H & T & U \\ {}^2\cancel{3} & {}^1\!4 & 5 \\ & 6 & 2 \quad - \\ \hline 2 & 8 & 3 \end{array}$$

Pupils practise decomposition questions. They write the question, model it on a place value grid using equipment, and record it under HTU headings.

452 - 36   136 - 65

Checklist - Decomposition on the place value grid

Pupils can:
- ☐ Subtract from 2-digit numbers involving decomposition from tens to units
- ☐ Subtract from 3-digit numbers involving decomposition from hundreds to tens
- ☐ Record reasoning steps to show the decomposition.

Introducing the thousands

Objectives
- Extend the place value grid to represent thousands numbers
- Build numbers to 9,999 on the place value grid
- Write numbers to 9,999 using place value headings
- Read numbers up to 9,999

Introduce the thousands numbers on a place value grid with six columns. It is important to make it clear that the word thousands refers to a group of 3 places in the place value structure. These places are called hundreds of thousands, tens of thousands and thousands. Make the repetition of HTU clear by writing the word thousands across the top of all 3 columns in the thousands positions on the place value grid. Often pupils think that the word thousands only refers to a 4-digit number.

Textbooks often introduce the thousands under 4 column headings: Th H T U. This representation obscures the repeated triple pattern of HTU. Some pupils develop the idea that the thousands occur in a single column, particularly as they rarely do concrete work with very large numbers. This can lead to difficulties calculating with larger numbers. It may lead to further confusion when the millions are introduced and they do not realise that the millions also include the categories of hundreds, tens and units.

Teaching
Use base 10 equipment tens and unit cubes to establish that the 1,000 block has the same value as a 1,000 ones.

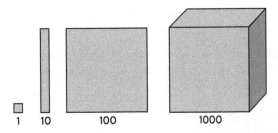

A large cube represents 1,000 in the base 10 system. Some pupils prefer to use the word 'block' rather than 'cube' for the thousand cube to avoid confusion with the unit cube. Interpreting the cube as 1,000 requires an understanding of three dimensions which many pupils find confusing. Take the time for pupils to count out 1,000 unit cubes in a line. This provides an opportunity to see how much larger 1,000 is than 100. Then pupils build a cube using the ones from the line so that they understand that 1,000 ones is the same size as a thousand block. For practical purposes it is best to provide a frame for this activity.

Ask pupils to build numbers using base 10 equipment. At this stage do not incorporate any zeros in the numbers.

Build 3,285. Tell me what you have done.

> *3,285 is made of 3 thousand blocks, 2 hundred squares, 8 tens and 5 units.*

Ask pupils to build several other numbers. Pupils describe what they are doing as they work. Many pupils have difficulty drawing and interpreting a diagram of a cube so it may be impractical to draw diagrams.

2,149   5,821

Thousands on the place value grid
Use a place value grid with 6 columns.

This is the thousands place value grid. Look at it and tell me what you see?

The thousands HTU columns are called hundred thousand, ten thousand and thousand.

Use base 10 equipment to show 2,345 on the place value grid.

Use digit cards to show 2,345 on the place value grid.
If the pupil has difficulty, suggest they show 345 and then put the digit card in the units column of the thousands section.

Write the place value headings and record the number 2,345 in the correct places.

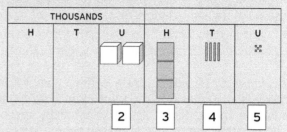

There are 6 columns. There are 3 columns in the thousands section headed HTU. Then there are 3 columns headed HTU for hundreds, tens and units.

2,345 is made of 2 thousands, 3 hundreds, 4 tens and 5 units.

Thous.
H T U H T U
   2,3 4 5

Introduce 0 into numbers when pupils can confidently build 4-digit numbers.

Build 4,027 on the place value grid.

Use digit cards to show 4,027 on the place value grid.

Write 4,027 under the correct place value headings.

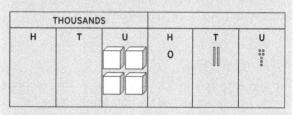

Pupil puts out 4 thousands, 2 tens and 7 units.

4,027 is made of 4 thousands, 0 hundreds, 2 tens and 7 units.

Thous.
H T U H T U
   4,0 2 7

| 4,361 | 9,780 | 6,504 |
| 3,027 | 2,003 | 1,060 |

Checklist - Introducing the thousands
Pupils can:
- Extend the place value grid to represent thousands numbers
- Build numbers to 9,999 on the place value grid
- Write numbers to 9,999 using place value headings
- Read numbers up to 9,999

Read, write and sequence numbers to 999,999

Objectives
- Read numbers to 999,999 using place value headings
- Write numbers up to 999,999 using place value headings
- Count flexibly forwards or backwards from any number in this range
- Continue a sequence from any number in this range.

It is impractical to do concrete work on numbers larger than 9,999. The purpose of working with concrete materials is to use them to develop cognitive models so that pupils can understand written numbers and work abstractly with them. By now pupils should understand the structure of the place value system and be able to reason about larger numbers without the support of concrete materials. Discuss and work with the larger thousands numbers, the 5-digit and 6-digit numbers, which are tens of thousands and hundreds of thousands.

Teaching
Pupils use digit cards to show a variety of 5-digit and 6-digit numbers and read them and record them under place value headings.

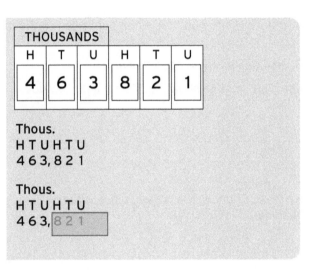

Show 463,821 on the place value grid using digit cards.

Write the place value headings, then write the number under the correct headings.

Read the number.

If the pupil has difficulty reading it, use a coloured overlay to cover up the section showing the HTU portion. Ask the pupil to read 463 as four hundred and sixty-three. Point out that these are thousands so they read it as 463 thousand. Then uncover the rest of the number.

Ask the pupil to show, write and read the following numbers:

56,437	60,521	865,493
709,853	230,479	999,999

Play the game, Card Wars, using 5 digits or 6 digits for each player. The instructions are on p106. Players use cards only. It is not possible to model large numbers using concrete materials.

The series of commercial card games called 'Top Trumps' has packs that use very large numbers. It is an enjoyable way to practise reading and comparing large numbers.

Checklist - Read, write and sequence numbers to 999,999
Pupils can:
- ☐ Read numbers to 999,999 using place value headings
- ☐ Write numbers up to 999,999 using place value headings
- ☐ Count flexibly forwards or backwards from any number in this range
- ☐ Continue a sequence from any number in this range

Introducing the millions

Objectives

- Extend the place value grid to represent millions numbers
- Read numbers to 999,999,999
- Write numbers to 999,999,999 using place value headings.

Million is a word that is often used with little sense of the size of it. Pupils may think that millions is the next column after thousands, not realising that the millions category also includes the HTU sub-groups.

Show pupils the millions place value grid, which has 9 columns. The millions columns are named hundreds of millions, tens of millions and millions. These columns can be headed H M, T M, and M. However the structure is clearer if the word 'millions' is written across the top of all 3 columns to show that this is a larger group which contains the sub-groups of HTU.

MILLIONS			THOUSANDS					
H	T	U	H	T	U	H	T	U

Teaching

Give pupil a place value grid with 9 columns.
This is the millions place value grid. Look at it and tell me what you see.

The millions HTU columns are called hundred million, ten million and million.

Use digit cards to show the number 2,459,678 on the place value grid and then read it.

Write 2,459,678 under place value headings.

There are 9 columns. There are 3 columns in the millions section headed HTU. In the thousands section there are 3 columns headed HTU. Then there are 3 columns headed HTU for hundreds, tens and units.

MILLIONS			THOUSANDS					
H	T	U	H	T	U	H	T	U
		2	4	5	9	6	7	8

2 million, 459 thousand, 6 hundred and seventy-eight.

MILL. Thous.
H T U H T U H T U
  2, 4 5 9, 6 7 8

Ask pupils to use digit cards to show a variety of numbers on the place value grid and read them. Pupils write the numbers in their books in a place value grid.

6,098,703	42,158,367	50,524,501
239,176,458	50,524,501	190,324,652

Checklist - Introducing the millions

Pupils can:

- ☐ Extend the place value grid to represent millions numbers
- ☐ Read numbers to 999,999,999
- ☐ Write numbers to 999,999,999 using place value headings

9

Formal written methods

Pupils need to understand and use standard written algorithms. The satisfaction in mastering a skill and using it to produce an attractive piece of work should not be underestimated. Before pupils embark on standard algorithms they need to know the key facts, be able to bridge through 10 and be able to partition and recombine numbers using appropriate mental methods and informal recordings. They also need to understand the structure of the place value system.

The standard written methods are very efficient procedures for calculation; however they compress a great deal of information and this can be confusing for some pupils. Traditionally the standard methods were taught as a sequence of steps to be applied to get the answer. Pupils with poor memories may not remember the steps nor be able to relate them to mental methods of calculation if they learn them by rote. Instruction on working with standard methods often emphasises the direction of working from right to left. Pupils with directional or spatial difficulties quickly become confused.

If they model the algorithms using base 10 equipment and record the information clearly and systematically from the start, pupils can use standard methods successfully. Instil the habit of making a rough estimate of the expected size of the answer before they do the formal calculation. Establishing this habit with work on whole numbers will help for later work with fractions. Effective calculator use depends on being able to estimate the expected answer in order to check the calculation.

It is best for pupils to learn the standard methods by modelling questions and reasoning to derive the steps in the calculation. The concrete models provide an exact representation of the standard written methods and make the meaning of the value of the numbers explicit. This approach is particularly helpful in making exchanging and decomposition understandable. Pupils build numbers on the place value grid, draw diagrams to illustrate their thinking and discuss what they are doing as they reason logically to calculate using the standard written method.

As soon as pupils can confidently solve algorithms, present them with word problems. Encourage them to make up their own word problems and share them with other pupils.

Equipment

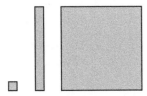 

Formal written addition

Objectives
- Use column addition to add multi-digit numbers with no exchange
- Use column addition to add multi-digit numbers with exchange between place value columns
- Use estimation to check answers to calculations

Pupils write the standard addition algorithm and model the question using base 10 equipment on a place value grid. They discuss their thinking at all stages. The base 10 equipment helps to remind them of the value of the numbers in the calculation rather than seeing them as individual digits. Pupils can arrange tens in a tally formation to make it easier to read larger groups of tens. When pupils can explain their reasoning confidently, they can work without the concrete materials.

Start with examples where no exchange (carrying) is required and give pupils plenty of practice so that they are comfortable with the format of the addition algorithm. Then introduce addition requiring exchange, first between units and tens, then between tens and hundreds and finally exchange in all columns. Make sure pupils round numbers to produce an estimate. Revise rounding if they are unsure about it. (See p111)

Teach pupils to set out their work clearly so that their workings are easy to follow. The formal algorithm is placed on the left hand side of the page and the workings shown on the right. It is important that pupils have plenty of space to make jottings and draw diagrams to show their reasoning. If the work is cramped because the pupil's handwriting is large, then they should work on a double page spread. Work on squared paper and write the place value headings above the relevant numbers until pupils are confident and accurate. Do not draw vertical lines to emphasise the place value columns – pupils need to see multi-digit numbers as a whole quantity not a collection of ones, tens and hundreds.

When pupils can confidently handle addition involving carrying with 3-digit numbers, encourage them to extend their thinking to larger numbers. Many pupils derive pleasure from realising that they can handle numbers in the thousands and millions, and more, by applying the same rules. Of course it is not practical to build or draw diagrams of very large numbers.

Teaching

Teach pupils to model the tens using the tally formation as tallies are compact and easy to record in diagrams. Demonstrate that vertical strokes are used for quantities up to 4. Number 5 consists of 4 vertical marks with a diagonal line across them. Larger numbers are composed of 5 plus some more.

Example: 7 is shown using tally marks.

Addition with no exchange
We are going to look at the formal written way of doing addition. What is 154 add 243? Write the place value headings HTU, then write the numbers you want to add underneath each other in the correct places. Write the addition sign to the right of the bottom number. Draw two lines underneath the bottom number. Leave a space between the lines. This is where the answer will go.

Demonstrate if the pupil has difficulty following the instructions.

Before you start to work out the addition, estimate what the answer will be. Round each number to the nearest 100 and write the estimate as an equation. Write it on the right hand side of the page. Explain what you are doing.

154 rounds up to 200, and 243 rounds down to 200.
My estimate is 200 add 200 which is 400.

H	T	U		Estimate: 200 + 200 = 400
1	5	4		
2	4	3	+	

Build 154 and 243 on the place value grid. Make 50 in the tally formation. Show the pupils how to lay 5 tens out in the form of the tally of 5 by putting out 4 tens and laying 1 ten diagonally across them.

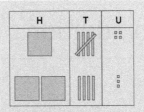

Draw a diagram to show the model. Do the addition starting with the units. Explain your thinking and write the answer in the correct place value columns.
Pupils do not need to write the HTU headings above the drawing of the equipment as the relative size of the pieces makes their meaning clear.

4 and 3 makes 7 so I write 7 in the units column.

5 tens and 4 tens make 9 tens so I write 9 in the tens column.

2 hundred and 1 hundred make 3 hundred so I write 3 in the hundreds column.

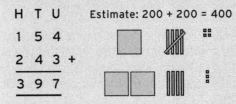

H T U   Estimate: 200 + 200 = 400

1 5 4

2 4 3 +
_____

3 9 7

Check your answer against your estimate.

Pupil adjusts the model to show 397.

154 and 243 makes 397. My estimate was 400 so my answer is close to my estimate.

Pupils work out the following addition calculations using the formal column method and explain their reasoning. They make an estimate before they start the addition. They may use base 10 equipment until they can give a confident explanation of their working.

HTU	HTU	HTU	Thous
256	317	471	HTU HTU
131 +	281 +	327 +	2 546
			7 422 +

Addition with exchange (from units to tens)

What is 236 add 357? Write the question as a formal addition and work out an estimate.

236 rounds down to 200 and 357 rounds up to 400.
My estimate is 200 add 400 which is 600.

Model the question on the place value grid and draw a diagram.

H T U   Estimate: 200 + 400 = 600

2 3 6

3 5 7 +
_____

_____

Do the addition starting with the units.

6 and 7 make 13. I need to exchange 10 of the units for 1 ten. There are still 3 ones in the units column.

Demonstrate your reasoning on the place value model and record it on the diagram.

Pupil does the exchange, and places 1 ten in the tens column underneath the other quantities.

Write the answers and explain your thinking.

You can say that you carry one 1 ten into the tens column. You write it underneath the line. Draw a small loop to 'hold' the 1 ten.

Teacher demonstrates how to write the 'carried' number. Drawing a loop under the carried number helps to focus attention on it so it is not forgotten in the calculation. Some pupils like to refer to the loop as a basket.

Complete the calculation.

Pupil records the exchange on the diagram as shown.

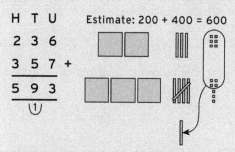

There are 3 tens and 5 tens and 1 ten in the basket so I have 9 tens altogether.

2 hundred and 3 hundred make 5 hundred.

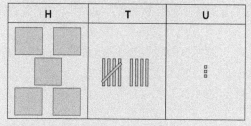

Pupil adjusts the model to show 593.

H	T	U

Check your answer against your estimate.

236 add 357 makes 593. My estimate was 600 so my answer is close to my estimate.

Pupils work out the following addition calculations using the formal column method and explain their reasoning. They make an estimate before they start the addition. They may use base 10 equipment until they can give a confident explanation of their working.

```
HTU              HTU              HTU
125              357              768
546 +            535 +            216 +
```

Addition with carrying (exchange from tens to hundreds)

What is 246 add 581?

This time the exchange will be from the tens column to the hundreds column. 1 hundred will be 'carried' from the tens to the hundreds. By now pupils should be able to explain their reasoning without prompting from the teacher, however if they struggle the teacher should encourage them by asking appropriate questions. They do the calculation and explain their reasoning before using the equipment to check their answer.

```
H T U      Estimate: 200 + 600 = 800

2 4 6

5 8 1 +
_____

_____
```

The pupil explains the steps in the calculation.
What is 246 add 581? I round 246 down to 200 and round 581 up to 600. Then 200 add 600 is 800.
My estimate is 800.

```
H  T  U        Estimate: 200 + 600 = 800

2  4  6
               40 + 80 = 120 = 100 + 20
5  8  1  +

8  2  7
  ⌣
  1
```

I start with the units. 6 add 1 is 7. Now I add the tens. 40 and 80 makes 120 so I need to exchange. I write 2 tens in the tens column and I exchange 10 tens for 1 hundred. I show that in a loop in the hundreds column. Now I add the hundreds. 200 add 500 add 100 makes 800.

246 add 581 makes 827. My estimate was 800 so my answer is close to my estimate.

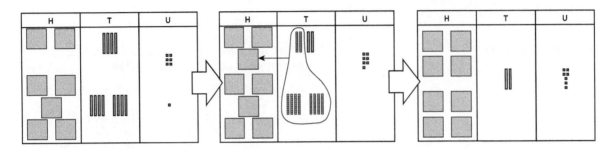

Pupils work out the following addition calculations using the formal column method.

```
756          645          721
163 +        182 +        195 +
```

Addition with exchanges between all columns

This question involves exchanges from units to tens, and from tens to hundreds.

```
H  T  U        Estimate: 500 + 400 = 900

5  3  4

3  7  8  +
```

The pupil explains the steps in the calculation.

What is 534 and 378? I round 534 down to 500 and round 378 up to 400. Then 500 add 400 is 900. My estimate is 900.

I start with the units. 4 add 8 is 12. I need to exchange 10 of the units for 1 ten. I show 1 ten in a loop under the tens column.

```
H  T  U        Estimate: 500 + 400 = 900

5  3  4
               4 + 8 = 12 = 10 + 2
3  7  8  +     30 + 70 + 10 =110 = 100 + 10

9  1  2        500 + 300 + 100 = 900
⌣ ⌣
1  1
```

Now I add the tens. 30 add 70 add 10 makes 110. I write 1 ten in the tens column and I exchange 10 tens for 1 hundred. I show 1 hundred in a loop in the hundreds column.

Now I add the hundreds. 500 add 300 add 100 makes 900.

534 and 378 makes 912. My estimate was 900 so my answer is close to my estimate.

Pupils work out the following addition calculations using the formal column method.

```
HTU          HTU          HTU          HTU
143          342          456          695
678 +        589 +        367 +        237 +
```

Checklist - Formal written addition

Pupils can:
- ☐ Use column addition to add multi-digit numbers with no exchange
- ☐ Use column addition to add multi-digit numbers with exchange between place value columns
- ☐ Use estimation to check answers to calculations

Formal written subtraction

Objectives

- Model formal subtraction using base 10 equipment
- Use column subtraction to subtract multi-digit numbers with no decomposition
- Use column subtraction to subtract multi-digit numbers with decomposition
- Use estimation to check answers to calculations

The subtraction algorithm was introduced when pupils worked on place value (see p187). The use of base 10 equipment makes the steps in the formal column method easy to follow. It is important that pupils set out their work clearly so that there is sufficient space to record the decomposition clearly.

Start with examples where no decomposition is required. Then introduce subtraction requiring decomposition, first between tens and units, then between hundreds and tens and finally between all columns. Take particular care with decomposition involving a zero place holder (see p181).

When pupils can confidently handle subtraction with 3-digit numbers, encourage them to extend their thinking to larger numbers.

Teaching

Subtraction with no decomposition

We are going to look at the formal written way of doing subtraction. What is 346 subtract 234?

Write the calculation as a formal subtraction and work out an estimate.

The teacher demonstrates the layout if necessary.

346 rounds down to 300 and 234 rounds down to 200. My estimate is 300 take away 200 which is 100.

```
H T U        Estimate: 300 - 200 = 100
3 4 6
2 3 4 -
_____

_____
```

Model the question on the place value grid and draw a diagram. Do the subtraction starting with the units. Demonstrate your reasoning on the place value model and show it on the diagram.

Write the answers and explain your thinking.

6 subtract 4 is 2. 4 tens take away 3 tens is 1 ten. 3 hundred take away 2 hundred is 1 hundred.

```
H T U        Estimate: 300 - 200 = 100
3 4 6
2 3 4 -
1 1 2
```

Check your answer against your estimate.

346 subtract 234 leaves 112. My estimate was 100 so my answer is reasonable.

Pupils work out the following subtraction calculations using the formal column method. They make an estimate, use base 10 equipment and draw diagrams as well as writing the standard algorithm.

HTU	HTU	HTU	HTU
234	576	634	862
123 -	342 -	412 -	641 -

Subtraction with decomposition (from tens to units)

What is 593 subtract 128?

Pupils write the question in the standard form and estimate the answer. They use base 10 equipment to help them explain their reasoning. Pupils worked with decomposition in subtraction in the work on place value. If they cannot remember how to decompose, the teacher explains how to proceed. (See p187)

What is 593 subtract 128? Write the question as a formal addition and work out an estimate.

H T U   Estimate: 600 - 100 = 500

5 9 3

1 2 8 -

Do the calculation and explain your thinking.

I start with the units column. 3 subtract 8. I cannot take 8 away from 3 so I need to change 1 ten into 10 units. Now there are 8 tens left and 13 in the units column.

H T U   Estimate: 600 - 100 = 500

5 ^{8}9 ^{1}3

1 2 8 -

13 take away 8 is 5. 8 tens take away 2 tens leaves 6 tens. 5 hundred minus 1 hundred leaves 4 hundred.

H T U   Estimate: 600 - 100 = 500

5 ^{8}9 ^{1}3

1 2 8 -

4 6 5

Check your answer against your estimate.

593 subtract 128 leaves 465. My estimate was 500 so my answer is reasonably close to my estimate.

Pupils work out the following questions using the formal column method.

HTU	HTU	HTU	HTU
953	752	286	543
524 -	235 -	147 -	327 -

Subtraction with decomposition (from hundreds to tens)

What is 638 subtract 254?

This time the decomposition will be from the hundreds column to the tens column. Pupils repeat the same subtraction procedure: write the formal algorithm, estimate the answer, and explain their thinking as they carry out the calculation. By now pupils should be able to explain their reasoning without prompting from the teacher, however if they struggle the teacher should encourage them by asking appropriate questions. Pupils should not need to use base 10 equipment, however they may use concrete material to check their answer when they have done the calculation.

```
H T U     Estimate: 600 - 300 = 300
6 3 8
2 5 4 -
_____
_____
```

```
 H T U     Estimate: 600 - 300 = 300
5 1
6 3 8
2 5 4 -
_____
3 8 4
```

The pupil explains the steps in the calculation. *What is 638 subtract 254? I round 638 down to 600 and round 254 up to 300. Then 600 take away 300 is 300. My estimate is 300.*

I start with the units column. 8 subtract 4 is 4. Then I need to do 30 take away 50. I cannot do this so I need to change 1 hundred into 10 tens. Now there are 500 in the hundreds column and 13 tens in the tens column. 130 take away 50 is 80.

Then I work out 500 subtract 200 which is 300. 638 subtract 254 is 384. My estimate was 300 so my answer is reasonable.

Pupils work out the following subtraction calculations using the formal column method.

```
HTU            HTU            HTU            HTU
925            867            635            462
343 -          373 -          451 -          281 -
```

Subtraction with decomposition in several place value columns

What is 531 subtract 278?

Pupils repeat the same subtraction procedure: write the formal algorithm, estimate the answer and explain their thinking as they carry out the calculation. This time the decomposition will be from the hundreds column to the tens column and from the tens column to the units column. Pupils should not need to use base 10 equipment.

```
H T U     Estimate: 500 - 300 = 200
5 3 1
2 7 8 -
_____
_____
```

```
H T U     Estimate: 500 - 300 = 200
  2  1
5 3 1
2 7 8 -
_____
      3
_____
```

```
H T U     Estimate: 500 - 300 = 200
4 12  1
5 3 1
2 7 8 -
_____
2 5 3
_____
```

What is 531 subtract 278? I round 531 down to 500 and round 278 up to 300. Then 500 take away 300 is 200. My estimate is 200.

I start with the units column. 1 subtract 8. I cannot take 8 away from 1 so I need to change 1 ten into 10 units. Now there are 2 tens left in the tens column and 11 in the units column. 11 take away 8 is 3.

Then I need to work out 20 subtract 70. I cannot do this so I need to change 1 hundred into 10 tens. Now there are 400 left in the hundreds column and 12 tens in the tens column.

120 take away 70 is 50.

Then I work out 400 take away 200 which is 200. 531 subtract 278 is 253. My estimate was 200 so my answer is reasonable.

Pupils work out the following subtraction calculations using the formal column method.

```
HTU            HTU            HTU            HTU
453            576            642            852
164 -          389 -          471 -          573 -
```

Checklist - Formal written subtraction

Pupils can:

☐ Model formal subtraction using base 10 equipment
☐ Use column subtraction to subtract multi-digit numbers with no decomposition
☐ Use column subtraction to subtract multi-digit numbers with decomposition
☐ Use estimation to check answers to calculations

Multiplication and division

Objectives
- Understand the box method of long multiplication
- Use the box method to multiply multi-digit numbers
- Explain reasoning and record it systematically as a diagram and equations
- Use the standard addition method for the addition part of the calculation

The traditional multiplication algorithm is very efficient but does not make the meaning of the calculation explicit. Pupils may not understand why a long multiplication requires both a multiplication calculation and an addition calculation. The box method, also known as the grid method, breaks the multiplication and addition into two distinct steps. It is called the box method because interim steps in the calculation are recorded in boxes in tabular form. Provided that it is taught in a multi-sensory way, it makes the stages of long multiplication and long division clear and leads on to the standard written method.

Start teaching with small numbers and work up to 3-digit numbers. Use the box method, which is based on the area model. Pupils demonstrate multiplication using concrete equipment, and record the calculation in a multiplication box. Once pupils understand the box method, they transfer this knowledge to the standard written method. When pupils can multiply 3-digit numbers they should be able to apply their skills to larger quantities by applying their reasoning skills.

The terms multiplier and multiplicand are used in order to simplify explanations in the instructions for teachers. However do not expect pupils to use this terminology. The multiplicand is the size of the group, or set, and the multiplier is the number of times it is repeated. The product is the result of a multiplication calculation. In the box method the multiplicand (quantity) is written along the top of the diagram and the multiplier (number of repetitions) is shown to the left of the boxes. It is important to maintain this structure as it lays the foundation for work on long division.

Teaching
Teach the box method in clear stages and do not move on until pupils have mastered each stage. Start with 2-digit numbers multiplied by a single digit, then a 2-digit number multiplied by a 2-digit number, and finally a 3-digit number multiplied by a 2-digit number.

The box method uses the area model to show multiplication by partitioning. The word 'box' is used because each place value product is recorded in a box diagram. This consists of a series of rectangles, or boxes, each of which represents a place value position. The product for the multiplication question is found by finding the total amount for all the boxes.

At each stage pupils:
- Write the multiplication question
- Partition the numbers into components
- Model multiplication using base 10 equipment or Cuisenaire rods
- Explain what the model represents
- Draw a box diagram and write the partitioned numbers in the appropriate places
- Calculate the quantity in each box
- Add up the products of all the boxes
- Write the answer in the form a x b = c

Remember to use transparent language. For example say '3 twelves' rather than '3 times 12'. Use of the form '3 twelves' is linguistically clearer: it emphasises that there will be 3 rows with 12 in each row.

2-digit x a single number
Teach pupils to draw the box diagram as well as recording their thinking in written form which can be transferred to the multiplication algorithm.

What are 4 fifteens? Write the question, then use base 10 equipment to build 4 fifteens using the area model. Describe it.

4 x 15 = ?
Pupil makes 15 using 1 ten and 5 units. They repeat this until they have 4 rows with 15 in each row.

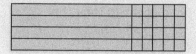

There are 4 rows with 15 in each row.

15 is made of 1 ten and 5 units.
15 = 10 + 5

What is 15 made of? Partition 15 into tens and units and write it as an equation.

Teacher demonstrates the box diagram whilst explaining. *Draw a diagram to show a box for the tens and a box for the units. Write 10 plus 5 at the top of the diagram with 10 above the tens box and 5 above the units box. This shows how many there are in each row. Write 4 to the left of the box to show how many rows there are. Write the multiplication sign at the top left of the box.*

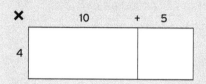

Ask the pupil to draw the box diagram.
What do 4 tens make? Write it in the tens box.
What do 4 fives make? Write it in the units box.

4 tens make 40.
4 fives make 20.

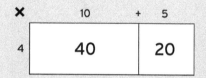

4 tens make 40 and 4 fives make 20. So what do 4 fifteens make?

I need to add 40 and 20 which makes 60.
4 fifteens make 60.

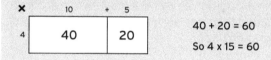

40 + 20 = 60
So 4 x 15 = 60

Pupils work out the following multiplication calculations using the box method.

3 x 24   4 x 54   5 x 36   6 x 23

2-digit x 2-digit numbers

Pupils use the same procedure for multiplying 2-digit numbers as they did with a single digit and a 2-digit number. Both the multiplicand and the multiplier must be partitioned into tens and units so now four boxes are required: two for the multiplicand and two for the multiplier. It is best if the teacher shows the pupil how the boxes are drawn below the existing boxes as the directional language becomes too complicated to explain it so it can be easily understood. Vary the language to include the word 'times'.

What is 12 times 34? Write the question, then model it using base 10 equipment. Describe it.

12 x 34 = ?
Pupils build 34 using a line of 3 tens and 4 units. They repeat this 12 times so that there are 12 rows with 34 in each row.

There are 12 rows with 34 in each row.

Partition 34 into tens and units and write it as an equation.
Partition 12 into tens and units and write it as an equation.

$34 = 30 + 4$

$12 = 10 + 2$

Draw and label a box diagram to show that 34 is partitioned into tens and units, and 12 is partitioned into tens and units.
Teacher demonstrates, then asks the pupil to draw the diagram.
When pupils understand what the boxes represent, they no longer need to make them proportional to the size of the quantities. Use a simple box with equal sized rectangles or squares.

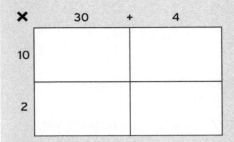

What does 10 times 30 make? Write it in the correct box.
What does 10 times 4 make? Write it in the correct box.
What does 2 times 30 make? Write it in the correct box.
What does 2 times 4 make? Write it in correct box.

10 times 30 makes 300.

10 times 4 makes 40.

2 times 30 makes 60,

2 times 4 makes 8.

✖	30	+ 4
10	300	40
2	60	8

When pupils have completed the calculation in each box, they add the quantities in each row and write the addition calculation as equations to the right of the box. Then they set the addition out as a formal addition as this will help them transfer to the traditional multiplication algorithm later. Even if pupils can do the calculations mentally they need to record it to establish the pattern for work with larger numbers.

Add the quantities in each row and write the equations. Then add the total for each row to work out 12 times 34.

✖	30	+ 4	
10	300	40	$300 + 40 = 340$
2	60	8	$60 + 8 = 68$

$$340 + 68 = 300 + 100 + 8$$
$$= 408$$

So $12 \times 34 = 408$

Show your addition calculation using the formal written method.

```
HTU
300
 40
 60
  8 +
408
```

Finally pupils need to write the answer to the original question as an equation.
What is 12 times 34? Write the answer.

12 times 34 makes 408.
Answer: $12 \times 34 = 408$

Pupils work out the following multiplication calculations using the box method. When pupils are confident about what the calculation represents, they can work directly with the multiplication box without using concrete materials.

25 x 43   34 x 52   56 x 74   68 x 83

2-digit x 3-digit numbers

At this point teachers may go directly to teaching standard long multiplication. However those pupils who cannot manage the traditional algorithm can continue to use the box method for calculation with multi-digit numbers.

The process for multiplying larger numbers is the same: now there will be 3 columns as the 3-digit number (the multiplicand) will be partitioned into hundreds, tens and units. By now pupils should be able to work directly into the structured box. Encourage them to set out the addition part of the calculation using the formal written method. Allow pupils to use concrete equipment if they wish to verify their answers as the size of the numbers means they are often quite intrigued and surprised by the scale of the concrete model.

Encourage the pupil to talk through their thinking without prompting. If they do need help, follow the steps used in the work with 2-digit numbers.

What is 35 times 256?
35 x 256 = ?

✖	200	50	6
30	6,000	1,500	180
5	1,000	250	30

6,000 + 1,500 + 180 = 7,680

1,000 + 250 + 30 = 1,280

```
       Thous.
       H T U H T U
           7 6 8 0
           1 2 8 0 +
           ---------
           8 9 6 0
             (1)
```

Answer: 35 x 256 = 8,960

Pupils work out the following multiplication calculations using the box method. They work directly with the multiplication box and record their thinking in diagrams, equations and use standard written addition. Allow them to use concrete equipment to model their answers if they are interested in seeing the size of the products.

256 x 34   416 x 36   689 x 53   709 x 75

Checklist - Multiplication and division
Pupils can:
- ☐ Understand the box method of long multiplication
- ☐ Use the box method to multiply multi-digit numbers
- ☐ Explain reasoning and record it systematically as a diagram and equations
- ☐ Use the standard addition method for the addition part of the calculation

Long multiplication

Objectives
- Use the standard written methods to multiply multi-digit numbers
- Link the standard written method to the box method
- Explain their reasoning
- Use estimation to check answers to calculations

The traditional multiplication algorithm, usually referred to as long multiplication, makes heavy demands on sequencing and memory but these can be reduced by teaching in a reasoning based way. At this stage pupils no longer use concrete materials but they may use informal jottings on the right hand side of the page to support their thinking.

Long multiplication relies on understanding partitioning. Pupils apply the strategies they learnt using the box method and record the results in a vertical format. It is reassuring to pupils to find that there is nothing new to learn about the calculations; it is merely a question of rearranging the layout on the page. However some pupils have developed such anxiety about long multiplication that it may be best to allow them to continue to use the box method.

Many pupils struggle with formal multiplication and find it extremely stressful. Long multiplication is often taught as a set of rules which pupils may not understand nor be able to remember. These instructions include 'add a zero' when multiplying by a tens number, and 'add 2 zeros' when multiplying by hundreds numbers. This is mathematically incorrect – adding a zero does not change the value of a number – and will not work when working with decimals.

Start teaching by multiplying a 2-digit number by a single digit. This is usually referred to as short multiplication and is an important step in learning to record multiplication in a vertical format. In the partitioning approach, 'the 2-digit number in a short multiplication question is broken down into its constituent values; each value is multiplied separately by the single digit multiplier and then the partial values are combined' (Yeo 2003). Initially pupils use place value headings (HTU) to reinforce the idea that whole numbers are being multiplied rather than a series of digits. Remember to write HTU even when only two digits are used as this reinforces the place value structure of the repeated triple.

Teaching

Pupils set their work out to allow sufficient space on the right hand side of the page for jottings and sketches to help their reasoning. It is important that they write the estimate before they start any calculation.

We are going to look at the formal written way of doing multiplication. You use the same layout as you did for addition using the HTU headings. Write the place value headings HTU. Write the numbers you want to multiply underneath each other in the correct places. You write the bigger number first, and then write the smaller number underneath. Draw a line underneath the bottom number. Write the multiplication sign to the right of the bottom number.

2-digit x single digit

What is 4 times 32? Set it out using the formal written method. Estimate the answer.

```
H  T  U        Estimate: 4 × 30 = 120
   3  2
      4 ×
   _____
```

32 rounds down to 30. I know 4 threes are 12 so 4 times 30 is 120. My estimate is 120.

Now work out 32 times 4. Start by working out 4 twos. Talk about what you are doing.

4 twos make 8. I write 8 in the units column.

```
H  T  U        Estimate: 4 × 30 = 120
   3  2
      4 ×
   ──────
      8
```

4 threes are 12 so 4 times 30 makes 120.

What is 4 times 30? Write the answer on the line underneath 8.

It is important to name the actual value of the numbers being multiplied. This avoids any confusion about where to write zeros in the partial products.

Now show your workings using the box method.

Look at the box method. What did you do after you multiplied 30 by 4?
The formal way of describing these answers is partial products but it is not necessary for pupils to use the term.

Now look at the long multiplication. What do you need to do next?
Write a plus sign next to 120. Draw a line underneath 120 to show where the answer will be. Do the calculation.

```
H  T  U        Estimate: 4 × 30 = 120
   3  2      ×   30   +   2
      4 ×   ┌──────┬──────┐
   ──────  4│ 120  │  8   │ 120 + 8 = 128
      8     └──────┴──────┘
1  2  0
```

I added 120 and 8 which makes 128.

I need to add 8 and 120.

```
H  T  U        Estimate: 4 × 30 = 120
   3  2      ×   30   +   2
      4 ×   ┌──────┬──────┐
   ──────  4│ 120  │  8   │ 120 + 8 = 128
      8     └──────┴──────┘
1  2  0 +
──────
1  2  8
```

Check your answer against your estimate.

32 times 4 is 128. My estimate was 120 so my answer is close to the estimate.

Pupils work out the following questions using long multiplication. They make an estimate before starting any calculation. Pupils may sketch the box method if they need it to help express their reasoning.

```
HTU            HTU            HTU            HTU
 21             43             32            123
  3 x            2 x            4 x            2 x
────           ────           ────           ────
```

2-digit x 2-digit

Pupils repeat the same multiplication procedure: write the long multiplication question, estimate the answer, and then use the standard long multiplication method. Pupils may sketch the box method to help them reason through the steps.

What is 23 times 16? Estimate the answer. Then work out the long multiplication and describe what you are doing.

It is essential that pupils say what value each number represents, not merely the name of the digit.

23 rounds down to 20. 16 rounds up to 20. 20 times 20 is 400. My estimate is 400.

```
H  T  U        Estimate: 20 × 20 = 400
   2  3
   1  6 ×
   ──────
```

Pupil records the answers on separate lines as they explain:
6 threes make 18, and 6 times 20 makes 120.

After that they multiply by the tens number and record the answers on separate lines.
10 threes are 30 and 10 times 20 makes 200.

```
H  T  U        Estimate: 20 × 20 = 400
   2  3
   1  6 ×
  _____
   1  8
1  2  0
   3  0
2  0  0
_____
```

Complete the calculation. Explain what you do.
Ensure that the pupil writes the addition sign.

Now I need to add the answers. There are 8 in the units column. 10 add 20 add 30 makes 60 Then 100 add 200 is 300.

```
H  T  U        Estimate: 20 × 20 = 400
   2  3
   1  6 ×
  _____
   1  8
1  2  0
   3  0
2  0  0 +
_____
3  6  8
```

Check your answer against your estimate.

23 times 16 makes 368. My estimate was 400. My answer is reasonably close to my estimate.

Pupils work out the following questions using long multiplication. They make an estimate before starting any calculation. Pupils may sketch the box method if they need it to help them express their reasoning.

HTU	HTU	HTU	HTU
26	32	42	67
13 x	26 x	35 x	48 x

Checklist - Long multiplication
Pupils can:
- ☐ Use the standard written methods to multiply multi-digit numbers
- ☐ Link the standard written method to the box method
- ☐ Explain their reasoning
- ☐ Use estimation to check answers to calculations

Formal division methods

Objectives
- Model short division using the area model
- Link division to the box method of multiplication
- Explain reasoning using sketches and equations to help
- Use estimation to check answers to calculations

Teach the formal division method in a multi-sensory way emphasising the inverse relationship between multiplication and division. The formal division algorithm can be directly related to both the array model of multiplication and the box method. The layout of the division algorithm is visually different to the other arithmetical operations and requires pupils to work in different directions – left to right, bottom to top.

It is not necessary for pupils to learn the formal names of the different parts of the division calculation, however the terms dividend, divisor and quotient are used here for ease of explanation. The quantity to be divided is called the dividend. The divisor is the number by which the dividend is divided. The quotient is the answer – the result of dividing the dividend by the divisor. For example in the equation $15 \div 3 = 5$ the dividend is 15, the divisor is 3 and the quotient is 5. In the written division algorithm the dividend is partially enclosed by a vertical and horizontal line. The divisor is written to the left of the dividend and the quotient is written above the dividend. A distinction is made between short division in which the divisor is a single digit number, and long division where the divisor is a multi-digit number.

The rectangular shape of the array in the concrete model makes the layout of formal division explicit; it is clear to see that the total number of objects represents the dividend, the number of rows represents the divisor and the quotient is the number of objects in each row.

The pre-skills required to work with formal division are:
- The ability to partition numbers flexibly
- Knowledge of time tables
- Understanding place value
- Understanding the box method of multiplication
- Understanding the inverse relationship between division and multiplication
- Understanding the array and area models of multiplication
- Understanding subtraction as finding the difference.

Teaching

Short division with no remainders
First teach pupils how to set out the formal division algorithm.

We are going to look at the formal written way of doing division.
What is $15 \div 3$? Use counters to make an array to show me what it means.
Pupils who cannot do this are not ready to tackle formal division and need to do more work on understanding the concept of division (see p168).
How many counters are there?
How many rows are there?

Draw a diagram like the one you used in the box method to show what you have done.
If the pupil has difficulty, the teacher draws the diagram to show the relationship between 3, 5 and 15.
Can you work out what 15 divided by 3 is?

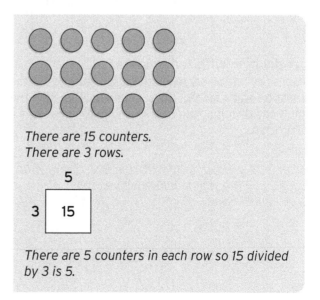

There are 15 counters.
There are 3 rows.

There are 5 counters in each row so 15 divided by 3 is 5.

Teacher demonstrates how to set out the formal division method.

Formal division is set out in a way that is similar to the box and the array. Now you only draw two sides of the rectangle – the top and the left. Write the quantity you have where the box would be. Write a question mark above the line to show where the answer will go.

$$\overset{?}{3\,|\,\overline{15}}$$

Encourage pupils to write the question mark to show where the answer will be found, until they are familiar with the structure of the division algorithm.

What is 128 divided by 4? Write the question in your book using the standard division method.

Work out an estimate for the answer.

I round 128 to 120. I know that 12 divided by 4 is 3 so 120 divided by 4 is 30.

$$\overset{?}{4\,|\,\overline{128}}$$ Estimate: 120 ÷ 4 = 30

Use base 10 equipment to model 128. Then divide it by 4. Explain what you are doing.

Pupil puts out 1 hundred square, 2 tens and 8 units. They need to explain in their own words that they need to exchange the 100 square for 10 tens. When they have done the exchange, they show the question as an array and explain their reasoning.

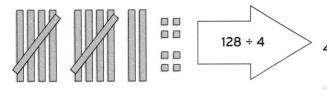

128 ÷ 4

4 rows

30   +   2

12 divided by 4 is 3 so 120 divided by 4 is 30. Then 8 divided by 4 is 2. There are 3 tens and 2 units in each row so 128 divided by 4 is 32.

Write the calculation as a formal written division.

$$\overset{3\;2}{4\,|\,\overline{128}}$$

Check your answer against your estimate.

128 divided by 4 is 32. My estimate was 30 so my answer is close to the estimate.

Pupils work out the following questions using short division. They do need to make an estimate before starting any calculation. They do not need to use concrete equipment if they can work without it.

39 ÷ 3   85 ÷ 5   132 ÷ 4   126 ÷ 6

Short division with remainders

Pupils repeat the same division procedure: write the division question, estimate the answer, model the question and work out the calculation. This time the recording is slightly different as pupils need to show the decompositions. They need to make sure that they allow sufficient space when they write the algorithm.

What is 74 divided by 3? Write the question in your book using the standard division method.
Give an estimate.

I round 74 down to 70. I can't divide 70 by 3 easily but I can divide 60 by 3. 6 divided by 3 is 2 so 60 divided by 3 will be 20. If I divide 70 by 3 my answer will be a bit more than 20.

$$\overset{?}{3\,|\,\overline{74}}$$ Estimate: 70 ÷ 3 = ?
                                          60 ÷ 3 = 20

Model the division and explain your thinking.

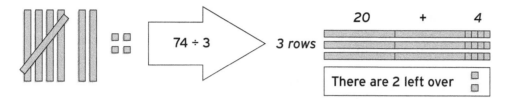

$74 \div 3$ 3 rows

20   +   4

There are 2 left over

Record your thinking and show the exchanges. If a pupil has difficulty doing this, the teacher demonstrates.

Check your answer against your estimate.

2 4 Rem. 2

$3\overline{)6\,7\,{}^{1}4}$

74 divided by 3 is 24 with remainder 2. My estimate was 20 so my answer is close to the estimate.

Pupils work out the following questions and record the calculations using the standard method. They need to make an estimate before starting any calculation. It is essential that pupils solve division word problems as the context dictates whether the remainder is 'left over' or has to be taken into account. For example:

There were 10 biscuits. 4 children ate 2 biscuits each. How many biscuits were left? Answer: 2 biscuits were left.

There are 7 people. How many cars do they need if 4 people fit in 1 car? Answer: They need 2 cars. (It is understood that the cars do not need to be full.)

$47 \div 2$ $78 \div 3$ $247 \div 3$ $354 \div 5$

Checklist – Formal division methods
Pupils can:
- ☐ Model short division using the area model
- ☐ Link division to the box method of multiplication
- ☐ Explain reasoning using sketches and equations to help
- ☐ Use estimation to check answers to calculations

Long division

Objectives
- Model long division
- Use the standard division algorithm
- Explain and record the calculations in the division algorithm
- Use estimation to check answers to calculations

Long division is used when the divisor has two or more digits. The algorithm is an efficient but very condensed method of recording the calculation. It relates directly to the area model of multiplication.

Pupils are often afraid of formal division because it involves a complex sequence of steps. This is compounded by directional difficulties caused by working from left to right, whereas in formal work with addition, subtraction and multiplication the calculation starts with the units which are on the right of the place value grid. It may be too difficult for pupils with directional, sequencing or memory problems to learn the set of instructions; however they can learn to use long division if they use concrete materials to help them reason through the steps logically.

Many pupils do not understand the role of subtraction in the division calculation. This may be caused by confusion between the chunking method of division and the area model. The chunking method involves repeated subtraction. Here the subtraction concept is 'take away'. The division algorithm links to the area model of multiplication. Here the subtraction part of the procedure is based on the concept of difference. Part of the dividend is divided, and then subtraction is used to find how much more is still to be divided.

Use base 10 equipment. Teach pupils to model, and informally record, each step of their reasoning as well as doing the formal recording, to make the underlying structure of the algorithm explicit. Only introduce long division with remainders once pupils have mastered long division without remainders. It is essential that pupils also work with numbers in context. In some cases the remainder will be left over, in others it needs to be taken into account.

Teaching

Long division with no remainder
Pupils write the division question, estimate the answer, model the question, describe their thinking as they work out the calculation and then record their working. Pupils use their knowledge of the inverse relationship between division and multiplication as well as rounding and adjusting to help them work out the calculation. They record their thinking informally in a box diagram and equations to make it clear how the information in the formal algorithm is derived. It can be helpful to write HTU headings above the algorithm in the initial stages.

What is 384 divided by 24? Write the question in your book using the standard division method. Give an estimate.
Pupils do not need to write the question mark if they know where the answer is to be found.

I round 384 up to 400. I round 24 down to 20. So 400 divided by 20 is 20. My estimate is 20.

$$24\overline{)384} \qquad \text{Estimate: } 400 \div 20 = 20$$

Model the division and explain your thinking. Record your thinking as a box diagram and in equations.

Pupil builds 384 using base 10 equipment. They explain in their own words how they divide the quantity of 384 by 24.

The pupil uses the equipment to model the question and show the first stage of the calculation.

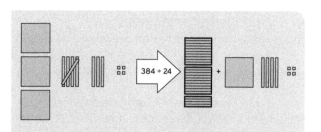

I need to divide 384 by 24. 24 tens make 240. I put out 24 rows with 10 in each row. I have used 240. There are 144 left.

When the pupil has recorded the calculation in the workings section, the teacher shows how it can be laid out in the long division algorithm in exactly the same form as the formal subtraction.

```
      1       Estimate: 400 ÷ 20 = 20
24 | 3 8 4    24 x 10 = 240 = 200 + 40
    2 4 0 -           10   +
    ─────          ┌──────┬──────┐
    1 4 4       20 │ 200  │      │
                   ├──────┼──────┤
                 4 │  40  │      │
                   └──────┴──────┘
```

Now you have to divide 144 by 24. Reason to work out the answer before you use the equipment.

Guide the pupil to use trial and error to work out the answer to 144 ÷ 24 by reasoning. They use the inverse relationship between multiplication and division to reframe the question as 24 x ? = 144. They record their trial and error attempts and show the answer in the box diagram.

Pupil uses trial and error and uses their own words. *I can write 144 divided by 24 as 24 times what makes 144? There are only 144 left so there will be less than 10 in each row. 24 tens are 240. Half of 10 is 5 so half of 240 is 120. That means 24 fives make 120. That is not enough. I need to try 24 sixes. 24 sixes are 144. So 144 divided by 24 is 6.*

```
    1 6      Estimate: 400 ÷ 20 = 20
24 | 3 8 4   24 x 10 = 240 = 200 + 40
   2 4 0 -        x    10   +   6
   ─────        ┌──────┬──────┐
   1 4 4     20 │ 200  │ 120  │
   1 4 4 -      ├──────┼──────┤
   ─────      4 │  40  │  24  │
       0        └──────┴──────┘

              24 x ? = 144
              24 x 5 = 120
              24 x 6 = 144
```

Adjust the model to check your answer.

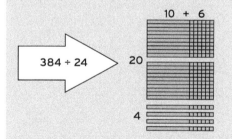

Check your answer against your estimate.

384 divided by 24 is 16. My estimate was 20 so my answer is close to the estimate.

Pupils work out the following questions using long division. They make an estimate before starting any calculation.

52 ÷ 26   75 ÷ 15   368 ÷ 16   117 ÷ 39

Long division with remainders

Pupils repeat the long division procedure as they did above. By now pupils should be able to explain their reasoning without prompting from the teacher. They do the calculation and explain their thinking before using the equipment to check their reasoning.

What is 335 divided by 23? Estimate the answer. Do the calculation showing your working. Do not use equipment until you have completed the calculation. Then model the question to check your answer.

23 | 335   Estimate: 300 ÷ 20 = 15

```
        1      Estimate: 300 ÷ 20 = 15
23 | 3 3 5     23 × 10 = 230 = 200 + 30
     2 3 0 -          ×    10
     1 0 5      20 | 200 |
                 3 |  30  |
```

```
      1 4      Estimate: 300 ÷ 20 = 15
23 | 3 3 5     23 × 10 = 230 = 200 + 30
     2 3 0 -         ×   10  +  4
     1 0 5      20 | 200 | 80 |
       9 2 -     3 |  30 | 52 |
       1 3
```

23 × ? = 105
23 × 5 = 115
23 × 4 = 92

The pupil explains the steps in the calculation. *What is 335 divided by 23? I round 335 down to 300 and round 23 down to 20. Then 300 divided by 20 makes 15. My estimate is 15.*

I need to find 335 divided by 23. 23 tens make 230. I can show this in a box diagram. 20 tens are 200 and 3 tens are 30. Now I need to find out how many I still need to divide by 23. I work out 335 take away 230 which is 105.

Once the pupil has established that 335 divided by 23 is 10 with 105 still to be divided, they use trial and error.

I need to find 105 divided by 23. 23 tens are 230. Half of 10 is 5 so half of 230 is 115. There are only 105 so the answer will be less than 5. 23 fours are 92 so 105 divided by 23 will be 4 with some left over.

I need to find the difference between 105 and 92. The remainder is 13.

335 divided by 23 is 14 remainder 13. My estimate was 15 so my answer is close to the estimate.

Modelling 335 divided by 23

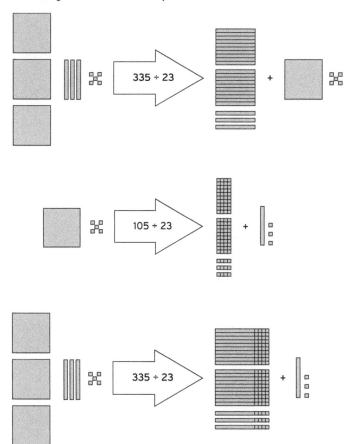

335 ÷ 23 = 14 remainder 13

Pupils work out the following questions using long division. They make an estimate before starting any calculation. It is essential that pupils solve division word problems as the context dictates whether the remainder is 'left over' or has to be taken in to account. (See p226)

57 ÷ 25	96 ÷ 23	142 ÷ 34	319 ÷ 53

173 men from Mars wanted to get on a star ship. Each star ship has 28 seats. How many men were left behind?

173 men from Mars wanted to go to earth. Each star ship has 28 seats. How many star ships did they need?

Checklist – Long division
Pupils can:
- ☐ Model long division
- ☐ Use the standard division algorithm
- ☐ Explain and record the calculations in the division algorithm
- ☐ Use estimation to check answers to calculations

10

Word problems

Word problems place numbers in contexts. Through tackling word problems, pupils learn the fundamental skills of problem solving which are: identify the components of the problem, plan effective action and review the result to make sure it makes sense. Even pupils who cannot read can tackle word problems. Read the questions to them and they can jot down information as drawings or diagrams in order to recall the information as they work on the solution.

The key to successful problem solving is being able to ask the relevant questions. It is helpful to provide a flexible framework to get pupils started. It is important that pupils present their thinking clearly both diagrammatically and in written forms.

- What do you want to find out?
- What information do you have?
- How can you summarise the relevant information?
- What is a sensible estimate?
- How do you express the problem in numerical terms?
- Which arithmetical operation is required? Is there more than one possibility?
- Does the answer make sense?

The aim is for pupils to develop confidence in their own ability to tackle word problems - being allowed to make mistakes is part of that process so it is important not to lead them step by step for too long.

Creating word problems

Good word problems will engage curiosity and encourage experimentation. Problem solving is about exploring how best to tackle the question, not merely finding the answer. 'Problems... should offer students a rich context for organisation and elaboration, not a context in which everything is already prepared and the only thing a student has to do is find the correct solution' (Van den Heuvel-Panhuizen, 2000).

Word problems may involve one step to find the solution, or two or more steps. Restrict questions to one-step problems until pupils are able to cope with detailed scenarios and can record their thinking clearly.

Construct word problems that are appropriate to the pupils' age and level of numerical understanding. It is easier to understand questions that are written in the simple past tense. Keep questions short initially with clear, transparent language that is not too condensed. Early word problems should contain a minimal amount of information so that there are few distracting details. Use letters rather than numbers when presenting a list of written word problems as some pupils are confused by the use of numbering as they are not sure if the list number forms part of the question.

Gradually introduce increasing complexity by giving more detailed scenarios so that pupils have to work to identify the question and extract the relevant information. Keep the numbers small whilst making the context more complex in order to prevent pupils guessing the operation from the size of the numbers. Sometimes pupils reason that larger numbers indicate that addition or subtraction is required as they are unlikely to be asked to multiply them. More complex calculations are introduced gradually as the pupils' confidence increases.

Make questions more complex by including different categories. In the example below cats and dogs both belong to the category of pets.

Kim had 5 cats and 5 dogs. How many pets did she have?

Gradually introduce more detail into the questions so that pupils have to think about the information in order to extract what is relevant.

Jon played 7-a-side rugby in the rain with some friends. Jon scored a try worth 5 points and then converted it to score another 2 points. How many points did Jon score for his team?

Pupils need to infer information that is not given and learn to draw upon their knowledge of the real world. In the following example the 'week' is 5 days long as school is not open at weekends.

Ben lives 3 km away from the school. He always walks. How far does he walk every week?

When pupils can confidently solve questions which require a single operation, introduce 2-step questions.

Emma runs around the park every week day. At the end of the week she has run 30 miles. Her dad sponsors her 30p per day. How much does she get for each mile?

Ensure that pupils also create their own word problems. Throughout this book pupils have used concrete equipment to support their thinking and develop visual images. Counters or unit cubes and tens rods have provided representations of numbers. It is then a small step to imagine that the equipment represents other items such as animals, cars, or cartoon characters. 'The fantasy world of fairy tales and even the formal world of mathematics can provide suitable contexts for a problem, as long as they are real in the student's mind' (Van den Heuvel-Panhuizen, 2000).

Types of word problems

Word problems can be classified into categories on the basis of their semantic structure (Anghileri 2006). It is helpful for teachers to be aware of the different types of word problems but pupils do not need to learn to identify them by naming the operation, although some pupils find this helpful.

Addition
- Combine: Two groups put together to create one new group.
- Change: Increase an initial quantity; change it by adding items.

Subtraction
- Change: Decrease an initial quantity; change it by subtracting items.
- Comparison: Two groups are compared by finding the difference between them.

Multiplication
- Repeated addition: Several same-sized groups can be added together.
- Array model: Objects are arranged in rows and columns to create a rectangle.
- Area model: Unit squares are arranged in rows and columns to create a rectangle.

Division
- Grouping: The quantity in each group is known. The number of groups is unknown. (The grouping model links directly with multiplication.)
- Sharing: The number of groups is known. The quantity of items in each group is unknown. The answer is found by sharing the items equally between the groups.

Avoid teaching cue or trigger words to identify the operation required as this can be misleading. For example, pupils are often taught that the word 'altogether' indicates addition, however that is not necessarily the case; it may require multiplication or subtraction. Consider the following questions:

- *Tom has 3 apples and Sam has 2 apples. How many apples do they have altogether?* (Addition)
- *There are 6 plates of biscuits. Each plate has 4 biscuits. How many biscuits are there altogether?* (Multiplication)
- *There were 10 people on a bus. 5 people got off at the first stop and 3 people got on. How many people altogether are now on the bus?* (Addition and subtraction)

Numbers to 10: basic problem solving

Objectives
- Identify what the question is asking
- Extract relevant information and draw clear diagrams to represent it
- Use number lines, triads, and equations to communicate thinking
- Write the answer as a full sentence
- Make up their own word problems

Introduce word problems as soon as pupils have some counting skills. Use varied language appropriate to the pupils' age and level of competency. Counting forwards and back a short distance is a form of early calculation. Adding 1 or 2 more, or finding 1 or 2 less than a quantity is the first stage in calculation. Then move on to problems using the key facts.

Teach pupils a basic structure of problem solving to help them get started. The key elements of problem solving are: What is the question asking? What do I know? How can I show the information in a diagram? How do I calculate the answer? Does the answer make sense?

Establish the habit of drawing diagrams to show what the question means. This enables pupils who cannot read or write to communicate their thoughts on paper as well as helping to develop visualisation skills. This work lays the foundations for later work using charts and graphs. Remind pupils that it is not an art lesson; they need to draw quick sketches to avoid time being wasted. As soon as pupils can write numbers ask them to label the diagrams by writing the number next to each group of objects. When they are ready to do so, ask them to write the equation that the drawings represent using the equals sign. Allow pupils to lay out their diagrams in any configuration as long as it is tidy and clear. It is important for pupils to learn that they have the freedom to communicate information in the way they wish to. If they are told to present their drawings in a particular format, an essential part of the investigative nature of word problems is lost and pupils may come to see them as formulaic (De Corte, 2000). Later they will learn to use pictograms, charts and graphs but the drawings should remain their own.

Give pupils written questions if they are able to read. Vary the format of the word problems. It is particularly important to include missing addend (mystery number) questions as well as addition and subtraction, as the missing addend helps to understand the inverse relationship between addition and subtraction. Pupils should create their own questions as well as answering set questions.

Teaching

Drawing to summarise information
Start with oral questions. Pupils draw sketches to summarise information. If necessary, pupils may use concrete equipment to model the questions before drawing the diagrams. Encourage pupils to produce work that is clear and easy to follow. Producing a simple yet clear diagram can have a dramatic effect on their level of confidence.

Jack has 6 cars. He gets 1 more. How many cars does Jack have?

We are going to work on some word problems. I want you to draw pictures to show what the question is about. Jack has 6 cars. He gets 1 more.

Jack has 7 cars.

How many cars does Jack have? Encourage pupils to point to each item in the picture as it is counted.

Anna had 3 stickers. Her teacher gave her 1 more. How many stickers did she have then?
There were 5 lettuces. A rabbit ate 2 of them. How many lettuces were left?

The process of enquiry: question the question

The teacher models questions to demonstrate how to examine a problem. Gradually encourage the pupils to ask the questions. Pupils set out their work so it is clear to a reader.

It is important that pupils write the answer as a full sentence. Experience has shown that they do not always relate the answer to the question being asked, even with simple, short questions.

John had 3 apples and his friend gave him 3 more. How many did John have then?

Read the question. What do you want to find out?

Summarise the question. That helps you remember what the question is asking. Write 'How many apples? Isolating the key feature of the question helps pupils to focus on what is relevant in the question.

What do you know?

Draw a diagram to show the apples.

How can you use numbers to find the answer? Encourage pupils to use a triad formation and write the equation.

What do you want to find out? Work out the answer.

Write the answer as a sentence.

How many apples John had in the end.

Pupil writes: How many apples?
Make sure the pupil writes the question mark even though it is a phrase not a full sentence.

John had 3 apples. He got 3 more.

How many apples?

🍎🍎🍎   🍎🍎🍎

?

3   3   3 + 3 = 6

I want to find how many apples there were in the end. 3 and 3 makes 6 so John had 6 apples altogether.

John had 6 apples.

Jake has 4 sweets. His sister gives him 5 more. How many sweets does Jake have now? (4 + 5 = ?)

Roger had 7 tennis balls. He lost 2. How many did he have left? (7 - 5 = ? or 5 + ? = 7)

Cod costs £6 per kilo and tuna costs £4 per kilo. Len bought 1 kilo of each fish. How much did he spend? (6 + 4 = ?)

Ian scored 7 goals. Ben scored 10 goals. How many fewer goals did Ian score? (10 - 7 = ? or 7 + ? = 10)

Tom had 5 crayons. His Mum gave him 3 crayons. How many crayons did dad give him? (5 - 3 = ? or 3 + ? = 5)

Two-step questions: Numbers to 10

Rob had 10p to spend at the school fair. He bought a biscuit for 3p and a drink for 4p. How much change did he get?

Tim gave half his conkers to his brother then he found 2 more. Now Tim has 6 conkers. How many conkers did Tim start with?

Checklist – Numbers to 10: basic problem solving

Pupils can:
- ☐ Identify what the question is asking
- ☐ Extract relevant information and draw clear diagrams to represent it.
- ☐ Use number lines, triads, and equations to communicate thinking
- ☐ Write the answer as a full sentence
- ☐ Make up their own word problems

Numbers to 20: addition and subtraction

Objectives

- Apply systematic problem solving skills
- Represent information in pictograms and tally charts
- Use number lines to compare quantities
- Write the equation and write the answer as a full sentence
- Make up their own word problems

Pupils analyse the information to work out the relationship between the components of the question. Are they combined, changed or compared? Start with questions in which 2 quantities are combined to create a single larger quantity. Here the outcome is unknown and the question is posed in the form a + b = ? Missing addend questions are also known as 'mystery number' problems. These are conceptually much more difficult as the outcome is known and pupils need to find one of the components. They are written in the form a + ? = c, or ? + b = c. Use triads to record 'mystery numbers' to make the relationship between the numbers clear. As pupils become more proficient they should use number lines to convey their thinking.

Change questions need to be carefully interpreted to work out whether the initial quantity is increased or decreased. Some pupils find change a very difficult concept to understand. In comparison questions, two quantities are compared in order to find the difference between them, or to equalise them. Equalising problems are useful for encouraging mental manipulations of the numbers. Comparison problems may be solved by subtraction or complementary addition.

Number lines are particularly appropriate for comparison questions and should be used to show the reasoning. Next teach pupils to formalise their diagrams by constructing pictograms. Pictograms are set out as a table in which one icon represents one item. (Later icons can represent groups of objects but that will be taught at a much later stage.)

Build pupils' confidence by posing a few questions using the number bonds to 10 before asking questions involving the number bonds to 20 as well as bridging through 10. Start with short questions containing minimal detail and gradually introduce more complex scenarios. It is important that pupils also construct their own word problems.

Teaching

Pupils work through each problem systematically. Encourage them to start posing the necessary questions by talking aloud as they go through the problem-solving process. What is the question asking? What information do I have? How can I show the information in a diagram? How do I record my reasoning on a number line? What is my estimate of the answer? How do I calculate the answer? How do I express the question as an equation? Write the answer as a full sentence. Teacher asks questions to prompt the pupil's thinking.

The teacher demonstrates how to draw a pictogram. Icons are arranged in a systematic way so that the correspondence between the items in both rows is clear.

Combine questions

Pat saw 14 crows in an oak tree and 8 ducks on the pond in the park. How many birds did she see?

Read the question. What do you want to find out?	Pupil reads the question aloud. *I need to find out 'How many birds?'*
What do you know?	*There are 14 crows and 8 ducks.*
How do you estimate the answer?	*I round 14 down to 10 and I round 8 up to 10. My estimate is 10 add 10 which is 20.*

Can you show the information as a pictogram?

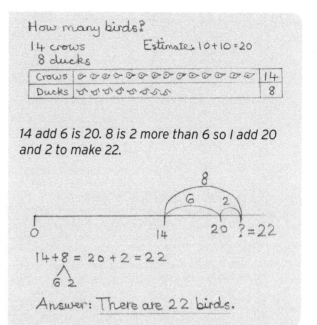

Can you show the question on a number line and explain your working?

14 add 6 is 20. 8 is 2 more than 6 so I add 20 and 2 to make 22.

Write the answer as a sentence.

Tom baked some loaves of bread. He needed 7 grams of yeast for the white loaf and 10 grams of yeast for the brown loaf. How much yeast did he use? (7g + 10g = ?)

Change questions (outcome is unknown)

Paul had 12 stickers and lost 6 of them. How many did he have left? (12 - 6 = ? or 6 + ? = 12)

Gemma made a daisy chain that was 12 cm long. She increased the length by 8 cm. How long was the daisy chain when she finished? (12 + 8 = ?)

Change questions (outcome is known)
These questions can be written as missing addend (mystery number) questions or as subtraction questions.

Carly has 8 DVDs. She bought 5 yesterday. How many did she buy today?
(5 + ? = 8 or 8 = 5 + ? or 8 - 5 = ?)

The temperature is 18 degrees. How much must the temperature decrease to get down to 8 degrees? (18 - ? = 8 or 8 + ? = 18)

Sam had some coins in his pocket when he left school and found 3 more coins on the way home. When he checked his pockets he found he had 10 coins altogether. How many coins did he have to start with? (? + 3 = 10 or 10 = ? + 3 or 10 - 3 = ?)

Comparison: difference
The teacher demonstrates how to record information in a tally chart.

Ben has 8 sheep and Sam has 14 sheep. How many more sheep does Sam have than Ben?

What do you do first?

I read the question. I need to find 'how many more sheep'.

What do you do next?

I look for information and write it down.
Ben has 8 sheep and Sam has 14 sheep.

How many more sheep?

Ben 8 sheep
Sam 14 sheep

How can you show the information?

I draw a tally chart to show the difference in the numbers of sheep. I draw 2 number lines so I can compare them.

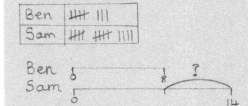

| Ben | ⵏⵏⵏⵏ ||| |
| Sam | ⵏⵏⵏⵏ ⵏⵏⵏⵏ |||| |

Ben
Sam

How do you write the question in numbers?
Can you explain your working?

I can write it as a mystery number question. I find the difference between 8 and 14. 8 and 2 is 10. Then I need to add 4 more to get to 14. So I need to add 6 to 8 to make 14.

$$8 + ? = 14 \qquad 14 - 8 = ?$$
$$14 - 8 = 10 + 4 - 8$$
$$10 \quad 4$$
$$= 10 - 4$$
$$= 6$$

Answer: Sam has 6 more sheep.

What is the answer?

Mary is 11 years old. Josh is 15 years old. How much older is Josh than Mary?
(11 + ? = 15 or 15 = 11 + ? or 15 − 11 = ?)

Abi cycled 18 miles. She cycled 12 miles further than Tom cycled. How much further did Abi cycle than Tom? (? + 12 = 18 or 18 = ? + 12 or 18 − 12 = ?)

Comparison equalising

Bill scored 15 goals. Ted scored 6 goals. How many more goals did Ted need to have the same score as Bill? (6 + ? = 15 or 15 = 6 + ? or 15 − 6 = ?)

Kevin grew a bean plant that was 16 cm high. Jake's bean plant was 9 cm high. How much more did Jake's plant grow to reach the same size as Kevin's plant?
(9 + ? = 16 or 16 = 9 + ? or 16 − 9 = ?)

Sam downloaded 14 songs on iTunes. If Amy downloads 8 songs on iTunes, she will have the same number of songs as Sam. How many songs does Amy have now?
(? + 8 = 14 or 14 = ? + 8 or 14 − 8 = ?)

Two-step questions: Numbers to 20

The farmer had 8 hens. She got 6 more. Half of the hens laid eggs yesterday. How many eggs did they lay?

Will had 13 sweets. He ate 3 then gave half of the rest to his sister. How many sweets did his sister get?

A sparkly necklace costs £20. Ann earned £7 for babysitting on Thursday and £6 for working last night. How much more does she need to buy the necklace?

Checklist − Numbers to 20: addition and subtraction

Pupils can:
- ☐ Apply systematic problem solving skills
- ☐ Represent information in pictograms and tally charts
- ☐ Use number lines to compare quantities
- ☐ Write the equation and write the answer as a full sentence
- ☐ Make up their own word problems

Numbers to 100: the four operations in context

Objectives

- Tackle questions without prompting from the teacher
- Select appropriate methods to communicate thinking
- Solve combine, change and compare questions
- Solve problems involving equal groups, arrays and the area model
- Make up their own word problems

Pupils need to develop confidence in their own ability to tackle word problems - being allowed to make mistakes is part of that process so it is important not to lead them step by step for too long. By now, pupils should take control of the investigative process in problem solving. They may continue to use equipment to model questions to support their reasoning.

Pupils work with larger quantities to solve problems in which numbers are combined, changed or compared. Then they use the operations of multiplication and division in contexts.

The concepts of multiplication and division as equal sized groups can cover a variety of situations. It is easiest to understand questions about equivalent groups, or equivalent measurement. Then move on to using the array and area models. These are similar in that elements are arranged in a rectangular formation. The area model is used to measure two-dimensional space. This is essential for practical real world situations, such as carpeting a floor. Understanding the area model is important for later work with fractions.

Teaching

Pupils should start to tackle the questions without prompting from the teacher. The script below is given as an example of the kind of thinking they might use. It is important that pupils use their own language and investigate the problem in their own way, even if it is different to the suggested structure. The aim is for pupils to explore numbers and develop their reasoning skills.

Pupils work through each problem systematically using questions to help them to reason logically. What is the question asking? What information do I have? How can I show the information in a diagram? How do I record my reasoning on a number line? How do I calculate the answer? How do I express the question as an equation? I must give the answer as a full sentence.

Combine, change or compare (addition and subtraction)

Jane scored 32 runs in the first innings and 27 runs in the second innings. What was her total score for the match?

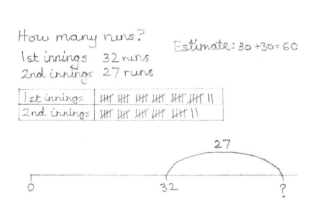

How many runs?

Estimate: 30 + 30 = 60

1st innings   32 runs
2nd innings   27 runs

| 1st innings | ᵁᴴᵀ ᵁᴴᵀ ᵁᴴᵀ ᵁᴴᵀ ᵁᴴᵀ ᵁᴴᵀ II |
| 2nd innings | ᵁᴴᵀ ᵁᴴᵀ ᵁᴴᵀ ᵁᴴᵀ ᵁᴴᵀ II |

$$32 + 27 = 32 + 20 + 7 = 52 + 7 = 59$$

Answer: Jane's total score was 59 runs.

Pupil reads the question aloud.
What do I need to find out?
How many runs she scored.

What information do I know?
1st innings 32 runs. 2nd innings 27 runs.

What is the estimated answer?
I round 32 down to 30 and I round 27 up to 30.
My estimate is 30 add 30 which is 60.

I can show the information on a tally chart and on a number line.

Now I write the equation and do the calculation.

I write the answer in a sentence.

Sam had 62 cms of ribbon. She cut off 37 cms. How much ribbon was left?
(62 - 37 = ? or 37 + ? = 62)

Dad is 56 years old. His son is 18 years old. What is their combined age? (56 + 18 = ?)

Pam had 75p. She went to the shops and spent 18p on an apple. How much money did she have left? (75 - 18 = ? or 18 + ? = 75)

There were 53 pupils at the swimming pool. 26 pupils were less than 8 years old. How many pupils were more than 8 years old? (53 - 26 = ? or 26 + ? = 53 or 53 = 26 + ?)

The family went on holiday to Devon. The camp site was 78 miles from their home. They drove 23 miles before lunch. How much further did they need to go after lunch?
(78 - 23 = ? or 23 + ? = 78 or 78 = 23 + ?)

Equivalent groups (multiplication and division)

6 children need 3 pencils each. How many pencils does the teacher give out to them?

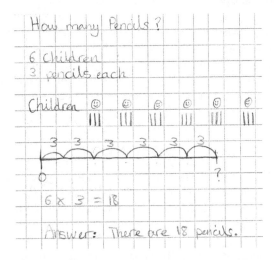

Pupil reads the question aloud.
What do I need to find out? How many pencils are there?

What information do I have? 6 children get 3 pencils each.

Can I show it on a diagram?

I can draw a picture, and I can show it on a number line.

Now I write the equation and do the calculation.
6 times 3 is 18. The teacher gives out 18 pencils.

70 girls played netball. There were 7 girls in each team. How many teams were there?
(70 ÷ 7 = ? or 7 x ? = 70 or ? x 7 = 70)

The teacher had 24 books. There were 4 pupils in the class. How many books did each pupil get? (24 ÷ 4 = ? or 4 x ? = 24 or ? x 4 = 24)

Pam took 6 puppies for a walk. They all played in the mud. How many muddy paws did she wash? (6 x 4 = ?)

Apples cost 8p each. Jane spent 48p. How many apples did she buy?
(48 ÷ 8 = ? or 8 x ? = 48 or ? x 8 = 48)

A doctor saw a patient every 6 minutes. How many patients did she see in 1 hour?
(60 ÷ 6 = ? or 6 x ? = 60 or ? x 6 = 60)

47 football players came to match practice. There were 4 teams. How many players did not play in a team? (47 ÷ 4 = ?)

Equal measures problems (multiplication and division)

Sam needs 3 pieces of string, each piece 10 cm long. How much string must he buy?
(3 x 10 = ?)

The shop sells planks of wood 12 metres long. Ben needs pieces of wood 4 metres long. How many pieces will he get from one plank? (12 ÷ 4 = ? or 4 x ? = 12 or ? x 4 = 12)

How many metres of ribbon will Lily buy? She needs to wrap 4 presents. Each present requires 3 metres of ribbon. (4 x 3 = ?)

Sally walked to school every morning. She caught the bus in the afternoon. At the end of the week she had walked 20 km. How far does she live from the school?
(20 ÷ 5 = ? or 5 x ? = 20 or ? x 5 = 20)

The array and area models (multiplication and division)

The array and area models are similar in that elements can be arranged in a rectangular formation. Arrays play a central role in communication in the modern world. For this reason it is important that pupils understand the basic structure of the array, and have plenty of practice in constructing arrays. At a later stage pupils will need to use the terms rows and columns when describing arrays, however they should continue to describe arrays in terms of the number of rows and the number of objects in each row. This was discussed on p163.

Introduce the concept of area in two stages. First ask questions that relate it to the array model so that the diagrammatic information is shown as a grid with individual squares. Then ask questions about the area of a space. Now pupils draw a rectangle and label the sides with the measurements; they do not show the individual squares. Pupils do not use number lines.

There are 4 rows of seats in the cinema. There are 8 seats in each row. How many seats are there in the cinema?

How many seats?

4 rows
8 seats in each row

8 seats in each row

4 rows

$4 \times 8 = 32$

Answer = There are 32 seats in the cinema.

> Pupil reads the question aloud.
> *What do I need to find out?*
> *How many seats are there?*
>
> *What information do I know?*
> *There are 4 rows with 8 seats in each row.*
>
> *Can I show it on a diagram? I can draw an array.*
>
> *Now I write the equation and do the calculation. 4 times 8 is 32.*
>
> *There are 32 seats in the cinema.*

A farmer planted 80 carrots in rows. There were 10 rows. How many carrots were in each row?

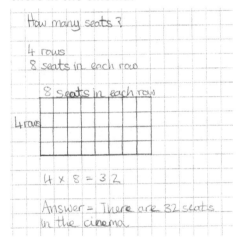

How many carrots?

80 carrots
10 rows

? carrots in a row

10 rows | 80 carrots

$80 \div 10 = 8$

Answer: There are 8 carrots in each row.

> Pupil reads the question aloud.
> *What do I need to find out? How many carrots in each row.*
>
> *What information do I know?*
> *80 carrots planted in 10 rows.*
>
> *Can I show it on a diagram? I don't need to draw each carrot. I can draw a rectangle to show the area the carrots take up.*
>
> *Now I write the equation and do the calculation.*
>
> *I know that 80 is made of 10 eights. So 80 divided by 10 is 8.*
>
> *There are 8 carrots in each row.*

Max tiled his bedroom floor. He used 5 rows of tiles with 6 tiles in each row. How many tiles did he buy?

Max tiled his bedroom floor. The room was 5 metres wide and 6 metres long. What was the area of the floor?

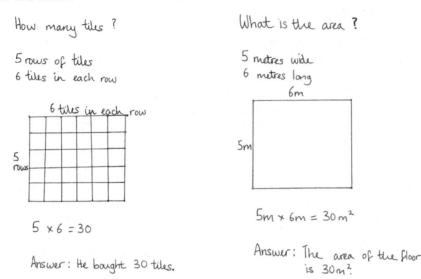

Each child at school planted a small tree for the Jubilee. There were 6 rows with 13 trees in each row. How many children planted trees? (13 x 6 = ?)

Tim drew a rectangle filled with 36 squares. There were 4 rows. How many squares were in each row? (36 ÷ 4 = ? or 4 x ? = 36 or ? x 4 = 36)

The swimming pool at school had a canvas cover over it in winter. The pool measured 5 metres by 14 metres. What size was the cover? (5 x 14 = ?)

Two-step questions: Numbers to 100

John is in Year 4. On Saturday he went to a football match with his uncle. The ticket price was £45 per person. A child's ticket costs £25 less. How much did his uncle pay for the tickets?

Jack is 80 cm tall. He planted a magic beanstalk which grew 20 cm on Monday and 25 cm the next day. By Wednesday night the beanstalk was the same height as Jack. How much did it grow on Wednesday?

The shop was open from 7am to 12pm and 1pm to 5pm on Saturday. On Sundays it was open from 10am to 5pm. Which day was it open longer? How much longer was it open on that day?

3 classes visited the Science Museum. Half of the students went to the dinosaur exhibition. 35 students looked at the space capsule and 13 played in the Launchpad. How many students visited the Museum?

Terry buys 3 bunches of rosemary and 2 pots of sage. The rosemary costs 15p a bunch and the sage costs 20p per pot. How much change does she get from £1?

37 people went to the football match. It costs £10 to take a taxi to go the football match. 5 people can fit into one taxi. What was the total cost to transport everybody?

Checklist - Numbers to 100: the four operations in context

Pupils can:

☐ Tackle questions without prompting from the teacher
☐ Select appropriate methods to communicate thinking
☐ Solve combine, change and compare questions
☐ Solve problems involving equal groups, arrays and the area model
☐ Make up their own word problems

Numbers to 1,000

Objectives
- Apply problem solving skills to numbers to 1,000
- Solve word problems involving measurement
- Make up word problems

Pupils apply their problem solving skills to questions which contain larger numbers. Introduce questions which involve measurement: length, area, mass, capacity.

Teaching
Give pupils written questions and also ask them to devise their own questions.

234 girls were in the school hall. 123 went out of the hall. How many were left?

There were 238 people on a train. At the next station 126 more got onto the train. How many people were on the train?

There were 26 rows of seats in the theatre with 32 seats in each row. How many seats were in the theatre?

Tom drove from London to Berlin, which is a distance of 648 miles. He drove 163 miles on the first day. How much further did he have to drive the next day?

Jane had £375. She spent £246 on a computer. How much money did she have left?

Emma had 224 grams of flour to bake cupcakes. Each cupcake needed 32 grams of flour. How many cupcakes did she bake?

2-step questions

A carton holds 750 ml of milk. Ruth poured 120 ml of milk into some glasses. There was 30 ml of milk left in the carton when she finished. How many glasses of milk did she pour?

A box of 24 cookies weighs 459 grams. The empty box weighs 27 grams. How much does each cookie weigh?

The caretaker sowed grass seed on the school football pitch. The pitch measured 34 metres by 21 metres. Each bag of seed is enough to cover 170 square metres. How many bags of grass seed did he buy?

Checklist - Numbers to 1,000
Pupils can:
- ☐ Apply problem solving skills to numbers to 1,000
- ☐ Solve word problems involving measurement
- ☐ Make up word problems

Appendix 1: Plan effective teaching

Successful numeracy teaching requires a systematic approach linking new knowledge to existing knowledge. Be clear about what you need to teach and how you are going to teach it using multi-sensory methods. Plan teaching in three stages:

- **Assessment:** find out what the pupil can do and where difficulties have arisen.
- **Medium term goals:** use the information from the assessment to set specific goals to be taught in a set time. List clear criteria for checking when those goals are achieved.
- **Individual Lesson Plan:** detailed instructions for teaching each lesson.

Assessment

Find out how the pupil thinks about numbers, what the pupil knows, and what they do not know, by doing a diagnostic assessment. Summarise this information in the Summary Numeracy Profile (Template p229) which provides an overview of the essential knowledge and skills for basic numeracy. *The Dyscalculia Assessment* is a detailed guide to conducting a diagnostic assessment and interpreting the results. (Emerson and Babtie 2013).

Medium term goals

Draw up a Teaching Plan Summary (Template p230) stating the topics to be taught in a specified length of time. It is important that teaching starts at a point of secure knowledge and then builds from there. Outline specific, medium term goals with clear criteria for checking when those goals are achieved. Keep the summary simple and focussed. A realistic guide is to allow about ten lessons to teach three topics. However the rate of progress will depend on the severity of the each pupil's difficulties. The topics should be related to each other, for example: place value, reading, and writing 2-digit numbers. When these are achieved, a new list of topics will be drawn up. Resist the temptation to move on too quickly. Remember that pupils need to have a firm grasp of a concept before they can progress.The Teaching Plan Summary also includes brief notes about other factors which need to be kept in mind when teaching lessons, such as attitude, literacy level, and any visual or language difficulty. Lack of confidence and anxiety affect learning. Teaching needs to take this into account by making sure that pupils start each lesson by reviewing something that they are able to do, before progressing to more difficult work. Note other pertinent information such as whether they know left and right. List information from other sources such as Educational Psychologists, Occupational Therapists, and Behavioural Optometrists.

Individual Lesson Plan

Draw up an Individual Lesson Plan (Template p231) with clear aims for the lesson, and details of specific tasks for multi-sensory learning. Keep the structure of each lesson consistent so that pupils know what to expect. Clearly state the concept being taught as well as any subsidiary aims. For example, for the concept 'Counting to 10' the initial goals are oral counting and counting objects into a line to reinforce one-to-one correspondence. Start by reviewing the previous topic, then consolidate understanding or introduce the next related topic, practice it and do an activity or play a game. Do not try to teach too much in one lesson. Be prepared to change the plan if the pupil has forgotten previous work, or is unsure.

Outline of an Individual Lesson Plan

- **Objectives:** set clear goals for the lesson
- **Equipment:** list all the equipment required for the lesson
- **Vocabulary:** key terms for pupils to use
- **Topic:** key skill or concept for lesson
- **Review:** quick oral or written starter to revise previous work
- **New Topic:** teach new skill or concept; pupils use concrete materials and record their thinking in diagrammatic and written form
- **Word problems:** present numerical information in contexts
- **Practice:** mental and written examples of the new information
- **Game:** reinforce new topic or revise previous work
- **Notes for next lesson:** what will need revision and what to teach next

Summary numeracy profile

Name _____

Date of assessment _____

Date of birth _____

Age at assessment _____

NUMBER SENSE AND COUNTING

☐ Subitising

Estimating
☐ up to 10
☐ more than 10

Counting forwards
☐ in 1s
☐ in 10s
☐ in 5s
☐ in 2s

Counting backwards
☐ in 1s
☐ in 10s
☐ in 5s
☐ in 2s

Reading
☐ two-digit numbers (TU)
☐ larger numbers

Writing
☐ two-digit numbers (TU)
☐ larger numbers

CALCULATION

Addition +1, +2
☐ one more +1
☐ two more +2

Subtract -1, -2
☐ one less -1
☐ two less -2

☐ Dot patterns 1-6

Doubles
☐ up to 10
☐ up to 20

Near doubles
☐ up to 10
☐ up to 20

Bonds of ten
☐ addition
☐ subtraction

Number bonds 1-9
☐ addition
☐ subtraction

Bonds of tens
☐ addition (e.g. 47 + ? = 50)
☐ subtraction (e.g. 70 - 6 = ?)

Bonds of multiples of 10
☐ addition (e.g. 30 + ? = 100)
☐ subtraction (e.g. 100 - 80 = ?)

PLACE VALUE

☐ Principle of exchange

10 plus a single digit/Tens plus
☐ 10 plus a single digit (10+ n)
☐ tens plus a single digit (20 + n)

Bridging
☐ units + units (e.g. 8 + 5)
☐ tens + units (e.g. 34 + 7)

Place value HTU
☐ value of each digit in a multi-digit number

☐ same units subtraction (e.g. 36 - 6)

Addition +10
☐ ten more

Subtraction -10
☐ minus ten

Subtraction strategies
☐ doubles
☐ bridging back
☐ counting on (shopkeeper's method)

MULTIPLICATION AND DIVISION

Multiplication
☐ demonstration of meaning

Key tables:
☐ x5   ☐ x10

Other tables:
☐ x2   ☐ x4   ☐ x6   ☐ x8
☐ x3   ☐ x7   ☐ x9

Division
☐ grouping concept
☐ sharing concept

WORD PROBLEMS
☐ addition
☐ subtraction
☐ multiplication
☐ division

FORMAL WRITTEN NUMERACY
☐ addition
☐ subtraction
☐ multiplication
☐ long multiplication
☐ short division

Teaching plan summary

Name _____

Date of assessment _____

Date of birth _____

Age at assessment _____

Summary of numeracy topics	Additional information
List topics to be covered based on the findings from the assessment.	Behaviour and attitude
Pupil needs:	Oral skills
	Writing numbers
•	Literacy levels
•	Other
•	Other assessments available

Individual lesson plan

Name _____   Date _____

Age _____   Teacher_____

Objectives:

Equipment:

Vocabulary:

Topics	Comments
Review:	
New Topic:	
Practice:	
Game:	
Homework:	Notes for next lesson:

Appendix 2: Templates

Caterpillar tracks
Print two copies. Join the sheets leaving a small space between one group of ten and the next.

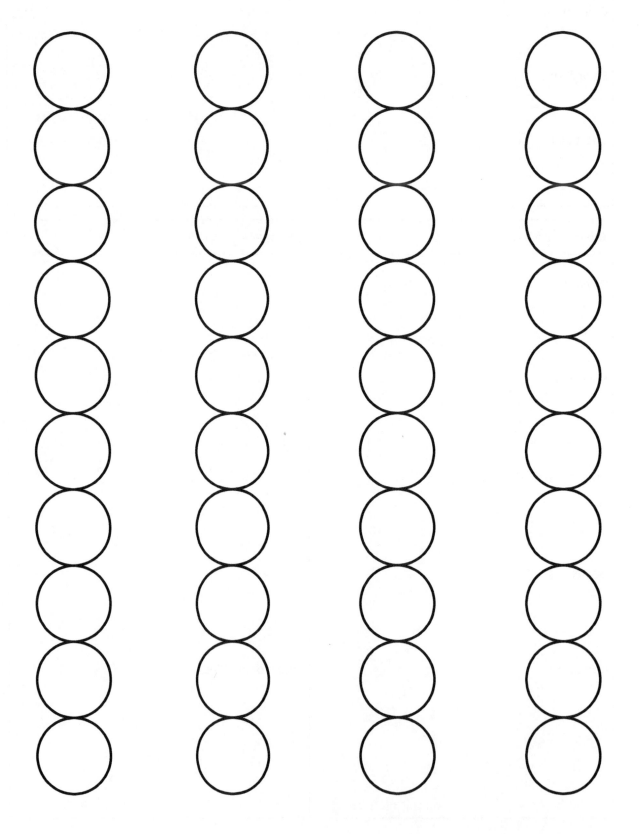

Numbered tracks (Numbers 1 to 20)

The Numbered Track: cut into strips and join the numbers 1 to 10 to 11 to 20. Do not leave a gap between 10 and 11.

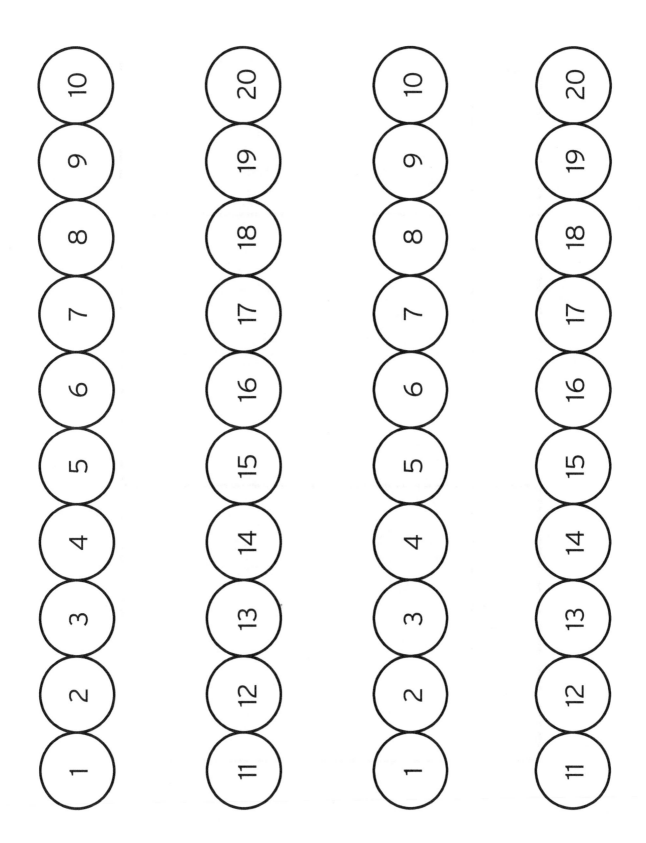

Place value grid
Hundreds, tens and units

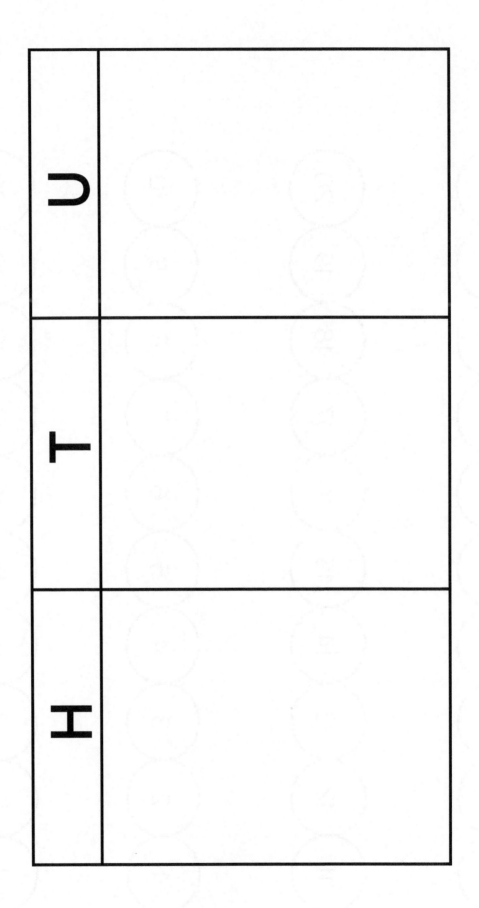

Place value grid for thousands
Enlarge to A3 to use with base 10 equipment

			Thousands		
U	T	H	U	T	H

Appendix 3: Worksheets

Look, say, cover, write
Say the first word. Copy it. Cover it up and write it. Check the spelling.
Write it again.

Say	Copy	Cover and write	Check and write
one			
two			
three			
four			
five			
six			
seven			
eight			
nine			
ten			

Learning to use Cuisenaire rods

Introduce the Cuisenaire rods in stages.

1. Free play

Allow pupils to play without giving any direction. Some may build structures, others prefer to make flat designs or patterns. It is important that pupils are allowed to discover the relationships between the rods for themselves. Learning to analyse information and make comparisons are important thinking skills. Pupils do not need to assign values to the rods to discover that Orange is twice the length of the Yellow, or 3 Light Green rods are equivalent to a Blue rod.

2. Make a design and ask pupils to copy it using Cuisenaire rods.

3. Give pupils a coloured picture of a design. Pupil uses Cuisenaire rods to replicate the design.

4. Pupils draw the design on squared paper and colour it in. (Squares should be 1 cm².)

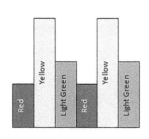  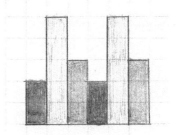

| Picture of rods | Design built with rods | Drawing of rods |

Further resources:
Davidson, P. (2002) *Idea book: Mathematics activities for Cuisenaire rods at the primary level* ETA Cuisenaire Publishing, Vernon Hills
This book uses a very clear, structured approach to teaching basic numerical concepts using Cuisenaire rods.

www.nrich.maths.org
The NRICH Project is run by the University of Cambridge. It offers free online maths resources.
For activities using Cuisenaire rods go to www.nrich.org and search for 'Cuisenaire'.

Bonds of 10 using Cuisenaire rods

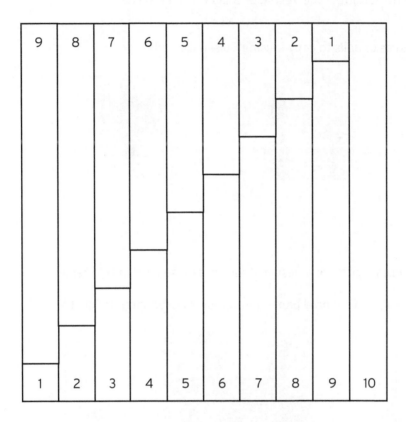

Bonds of 10

Colour the rods. Use the colour that matches the Cuisenaire rod for each number.
Fill in the mystery numbers in the boxes. The first one has been done for you.

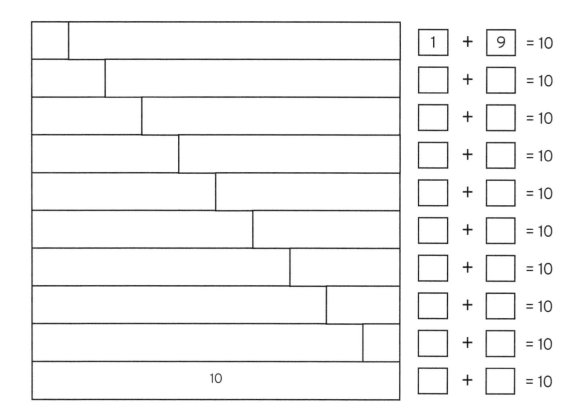

10 = 5 + ☐	☐ + 7 = 10	10 - ☐ = 6
10 = ☐ + 3	9 + ☐ = 10	10 - 7 = ☐
10 = 6 + ☐	☐ + 5 = 10	2 = 10 - ☐
10 = ☐ + 2	☐ + 4 = 10	☐ = 10 - 5
10 = 1 + ☐	☐ + 8 = 10	1 = 10 - ☐

Tracking for 10

Work from left to right.
Use a pencil to track the numbers in each row.
Circle each pair of numbers that make 10.

e.g. 5 + 6   (5 + 5)   3 + 4

6 + 4	7 + 5	9 + 2	7 + 3	8 + 4
5 + 4	3 + 7	2 + 9	2 + 8	4 + 3
5 + 5	6 + 5	4 + 6	3 + 8	9 + 1
7 + 3	8 + 1	4 + 9	5 + 3	9 + 3
8 + 2	4 + 7	1 + 9	6 + 2	5 + 5

Appendix 4: Card templates

Dot pattern cards: 1 to 10

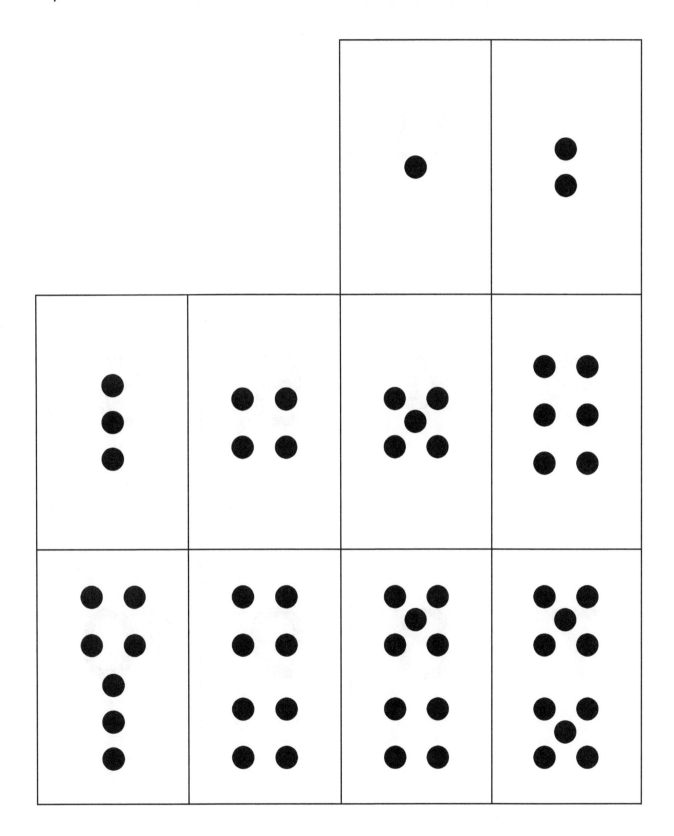

Number cards: 0 to 10

0	1	2
3	4	5	6
7	8	9	10

Word cards: 1 to 10

Smallest	Largest	**one**	**two**
three	**four**	**five**	**six**
seven	**eight**	**nine**	**ten**

Doubles and near doubles cards

1 + 1	1 + 2
2 + 2	2 + 3
3 + 3	3 + 4
4 + 4	4 + 5
5 + 5	

Cards bonds of 10

Print one set of question cards plus two sets of number cards 1 to 9.

Missing addend question cards

$1 + \boxed{} = 10$	$2 + \boxed{} = 10$	$3 + \boxed{} = 10$
$4 + \boxed{} = 10$	$5 + \boxed{} = 10$	$6 + \boxed{} = 10$
$7 + \boxed{} = 10$	$8 + \boxed{} = 10$	$9 + \boxed{} = 10$

Subtraction question cards

$10 - 1 =$	$10 - 2 =$	$10 - 3 =$
$10 - 4 =$	$10 - 5 =$	$10 - 6 =$
$10 - 7 =$	$10 - 8 =$	$10 - 9 =$

Untangling -teen and -ty

'-teen' cards and 'ty' cards

Print one set of '-teen' number cards. Write the suffix '-teen' on the back of each card.
Print one set of 'ty' number cards. Write the suffix 'ty' on the back of each card.

13	14	15	16	17
18	19	113	114	115
116	117	118	119	20
30	40	50	60	70
80	90	120	130	140
150	160	170	180	190

Multiplication cards x10

Question cards

1 x 10	2 x 10
3 x 10	4 x 10
5 x 10	6 x 10
7 x 10	8 x 10
9 x 10	10 x 10

Multiplication cards x10

Answer cards

10	20

30	40	50	60

70	80	90	100

References and further reading

Anghilieri, J. (2006) *Teaching Number Sense (2nd Edition)* London: Continuum

Anghilieri, J. (2007) *Developing Number Sense* London: Continuum

Askew, M. (2004) *Teachers' Notes for BEAM's big Book of Word Problems* London: Beam

Askew, M. et al (2001) *Raising attainment in primary number sense: from counting to strategy* London: BEAM Education

Ashlock, Robert B. (2006) *Error Patterns in Computation.* New Jersey: Pearson Merrill Prentice Hall

Emerson, J. and Babtie, P. (2013) *The Dyscalculia Assessment* London: Bloomsbury

Bird, R. (2007)*The dyscalculia toolkit: supporting learning difficulties in maths* London: Paul Chapman

Bird, R. (2009) *Overcoming Difficulties with Number* London: Paul Chapman

Butterworth, B. (2003) *Dyscalculia screener: highlighting children with specific learning difficulties in maths,* http://www.gl-assessment.co.uk/products/dyscalculia-screener-digital-0

Butterworth, B. (1999) *The Mathematical Brain* London: Macmillan

Butterworth, B. and Yeo, D. (2004) *Dyscalculia Guidance* London: nferNelson

Came, F. and Reid, G. (2007) *Concern Assess Provide It All* Marlborough: Learning Works

Chinn, S. and Ashcroft, R. (1993) *Mathematics for dyslexics: a teaching handbook* London: Whurr

Chinn, S. (2004) *The Trouble with Maths* Abingdon: Routledge Falmer

Chinn, S. (2012) *More Trouble with Maths: A complete guide to identifying and diagnosing mathematical difficulties* London: David Fulton/Nasen

Christmas, J. (2009) *Hands on Dyspraxia* Milton Keynes: Speechmark

Clausen-May, T (2005) *Teaching Maths to pupils with different Learning Styles* London: Paul Chapman

Clayton, P and Barnes, R (2004) *How to develop Numeracy in children with Dyslexia* London: LDA

Davidson, P. (2002) *Idea book: Mathematics activities for Cuisenaire rods at the primary level* Vernon Hills: ETA/Cuisenaire Publishing

Dehaene, S. (1997)*The Number Sense: how the mind creates mathematics* Oxford: Oxford University Press

Dept for Education (Archive) Department for Education and Employment (1999) *The national numeracy strategy framework for teaching mathematics from reception to year 6,* DfEE Publications, Sudbury

Dept for Education (Archive) Department for Education and Skills (2001) *Guidance to support pupils with dyslexia and dyscalculia (DfES 0521/2001)* London: DfES

Dowker, A. (2009) *What works for children with mathematical difficulties.* Nottingham: DCSF Publications

Gattengno, C. (1963) *Now Johnny can do arithmetic: a handbook on the use of Cuisenaire Rods* Reading: Educational Explorers

Gawande, A. (2011) *The Checklist Manifesto: How to Get Things Right* London: Profile Books

Gifford, S. (2005) *Young children's difficulties in learning Mathematics: Review of research in relation to dyscalculia* Qualifications and Curriculum Authority (QCA/05/1545)

Gillham, W. and Hesse, K. (2001) *Basic Number Screening Test* London: Hodder Murray

Grauberg, E. (1998) *Elementary mathematics and language difficulties* London: Whurr

Grey, E. (1997) 'Compressing the counting process: developing a flexible interpretation of symbols', in Thompson, I. (ed) *Teaching and Learning Early Number* Buckingham: Oxford University Press

Hannell, G. (2005) *Dyscalculia: Action Plans for Successful Learning in Mathematics*. London: David Fulton

Haylock, D. (2006) *Maths explained for primary school teachers* London: Sage

Henderson, A. (1998) *Maths for the Dyslexic: A Practical Guide* London: David Fulton

Henderson, A. (2012) *Dyslexia, Dyscalculia and Mathematics: A practical guide* London: Routledge

Kirby, A. (1999) *Dyspraxia: Developmental Co-ordination Disorder* London: Souvenir Press

Kosc, L. (1974) 'Developmental dyscalculia' in *Journal of learning disabilities*, vol. 7(3) pages 164-77

Mareschal, D. Butterworth, B. and Tolmie, A. (2013) *Educational Neuroscience* Chichester: Wiley Blackwell

Messenger, C. Emerson, J. and Bird, R. (2007) 'Dyscalculia in Harrow' Journal of Mathematics Teaching, The Association of Teachers of Mathematics

Miles, TR. and Miles, E. (1992) *Dyslexia and mathematics* London: Routledge

Nash-Wortham, M. and Hunt, J. (1997) *Take Time* Stourbridge: The Robinswood Press

Simmons, FR. (2011) *Mathematics difficulties: Current research and future directions. Dyslexia Review*, vol. 22(1), 18-19

Sharma, M. (2003) 'Dyscalculia' DVD *BBC Skillswise* Berkshire Mathematics

Tapson, F. (2006) *Mathematics Study Dictionary* Oxford: Oxford University Press

Thompson, I. (1999) *Issues in teaching numeracy in primary schools* Buckingham: Open University Press

Wilson, A. (2004) *Dyscalculia Primer and Resource Guide* OECD Organization for Economic Cooperation and Development, Directorate for Education (online) http://www.oecd.org/document/8/0,3343, en_2649_35845581_34495560_1_1_1_1,00.html (Accessed 2 March 2013)

Yeo, D. (2003) *Dyslexia, dyspraxia and mathematics* London: Whurr

Resources

Useful websites

Anna Wilson, University of Auckland
www.aboutdyscalculia.org
A public information website which is designed to bring scientific information about Dyscalculia to parents, teachers and policy-makers.

Brian Butterworth, University College, London
www.mathematicalbrain.com
Updates on the latest research into Dyscalculia, and links to resources.

Cambridge University
www.nrich.maths.org
Free enrichment material (Problems, Articles and Games) at all Key Stages for mathematics.

Dept for Education (Archive)
http://webarchive.nationalarchives.gov.uk/20130401151715/http://www.education.gov.uk/publications/eOrderingDownload/Assessing_pupils_progress.pdf 'Getting to Grips with Assessing Pupils' Progress' DfCSF 2008
A pamphlet created by the DCSF (Department of Children, Schools and Families) containing a three-step guide to Assessing Pupils' Progress (APP) and guidance on using APP to benefit pupils.

Diana Laurillard and Hassan Baajour, Institute of Education (IOE) and Birkbeck College, London
http://number-sense.co.uk/
Free interactive games to practice basic numeracy, including counting, bonds of 10, locating points on a number line and telling the time developed at the London Knowledge Lab, IOE and Birkbeck College

www.low-numeracy.ning.com
The research site and discussion forum 'Developing Number Sense' for the project *'Digital interventions for dyscalculia and low numeracy'*.

Dynamomaths
www.dynamomaths.co.uk
Online profiler to assess number strengths and weaknesses in children age 6 to 9 years old. Online intervention programme for pupils with dyscalculia and low numeracy.

DysCalculiUM
https://shop.tribalgroup.co.uk/vmchk/Assessment-screening/DysCalculiUM.html
DysCalculiUM is an online screener specifically designed to screen for dyscalculia in adults and learners in post-16 education.

Dystalk
www.dystalk.com
Discussion forum for parents and professionals to discuss issues related to Dyslexia, Dyspraxia and Dyscalculia. Interviews with professionals in the field and lists of resources.

Every Child Counts
https://everychildcounts.edgehill.ac.uk/
Every Child Counts helps schools to raise achievement in mathematics. It is run by Edge Hill University on a not-for-profit basis, with support from the Department for Education. Local ECC Providers give training and support to schools.

Learning Works
www.dyscalculia-maths-difficulties.org.uk
An educational consultancy with a forum for discussing Dyscalculia and maths learning difficulties.

Mahesh Sharma
Math Learning Disability Resource
www.dyscalculia.org
Dyscalculia.org is a nonprofit educational organisation dedicated to advancing understanding and treatment of specific learning disabilities in mathematics also known as dyscalculia.

Stanislas Dehaene, INSERM-CEA Cognitive Neuroimaging Unit
www.unicog.org (See the 'Numbers' page)
Updates on the latest research and lists of further academic articles to read.

http://www.thenumbercatcher.com/nc/home.php
Free online game involving basic arithmetic concepts – calculation, sets, and the logic of multi-digit numbers

Equipment suppliers

Counters: glass nuggets
Available from florists and decorative arts suppliers.
Online from:
House of Marbles
The Old Pottery
Pottery Road
Bovey Tracey
Devon TQ13 9AL
www.houseofmarbles.com
Tel: 01626 835285

Cuisenaire rods
The Cuisenaire Company
Unit 5, Feidr Castell Business Park
Fishguard
Pembrokeshire SA65 9BB
www.cuisenaire.co.uk
Tel: 01348 874890
Fax: 01348 874925
(Mini set contains 126 rods, International set contains 310 rods)

Base 10 place value material
(also called Dienes equipment)
Hands On
Arkwright Road
Bicester
Oxfordshire OX26 4UU
www.handson.co.uk
Tel: 01869 366160
Fax: 01869 320312

Hope Education
Hyde Buildings
Ashton Road
Hyde
Cheshire SK14 4SH
www.hope-education.co.uk
Tel: 08451 202055
Fax: 0800 929139

Learning Resources®
51 Bergen Way
King's Lynn
Norfolk PE30 2JG
www.learningresources.co.uk
Tel: 0845 241 0484

Stern blocks and Stern dual board
Vikki Horner Consultancy
Email: vikkihornerconsultancy@gmail.com
Tel: 01747 861503

Stern Math
754 N Hollow Rd
Box 172
Rochester
VT 05767
USA
www.sternmath.com
Email: sternmath@gmail.com

Stickers
Stickers are available from high street shops. For bulk purchases try:
Superstickers
PO Box 55
4 Balloo Avenue
Bangor
Co Down
Northern Ireland BT19 7PJ
www.superstickers.com

Transparent spinners
Crossbow Education Limited
Tollgate Court Business Centre
Tollgate Drive
Stafford ST16 3HS
www.crossboweducation.com
Tel: 0845 269 7272
Fax: 0845 269 7373
(Crossbow is run by Bob Hext, a former special needs teacher.)

10 sided dice
Hope Education (see above)

Useful organisations
Attention Deficit Disorder Information and Support Service (ADDIS)
Premier House
112 Station Road
Edgware
Middlesex HA8 7BJ
Tel: 020 8952 2800
www.addiss.co.uk
ADDIS provides information about Attention Deficit Hyperactivity Disorder to anyone who needs
assistance - parents, sufferers, teachers or health professionals.

British Association of Behavioural Optometrists
1 Bergamot Drive
Meir Park
Stoke-on-Trent ST3 7FD
Tel: 07443 569021
www.babo.co.uk
Behavioural optometrists use lenses and vision training to facilitate the development of a more efficient
and complete visual process.

The British Dyslexia Association (BDA)
Unit 8 Bracknell Beeches
Old Bracknell Lane
Bracknell
RG12 7BW
www.bdadyslexia.org.uk
Tel: 0845 251 9003
National Helpline: 0845 251 9002
The BDA campaigns for a dyslexia friendly society. It offers support and advice through a network of local Dyslexia Societies and has a network of volunteer befrienders.

Contact a Family
209-211 City Road
London EC1V 1JN
Tel: 020 7608 8700
Helpline 0808 808 3555
Text phone 0808 808 3556
www.cafamily.org.uk
Contact a Family provides a range of fact sheets and has a network of volunteer reps to help families with disabled or special needs children.

CReSTeD
Old Post House
Castle Street
Whittington
Shropshire SY11 4DF
Tel: 01691 655783
0845 601 5013
www.crested.org.uk
CReSTeD (The Council for the Registration of Schools Teaching Dyslexic Pupils) Helps parents, and those who advise them, to choose schools for dyslexic children. All schools included in the Register are visited regularly.

Dyslexia Action
Park House
Wick Road
Egham
Surrey TW20 0HH
Tel: 01784 222300
www.dyslexiaaction.org.uk
Dyslexia Action is the UK's leading provider of services and support for people with dyslexia and literacy difficulties. Dyslexia Action provides assessment, education and training.

The Dyspraxia Foundation
8 West Alley
Hitchin
Herts SG5 1EG
Tel 01462 454986
www.dyspraxiafoundation.org.uk
The Dyspraxia Foundation offers support and resources to dyspraxics and their families.

Dyslexia Teaching Centre
23 Kensington Square
London W8 5HN
Tel: 020 7361 4790
Fax: 020 7938 4816
www.dyslexiateachingcentre.co.uk
Dyslexia Teaching Centre provides assessment and teaching tailored to individual needs. It offers a range of therapies to people of all ages.

Emerson House
40 Redmore Road
Hammersmith
London W6 0HZ
Tel: 020 8741 4554
www.emersonhouse.co.uk
Emerson House is a specialist centre for children aged 5 to 11. It offers assessment and teaching for dyscalculia, dyslexia and dyspraxia.

I CAN
8 Wakley Street
London EC1V 7QE
Information: 0845 225 4073 or 020 7843 2552
Tel: 0845 225 4071 or 020 7843 2510
www.ican.org.uk
I CAN is an educational charity for children with speech and language difficulties. It provides training and information for parents, teachers and therapists. It runs special schools and nurseries and centres within local schools.

NASEN
Nasen House
4/5 Amber Business Village
Amber Close
Farmington
Tamworth
Staffordshire B77 4RP
Tel 01827 311500
www.nasen.org.uk
NASEN (National Association for Special Educational Needs) promotes the education, training, advancement and development of all those with special and additional support needs.

PATOSS
South Worcestershire College
Davies Road
Evesham
WorcestershireWR11 1LP
Tel: 01386 712 650
www.patoss-dyslexia.org
Patoss (Professional Association of Teachers of Students with Specific Learning Difficulties) represents the interests of teachers and students in matters that affect individuals with SpLD. It provides training and advice for teachers and maintains a directory of tutors and assessors.

Royal College of Speech and Language Therapists
2 White Hart Yard
London SE1 1NX
Tel: 020 7378 1200
www.rcslt.org
The Royal College of Speech and Language Therapists is the professional body for speech and language therapists and support workers.

Glossary

Algorithm: A step-by-step procedure used to perform a calculation.

Area model in multiplication: The multipliers are displayed as unit squares in rows and columns to form a rectangle. The product is the area of the rectangle.

Arithmetic: The branch of mathematics concerned with computation of numbers using the four operations of addition, subtraction, multiplication and division.

Array model: Counters are arranged in rows and columns to create a rectangle where the multipliers are the length of the rows and columns.

Assessment, informal diagnostic: Not timed or standardised, it is conducted in a friendly, relaxed way. The aim is to explore how a pupil is thinking in order to work out why they are having difficulties and underachieving so that a personalised teaching plan can be developed.

Attention deficit disorder (ADD): Causes inattention and distractibility making it difficult to concentrate. Children with ADD rarely experience pauses in their thoughts, actions or responses to questions and tend to be impulsive. If a degree of hyperactivity is also involved, the condition can be described as attention deficit hyperactivity disorder (ADHD).

Bridging: A strategy that applies bonds of ten knowledge to work out calculations. Ten, or a multiple of 10, is used as a 'stepping stone' to add two numbers where the answer will be more than 10. Example: 5 + 8 = (5 + 5) + 3 = 10 + 3 = 13.

Bridging back: Using ten or a multiple of ten as a 'stepping stone' to subtract a number. Example: 23 – 5 = (23 – 3) – 2 = 20 – 2 = 18.

Cardinal number: Denotes the quantity or size of a set of objects. The last number in a count represents the quantity in the group (e.g. 1, 2, 3, 4 so there are 4).

Chunking: Putting numbers or objects together to form a group in a calculation rather than calculating using ones.

Co-morbidity: A condition that occurs at the same time as another condition but is not related to it.

Commutative: Describes an arithmetical operation in which the order of the numbers does not change the outcome. Addition and multiplication are commutative. Example: 2 + 3 = 5 and 3 + 2 = 5 or 7 x 8 = 56 and 8 x 7 = 56. Subtraction and division are not commutative.

Complement of a number: The number that is added to another number to complete a specified quantity. Example: If the specified quantity is 10 and you have 2, the complement of 2 will be 8.

Complementary addition: The difference between two numbers is found by counting on from the smaller number up to the larger number in ones or in groups. (Also known as the 'shopkeeper's method'.) Example: 73 – 65: start at 65 and count on in ones until you reach 73. The difference is the number counted on, which is 8.

Component number: A constituent part of a specified number. Example: 7 = 4 + 3 where 3 and 4 are the components of 7.

Counting: Enumerating objects by matching each object to a specific number name in a sequence.

Counting all: Starting counting in ones from the first number in a calculation. If this is used as a calculation strategy it is evidence of very poor number sense.

Counting on: Starting with a number and counting on from that number in ones. Children need this ability but they should develop more efficient calculating strategies over time.

The Counting Trap: Numbers are seen as a collection of ones so each operation is seen as an instruction to count. Number facts never become known automatically and the very counting becomes a 'trap'.

Crossover point: A term used to describe the point in a counting sequence when the name of the tens number changes. For example, in the sequence ... 28, 29, 30, 31, 32 ... the crossover point is 30 because the tens name changes from twenty in twenty-nine to thirty.

Decade boundary: In counting, this is the point in the number system at which one group of tens ends and another begins. For example, in the sequence ... 28, 29, 30, 31, 32 ... the decade boundary falls between 30 and 31. This causes confusion for some children as the 30 is at the end of the twenties decade, not the beginning of the thirties in counting terms. The next decade starts with 31. (Compare this with crossover points.)

Dice patterns: The patterns for the numbers 1 to 6 found on a conventional dice.

Dot patterns: Number patterns to 10 derived from the conventional dice patterns. The dot patterns make the doubles and near doubles facts explicit.

Doubles facts: The number bonds created by doubling a number, also expressed as adding a number to itself. Example: 8 = 4 + 4.

Dyscalculia: Developmental dyscalculia is a condition that affects the ability to acquire arithmetical skills. Dyscalculic learners may have difficulty understanding simple number concepts, lack an intuitive grasp of numbers and have problems learning number facts and procedures. Even if they produce a correct answer or use a correct method, they may do so mechanically and without confidence (DfES 2001).

Dyslexia: 'Dyslexia is a learning difficulty that primarily affects the skills involved in accurate and fluent word reading and spelling. Characteristic features of dyslexia are difficulties in phonological awareness, verbal memory and verbal processing speed. Dyslexia occurs across the range of intellectual abilities. It is best thought of as a continuum, not a distinct category, and there are no clear cut-off points. Co-occurring difficulties may be seen in aspects of language, motor co-ordination, mental calculation, concentration and personal organisation, but these are not, by themselves, markers of dyslexia. A good indication of the severity and persistence of dyslexic difficulties can be gained by examining how the individual responds or has responded to well-founded intervention.' (Rose 2009)

Dyspraxia: Developmental dyspraxia, also known as developmental coordination disorder (DCD), is characterised by the inability to carry out and plan sequences of coordinated movements to achieve an objective. (Kirby 2009)

Enumeration: Finding out how many items there are in a group by synchronising one number name with each object in the count.

Estimate: The ability to guess roughly how many items there are in a group without counting, or to round numbers in a calculation to give the approximate size of the answer. Estimation is particularly important for successful use of calculators.

Exchange, principle of: A specific number of items can be exchanged for a single item which then represents those initial numbers or quantities, e.g. 10 one pence coins equals 1 ten pence coin, 7 days equals 1 week.

Finger agnosia: Not knowing where your fingers are in space.

Finger counting: Moving and touching fingers to aid counting. Children need to use their fingers to count initially as this is 'an important precursor to learning base ten' (Dehaene 1997). However, persistent use of fingers to count large quantities of ones often leads to inaccuracies. Finger counting can be used effectively if it is used to keep track of groups of numbers as in multiplication.

Formative assessment: An interactive assessment in which the teacher identifies the difficulties a pupil is having and uses the information to prepare a teaching plan to assess those difficulties. This approach is also called assessment for learning.

Individual education plan (IEP): Sets out the long-term goals and the short-term targets needed to achieve those goals, as well as detailing the additional teaching or support that will be needed. Now increasingly being superseded by provision maps or School Action Plans.

Key number bonds: Number bonds, or number components, are two numbers that are added together to make another number. The key number bonds are: doubles, near doubles, bonds of ten.

Key number facts: Bonds of ten, doubles and near doubles bonds, and multiplication by 10. Number facts need to be known 'off by heart' as they underpin calculation. Other number facts can be derived from the key facts.

Left-right orientation: Understanding the concept of the relationships between objects in spatial terms and being able to correctly apply the terms left and right to your own orientation and that of other people and objects.

Long-term memory: The ability to store information which can be retrieved again over a reasonably long period of time.

Mantra: A phrase or instruction that is learnt by rote and repeated to help remember facts or carry out calculations. This may be helpful if remembered correctly. However, some can be quite complicated and lead to problems if parts are forgotten or misapplied. Example of a mantra for mental calculation: 'Five in my head (points to head and touches it) and three fingers up (puts hand with three fingers up)'. Says again: 'Five in my head (touches head) six, seven, eight (touches each finger as counts 6, 7, 8)'.

Maths anxiety: Fear of mathematics which creates a psychological barrier, making it difficult, or impossible, for the person affected to solve mathematical problems.

Memory weaknesses: Auditory memory weakness will affect mental maths. Visual memory weakness may cause difficulties working from the board or from textbooks with a busy layout. Memory weaknesses make it difficult to learn new information and to remember it in the long term.

Missing addend: An addend is a number that is added to another number. For example, 2 and 3 are both addends in the equation 2 + 3 = 5. If one of the addends is unknown, it is called a missing addend question. For example, 2 + ? = 5.

Multi-sensory teaching: Involving all the senses of touch, sight, hearing and speech.

Near doubles facts: The number bonds that are created by adding adjacent numbers. Example: 4 + 3 = 7.

Number bonds: The fixed relationship between a number and its constituent parts. Usually taught as pairs of numbers which are combined to make another number. Example: 9 = 5 + 4 which can also be expressed in a variety of ways such as 9 – 4 = 5, 9 – 5 = 4, 5 + 4 = 9.

Number line: A number line shows measuring numbers. Numbers are marked on a line at regular intervals. Fractions can be shown in the intervals between the whole numbers. Number lines can be a useful aid in calculation and are essential for understanding graphs. Pupils need to understand how the number line relates to the number track. The difference between a number track and a number line is that a number track only shows whole numbers.

Number sense: A 'feel' for numbers which involves understanding that a number represents a specific quantity or value which is part of a sequence and can be compared with other numbers.

Number track: A number track shows counting numbers. Each number occupies a defined space on the track. The easiest way to show the difference between a number track and a number line is to measure unit cubes against a ruler where the cubes are comparable to a number track and the ruler is a number line.

Numerical operations: Addition, subtraction, multiplication and division.

Numerosity: The acquisition of the concept of numerosity means that you can decide whether two collections do or do not contain the same quantity. It also involves the ability to detect a change in quantity.

One-to-one correspondence: Each number word is mapped onto, or associated with, one object in a group being counted.

Ordinal number: Describes the position of a number in a sequence, e.g. first, second, third, fourth.

Partitioning: Breaking a number into constituent parts to make it easier to perform calculations. Numbers can be partitioned in various ways but early on it is best to use the term when partitioning numbers into hundreds, tens and units to reinforce place-value knowledge. Example: 435 + 62 = 400 + 30 + 5 + 60 + 2 = 400 + 90 + 7 = 497.

Place value: The value of a digit is determined by its position or place in a number. For example, in 635 the 6 represents 6 hundreds (600), the 3 represents 3 tens (30) and the 5 is worth 5 ones or units (5). The place-value pattern of hundreds, tens and units is repeated throughout the number system to build up larger numbers.

Processing speed: How quickly pupils can take in oral or visual information. If they process the information slowly the pace of lessons in a classroom may be too fast for them so that they cannot understand or remember what has been taught.

Provision map: A chart drawn up by a SENCO showing what help a pupil is receiving in each area of the curriculum and who is providing the support.

Recitation: Learning the number names and reciting them in sequence.

SENCO: Special Educational Needs Coordinator who is responsible for ensuring that children with special needs have their needs assessed and met through appropriate provision.

Sequences of numbers: An ordered list of numbers that is governed by a rule which defines the relationship between them. The rule might be 'add one' as in the counting sequence 1, 2, 3, 4, 5. Or it might be 'add 5' as in the sequence 25, 30, 35, 40.

Shopkeeper's method: See complementary addition.

Short division: Dividing by a single-digit number.

Short-term memory: Recalls things that are only needed temporarily for immediate use, such as remembering a new telephone number. Once the information has been used it can be forgotten without adverse effects.

Step counting: Counting forwards or backwards in groups. Pupils should be able to step count in tens, fives and twos. It is useful but not essential to be able to step count in threes and fours. Step counting in higher numbers will probably be too difficult for pupils with a memory weakness. Example: To calculate 4 x 5 step count 5, 10, 15, 20.

Subitising: The ability to take in the quantity of a random array of objects at a glance and without counting.

Subtraction strategies: The subtraction strategies suggested in this book are: doubles subtraction – recognising number combinations as part of doubles patterns, bridging back through ten, and complementary addition, which is often known as the shopkeeper's method.

Subvocalising: Talking to yourself under your breath about what you are thinking. Sometimes there is slight lip movement. Subvocalising is not wrong. Talking through what they are doing is exactly what you want the pupil to do. However, they should be reasoning to help develop their thinking, not simply repeating information or procedures learnt by rote.

Tally marks: Recording a number of items by writing one symbol, usually a line, for each item in the count. To make it easier to read, four vertical lines are recorded and the fifth is a diagonal that crosses the four. This makes it easy to compute the total tally at the end of the count. Tally marks are efficient for recording data for statistical analysis. However, some pupils persist in using them to do calculations with large numbers which is inefficient and prone to errors.

Teaching plan: A detailed plan of what to teach and how to teach it, taking into account the pupil's level of knowledge and style of learning.

Unit subtraction: Subtracting a single digit from a multi-digit number where the number to be subtracted is the same as the unit digit in the larger number.

Universal strategy: A strategy that can be applied in a variety of situations. Example: Bridging through ten can be applied to both addition and subtraction and adapted for larger numbers.

Visual perception: The ability to interpret what you see in a meaningful way.

Visual and spatial awareness: The ability to see the distances between objects and the relationships among them. The pupil who cannot do this may get lost finding their place on a page and returning to it.

Visualising: Thinking in pictures or images. If a pupil is silent and appears to be staring into space they may be seeing still or moving pictures in their head. The ability to retain a mental image to recall when needed plays an important part in memory.

Working memory: The memory needed to carry out step-by-step procedures and to reason.

Zero: The place-value holder that denotes an empty position in a multi-digit number.

Index